15TH December 2010

Thanks for supp

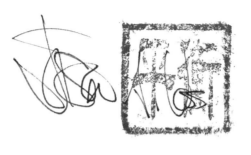

THE
INTUITIVE
INVESTOR

THE
INTUITIVE
INVESTOR

A radical guide for manifesting wealth

Jason Apollo Voss

SelectBooks, Inc.
New York

This edition published by SelectBooks, Inc.
For information address SelectBooks, Inc., New York, New York.

First Edition

ISBN 978-1-59079-206-3

Library of Congress Cataloging-in-Publication Data

Voss, Jason Apollo.
The intuitive investor : a radical guide for manifesting wealth / Jason Apollo Voss. – 1st ed.
p. cm.
Includes index.
Summary: "Successful Wall Street fund manager retired at age 35 guides investors to use intuitive and creative right-brained processes to complement traditional left-brain financial analysis. Author describes his principles based on spiritual insights and provides professional anecdotes to support his theories"–Provided by publisher.
ISBN 978-1-59079-206-3 (hardbound : alk. paper)
1. Finance, Personal–Psychological aspects. 2. Investments–Moral and ethical aspects. 3. Creative ability–Psychological aspects. I. Title.
HG179.V67 2010
332.601'9–dc22
2010014826

Interior Design by Janice Benight

Manufactured in the United States of America
10 9 8 7 6 5 4 3 2 1

DEDICATED TO EVERY PERSON
WHO BELIEVES IN HIS OR HER EXPERIENCES
ABOVE ALL ELSE

Contents

PART ONE

Preparing the Ground for Your Creativity, Intuition, and Wealth Manifestation   1

PART TWO

Activating Your Creativity and Intuition
for Wealth Manifestation   95

PART THREE

Putting the Four Principles to Maximum Use   165

Acknowledgments

My life has been blessed with many wonderful people who have each shared themselves with me. Thank you...

Family

Mom, for raising me and teaching me so many of my life's lessons. Clyde, for your example of integrity and honesty. Evelyn, for being the family glue. Phil, for being such a great friend when I was young. Kate, for teaching me humility. Dawn, for teaching me the missing lessons, for your enduring support, for such pure love, you are my custom-made wife—I love you! And to any family members I didn't name, your influence is honored and appreciated. I love all of you.

Friends

George, for your original elegant inspiration. Marco T., for having been there so many times; I consider you to be a brother. Rick W., for being such a powerful influence when I was young. Shai S., for your continued friendship, laughter and support for my life. Natalie V., for being my unswerving champion. Raymond and Isaac, for being my furry friends. Bob P., for being one of the best examples of a loving man. Fiona P., for changing everything. Chai, for teaching me patience. Jon F., for your sincerity, erudition, and love of animals. Jon A., for being an example of an adult and for your continued seismic influence. Stephen J., for suggesting that a single book could be about investing and spirituality. David W., for being my Brother. Tigtigo, for demonstrating what a living god looks like. Puka, thanks for showing others who I am. Tug, thanks for being a bodhisattva. Paula M., for being a living embodiment of profundity, your courage is an inspiration. Kelly H , for your frivolity and support. Michael J. Gelb, for providing the outstanding structure of the book that I am certain will ensure its prosperity and perpetuity. My beloved Friday Group, for the loving support and invaluable mirroring. I apologize in advance if I have been remiss by excluding any of my spectacular friends.

Professional

Joseph Piper, for your example of intuitive choices trumping analysis, your loving example, and your support. Andrew Davis, for championing me, for your hands off management style, and for your living example of intelligence and heart in a business person. Chandler Spears, thanks for being Statler to my Waldorf. Lori D., thanks for your professional friendship and grace under fire. Angelica V., for your sweet sincerity. Christopher Davis, for carrying the Davis torch, your example of intelligence, and your efforts to always be better. Andy Pritchard, for hours of conversations and for being one of Wall Street's most decent human beings. John Van Oast, for your levity and professional friendship. William Eager, for the opportunity of a lucrative future.

Literary
Stephan Pollan, for your initial "tipping point" support for my work. Jeremy Katz, for insisting that this book be centered on principles. Bill Gladstone, for your unswerving support, professional acumen, good nature, and deep desire to change it all. Kenzi Sugihara, for your enduring belief in the possible. Nancy Sugihara, for turning a manuscript into a book. Kenichi Sugihara for introducing me to you.

Teachers
Becky Myer, for your compassion. Jeff Belf, for being one of the earliest examples of Manhood that I could respect. Stephen Hayes, for showing me who I was and who I wasn't. Carolee Hayes, for your powerful support for who I am. Ginny Wilkins, for being willing to say "no" to me as you were supporting me. Ruben Zubrow, for helping me to see that I was an economist at heart and for pulling my tail. Bob Pois, for passionate involvement and love. Wayne Boss, for opening my heart to God. Quite honestly, everyone in my life has been a teacher—everyone.

Inspiration
The Rolling Stones, for "Gimme Shelter," the original Inspiration, and all the rest, too. Tommy Bolin, for your Direct Connection to Source. Prince Rogers Nelson, for being yourself, so I could be myself. Ivo Watts Russell, for your choices. Bauhaus, for your creative inspiration. Echo and the Bunnymen, for harmonizing so strongly with who I am. Tones on Tail, for Pop! James Marshall Hendrix for being you. Smashing Pumpkins, for "Siamese Dream"—it saved my life. All of the artists of the Asian Massive movement. The Chemical Brothers, for channeling It. Sly and the Family Stone, for "There's a Riot Goin' On." Lonnie Liston Smith and Isaac Hayes for being the right channels. Fela Kuti, for your courage and for Afrobeat.

Anupama Bhagwat, for your sitar. Albert Camus, for The Stranger. Michael Moorcock, for Elric. Deborah Tannen, for "You Just Don't Understand." Martin Luther King, Jr., Malcolm Little, and Mohandas K. Gandhi for fighting for positive change. Kmt, for being like no other place on Earth. Medjedu, for your pyramid. Ptah, for your Word. Sekhmet, for your femininity. Apollo, for your intuition. Nebt Het for your wings. $0 + 1 = \infty$.

WATOA

Preface

The date is October 21, 2004. The place is 1355 Avenue of the Americas in New York City at the Hilton Hotel. As the co-Portfolio Manager of the successful Davis Appreciation and Income Fund, I am one of the key note speakers presenting to a group of top-producing brokers at the Union Bank of Switzerland Investor Forum. After a tedious and boring cocktail mixer I retreat to my room where I begin meditating to calm my nerves and prepare for my discussion the following day. But this meditation is unlike any I have ever experienced; it is much deeper. Profound magic proceeds to unfold.

I can clearly see my future and can clearly foresee that within several years a financial markets' meltdown is likely to occur. Once started the convoluted, incestuous structures of Wall Street that have led to tremendous corruption are going to unwind rapidly, leading the financial markets, the country, and the world into near economic ruin. My strong intuitive sense is that it is time to retire with my performance record and sanity intact, and to pursue spiritual interests.

So what do I do with my clear vision of the future? I do what I have almost always done in my investment career: I trust my inner voice and on August 18, 2005, I walk away from the enviously successful life that I spent over a decade cultivating. By no means is it an easy choice, but it is the right choice.

Fast-forward to 2007 when cracks first begin to appear in the worldwide financial system. Businesses, especially those that lend money, are willing to do anything to earn an extra dollar. They ignore the ridiculous and unwarranted rise in real estate values, and they ignore the poor creditworthiness and unsophisticated nature of many of their borrowers. But then you know the rest. Beginning with the rapid collapse of the "first domino," Bear Stearns, the banking industry falls hard on its face. Soon after that, the massive real estate bubble bursts, taking the global economy with it.

So who am I? I am Jason Apollo Voss, the retired co-Portfolio Manager of the Davis Appreciation and Income Fund (DAIF). Over the course of my investment career the DAIF bested the NASDAQ Composite index by 77.0%, the Standard and Poors 500 index by 49.1% and the Dow Jones Industrial Averages index by 35.9%.[1]

Importantly, these returns were earned even in recessionary, and financial-market-bubble-bursting, times. And these returns were earned with significantly less volatility than that of the overall stock market. The DAIF was one of Morningstar's first 10 mutual funds (of 10,000) to receive its Stewardship Award for ethical treatment of investor monies.

The firm I worked for, Davis Selected Advisers, was at the time of my retirement, one of the nation's top 50 largest money management firms and was among the largest shareholders for a number of household name companies, such as American Express, Costco, Altria (i.e., Philip Morris), and Sealed Air (makers of bubble wrap).

Furthermore, the DAIF was regularly ranked in the top decile of its investment category and earned a Lipper #1 ranking in its investment category. The fund was named a Lipper Leader, and was a perennial Morningstar Analyst Pick. Over the years I gave numerous press interviews to: the *Wall Street Journal, Barron's, Business Week*, Bloomberg, Reuters, *Money*, the *Wall Street Transcript, Smart Money, Red Herring, Value Line*, etc. I gave many speeches to investor groups, stock brokers, and undergraduate and graduate students. I thank them for being the guinea pigs for what I will share with you in *The Intuitive Investor: A Radical Guide for Manifesting Wealth*.

In addition to my timely retirement decision to avoid the financial markets meltdown of 2008–2009, in the midst of that spring 2009 panic, one of the greatest in history, I publicly called the market low of March 9, 2009, a mere three days after the fact on my blog: http://jasonapollovoss.blogspot.com.

I earned both my bachelor's degree in economics, and my master of science degree in business administration, with an emphasis in finance and accounting, from the University of Colorado (go Buffs!). Additionally, I am a chartered financial analyst (CFA) as designated by the CFA Institute. At the age of 35 I retired from my career as the guardian of people's fortunes, both large and small.

But this is all in the past. Some of the important questions to be answered by reading this book are: What can I share with you *now* that

---

[1] Results include the effects of dividends and stock splits on total return. Results were calculated based on data published by *Yahoo!* Finance; DAIF ticker symbol is DCSYX and covering the period of September 22, 2000 to August 18, 2005.

will make you money? Or, what skills led me to making such a timely and perfect retirement choice? And the best question: What led to my large outperformance relative to my investment peers? In short, the answer is that I am a decided *outsider* who does things that few others know how to do. Want to know the secret? The majority of the wealth I have created for investors, and for myself, comes from knowing how to use my right brain and its creative and intuitive functions.

In your hands is a radical new way of investing that maximizes the power of your right brain. I can show you how to more fully activate your creativity and intuition because it is the right, creative, intuitive brain that is the primary source of wealth manifestation in the economy. Bennett W. Goodspeed articulated this well when he said:

> "Why do investment professionals get such poor marks? The main reason is that they are victims of their own methodology. By making a science out of an art, they are opting to be precisely wrong rather than generally correct."[2]

Before embarking on this journey I want to remind you of several things:

> ➤ Alignment of money with higher purposes is a potent combination.

> ➤ All successful investing may be boiled down to four words: "buy low, sell high." Never lose sight of that. And …

My sincerest wish is that you enjoy our journey together. Good luck and good skill!

---

2 Bennett W. Goodspeed, *The Tao Jones Averages: A Guide to Whole-Brained Investing* (New York: Penguin, 1984), 3.

Introduction

Welcome to the *Intuitive Investor: A Radical Guide for Manifesting Wealth*. It is my feeling that every investor is capable of earning outstanding returns on their investments. Yet, to my knowledge, no investment book has yet been written that fully addresses the most critical topic for generating those outstanding returns, namely the right brain's creative and intuitive functions.

To be clear, the right brain is understood to be the portion of the mind that handles organic, multi-dimensional, creative, and intuitive processes. Whereas, it is understood and accepted that the left brain is the portion of the mind responsible for linear and analytical processes.

✦ Functional Differences Between What has Been ✦ Termed the Left and Right Brain

The rigid divide once believed to exist between the left and right hemispheres of the brain has been convincingly demonstrated to not exist. In fact, full functionality is spread throughout the entire brain. Specific functions are not limited only to one hemisphere or another. However, the functional distinction suggested by the terms left and right brain are still important. Thus, in *The Intuitive Investor* the common definitions of left and right brain are used.

It turns out that some of the greatest problems faced by investors are neatly addressed by a fully functional right brain. For example:

➤ Developing new investment ideas

➤ Identifying
  ○ *information that will truly affect your investments*
  ○ *investment risks before they occur*
  ○ *financial market bottoms*

➤ Evaluating
  ○ *the future competitiveness of a business*
  ○ *the products of a business*

○ *the management executives of a business*
○ *the "mood" of the financial markets*

➤ Knowing when to buy and when to sell an investment

If you have been investing for any length of time, you know that these are all critical challenges for the investor that can stand in the way of your success. In fact, it's my estimate that these issues are fully 95% of the "analysis" that is important for making good investment decisions. What's more, they have nothing to do with crunching numbers. Instead, it is the capacities of the right brain that are utilized to evaluate these factors in a carefully discerning way. Rest assured these are the considerations, among others, that lay at the heart of this book. So why hasn't the right brain received its due respect?

One of the reasons that the right brain has not received its due respect is because of the seemingly ephemeral nature of the right brain and its creative and intuitive functions. Because creativity and intuition have defied easy description, business school professors, business executives, investment managers, asset traders, stock brokers, and authors of books on investing steer clear of talking about and working with the tremendous capacities of the right brain. This prejudice means that the majority of investment analysis is done using "hard" data. That is, the stuff that is more tangible and that seems more real.

Massive overemphasis on hard data analysis and its generic, boilerplate answers means there is tremendous expert scrutiny of a very limited amount of numerical and, in some cases, verbal data. Within moments of uncovering any perceived financial advantage in this process, any potential for outsized returns is lost by the individual investor because the scrutinizing pros bid up the price of investment opportunities through rapid-fire buying, often involving super computers. This rabid competition is even difficult for most investment professionals, who ironically underperform the stock markets routinely. But by definition, if you want to earn returns better than everyone else, you can't do what everyone else is doing. You must do something that is unique. Luckily, the critical investment tasks I identified as the greatest challenges for the investor are impossible to evaluate computationally, both for computers and for human-beings.

Therefore, the creative and intuitive powers of your right brain deserve some exploration—since very few people are consciously competing in the domain of the right brain. The ingredient missing for investors is a guide for how to use your right brain in a systematic way so that creativity and intuition move beyond unexpected serendipity to on-demand tools.

Who This Book Is For

ANYONE NERVOUS ABOUT MONEY One of the reasons you are likely to be nervous about your money and about investment decisions, is that there are so many things in the future that can happen, including bad things. Anxiety about these bad things stands in the way of your ability to clearly access your creativity and intuition and leads to too much mental noise. In turn, this diminishes your ability to make prescient, timely, and accurate intuitive decisions. I will specifically teach you techniques for not only how to mitigate your anxieties, but also how to take advantage of them.

ANYONE WHO HAS EVER HAD DIFFICULTY MAKING A DECISION ABOUT MONEY Besides nervousness about money, there is also a bewildering amount of information surrounding investment decisions. Often this leads to paralysis in decision making. I will demonstrate specific techniques for identifying which information is pertinent and impactful to your decisions. Additionally, I will describe methods for how to take advantage of the situation when you feel ignorant and overwhelmed during the making of an investment decision.

ANYONE WHO FEELS AS IF THERE IS SOMETHING MISSING FROM THE CURRENT INVESTMENT LITERATURE The current investment literature either completely ignores right-brain investment issues or actually goes out of its way to get rid of the influence of the right-brain. Yet having comfort with these unaddressed issues, such as your emotions and how to take advantage of them, and also how to take advantage of your creativity and your intuition, is most of what it takes to win the investment battle. Addressing this imbalance is the central focus of this book.

ANYONE WHO HAS HAD INTUITIVE INSIGHTS BUT DIDN'T FOLLOW UP ON THEM Creativity and intuition are natural functions of your brain. You have had creative and intuitive insights that have benefitted you. But it's also likely that you have ignored your creative and intuitive insights at least once and ended up regretting it. To gain trust in your creativity and intuition is thus critical for investment success. I will be sharing powerful techniques for accomplishing both of these tasks.

ANYONE WHO TRUSTS HIS OR HER INTUITION BUT WANTS IT TO MOVE BEYOND MERE SERENDIPITY AND INTO A POWERFUL INVESTMENT TOOL Perhaps you already trust your creativity and intuition, but you would like access to these brain functions as on-demand tools. Methods for doing just this are a major portion of the book.

ANYONE WHO WANTS A NATURAL COMPLEMENT TO HIS OR HER LEFT-BRAINED ANALYTICAL PROCESS While the singular focus of *The Intuitive Investor: A Radical Guide for Manifesting Wealth* is on the right brain and its creative, intuitive, and wealth manifesting powers, the right brain is simply the natural equal partner of the left, analytical brain. This book is definitively not an argument against the left brain and its many capabilities. Instead, the book addresses the imbalance of respect given to the left brain, as opposed to the right brain when making investments. So if you already have an arsenal of left-brained, analytical tools you will be dramatically increasing your capabilities by folding right-brained, intuitive tools into your repertoire.

THE EXPERIENCED INVESTOR WHO WANTS TO MAKE MORE IN-SPIRED DECISIONS If you have many years of investing under your belt, then you know that investment success relies on more than just an understanding of the "hard" data; it frequently relies on something unquantifiable. Moving beyond mere heuristics, *The Intuitive Investor* firmly maps out the previously unquantifiable and mostly indescribable aspects of investing: using your creativity and intuition to manifest wealth. I am certain that whatever your level of investment expertise is, you will walk away from your experience of this book as a better investor, and feeling as if you have more than gotten your money's worth.

Overview of the Intuitive Investor

Because creativity and intuition are often ephemeral I have carefully structured this book to provide it with a firm grounding. Here is an overview of the book's structure:

ANECDOTES

Throughout the book are anecdotes from my career. These stories demonstrate the book's concepts in action and also serve to introduce frequent investment problems you may have.

SELF-ASSESSMENTS AND EXERCISES

At the end of each chapter you will find self-assessments and exercises. These are designed to directly connect you with the knowledge and techniques demonstrated in the book. I strongly encourage you to do as many of the self-assessments and exercises as you can. Your active participation will ensure increased potency for your creative and intuitive abilities, ultimately leading to greater investment success for you. I recommend that you keep a notebook and pen nearby as you read through the book. This will quickly facilitate doing the self-assessments and exercises.

The following describes the order of the major sections of *The Intuitive Investor:*

PART I: PREPARING THE GROUND FOR YOUR CREATIVITY, INTUITION & WEALTH MANIFESTATION Given the unique nature of *The Intuitive Investor* I begin by reviewing the book's foundations to maximize your success with the material. Next, much of why creativity and intuition remain elusive is the massive overemphasis in our culture on preparing, educating, and cultivating your left, analytical brain. Unfortunately, this prejudice is the very thing that stands in the way of fully utilizing the right, creative, and intuitive brain. So getting an immediate handle on the obstructions created by the left brain is critically important for investment success. The focus is to overcome the unconscious use of your left brain so that it works with, and not against, your right brain. At two strategic moments the first two of the Four Principles of Intuitive Investing, *Infinity* and *Paradox,* will be introduced. Last in this section I address the who, what, where, when, and why of investing. This will provide you with "A Map for the Investor" that will help you to mentally place yourself within the investment landscape with more confidence and expertise.

PART II: ACTIVATING YOUR CREATIVITY AND INTUITION FOR WEALTH MANIFESTATION Greater conscious control of the left brain allows the layering in of both the Seven Attitudes and Seven Behaviors of Intuitive Investing. Once in place the Seven Attitudes serve as a form of subconscious immune system to help in the prevention of common obstacles to your creative and intuitive investment process. Meanwhile, the Seven Behaviors, once in place, are the unshakeable foundations on which you actively engage your creative and intuitive investment capabilities. The final two of the Four Principles of Intuitive Investing, *Harmonizing* and *Action,* will be introduced. I conclude this section by sharing three of the most powerful right-brain investment tools I developed over the course of my career.

PART III: PUTTING THE FOUR PRINCIPLES TO MAXIMUM USE This last section of the book teaches you how to access your right brain at will. This access, in turn, leads you to more creative and intuitive investment decisions. Using these new talents in sequence, I then share with you techniques for radical wealth manifestation. This final section concludes with a series of stories from my investment career that definitively assist you to make "The Intuitive Investor" tools a part of your investor's toolkit.

You Can Do This, Too

I have expectations for you. While I will be sharing with you many of the secrets that I used to help steer the Davis Appreciation and Income Fund to noteworthy success, I expect you to maintain an open mind, as well as to take responsibility for your learning. If you do this, I can assure you that you can be a successful investor, too. This is because creativity and intuition are *natural* functions of the human brain and we all have access to them. But what has been missing for most are systematic techniques to access creativity and intuition, which turns them into powerful tools. The information I provide, combined with your active participation in the self-assessments and exercises will radically increase your ability to manifest wealth.

Yes, you are going to have to earn your investment returns by shrewd application of these principles and ideas. But even more, by your ability to integrate the secrets I share with you into your already talented self, and thereby owning my skills, you also make them grander and greater by contributing the ineffable YOU to the equation. Nothing would make me happier than to know that many of you out there are "spanking" my investment returns. That would be incredible and I would take absolutely no credit for it. You see, I cannot be there with you each and every day. I cannot pull the trigger for you when it comes time to buy, or sell, investments. That is your job. All of the responsibility for putting what I teach you into action is on your very able shoulders. My insights and methods will probably require change on your part.

Additional access to me and my thoughts and feelings about investing can be found at:

Home page: www.jasonapollovoss.com
Blog: jasonapollovoss.blogspot.com
Book home page: www.intuitiveinvestor.com
Workshops: www.intuitiveinvestingworkshop.com

Preparing the Ground for Your Creativity, Intuition, and Wealth Manifestation

GIVEN THE UNIQUE NATURE of *The Intuitive Investor* in Part One, "Preparing the Ground for Your Creativity, Intuition, and Wealth Manifestation," I first explain the underlying assumptions of the book. The goal is to provide you with reliable foundations for maximum success with the material. Next I give a brief description of the Four Principles of Intuitive Investing that naturally flow from my underlying assumptions. Lastly, I provide you with a new, preferable definition of investing. This is to significantly increase the impact of the material on all aspects of your life, but especially on your ability to be a good investor.

I will then share with you the most important investment skill: understanding information. Following that is a discussion about the surprising limitations of facts in investing. From there we will move on to an exploration of the primary tools most people use to communicate and understand information: numbers and words. The limitations of these tools leave gaps in your ability to understand information and argue for an investment in the right brain. The right brain is your source for creativity, intuition, and wealth manifestation. What's more, the right brain nicely compensates for the gaps in solely fact-based investment analysis. Next is a discussion about the currency of the right brain: feelings. Our feelings from signals received in our general state of consciousness differ in important ways from their manifestation as emotions.

Principle I: Infinity is then introduced, which addresses the "information" half of "understanding information." This first principle is about the vastness and interconnectedness of the universe and its information. In order to be in accord with Principle I, an investor must be as free of boundary as possible. To this end, two primary sources of investor limitations are discussed: emotional responses occurring from our feelings of ignorance and emotional states resulting from fear. Techniques for turning both of these into investment allies are shared.

Principle II: Paradox addresses the "understanding" half of "understanding information." This principle acknowledges the need for investors to begin to narrow down infinite investment *possibilities* to narrow investment *probabilities* by making distinctions. Three tools are used for doing just this: contexts, scales, and continuums. Contexts allow the investor to switch from the infinite information map down to a smaller, more digestible map. Adjusting scales helps the investor in revealing prominent features of the information map. Lastly, continuums allow you to really zero-in on relevant information and detail.

Each of the mapping tools addresses the external, rather than the internal environment. Thus, an internal map, a Map for the Investor, is necessary. Knowing what investing is, and who the investor is, allows you to place yourself in relation to the information landscape in a more effective manner.

Each section will help to reshape you in preparation for greater activation of your right brain's potency. In effect, part one is about erasing the chalk that is written on your mental slate, in preparation for new understanding.

1

Foundations

MANY READERS WILL TAKE the information contained in *The Intuitive Investor* at face value and do not need any convincing as to the validity of the underlying assumptions. However, I am well aware that some of what I will be sharing with you is considered to be of a radical nature, especially in the context of our modern, rightfully skeptical, scientifically-based culture. I can assure you that I am a firm believer in scientific method. I can also assure you that I have personally experienced and made use of the techniques demonstrated in this book, and as the investment record of the Davis Appreciation and Income Fund demonstrates, those techniques have led to outsized wealth creation. While a thorough discussion of these topics appears in chapter nine, "Increasing the Potency of the Four Principles," here is a brief overview of the underlying assumptions of *The Intuitive Investor*.

The Underlying Assumptions

ASSUMPTION 1. That consciousness and energy are the ground of reality and not matter.

For most of the history of science, matter, or that which you can experience with your five senses, has been taken as the basis of reality. However, beginning with the scientifically observed phenomena of the late 19th century that led to the development of quantum physics, scientists have begun to question this assumption. For the purposes of *The Intuitive Investor* I will assume, as many physicists are beginning to assume, that consciousness and energy are the ground of reality. Ironically, some of the oldest belief systems on the planet have historically believed this same thing;[3] meaning

---

[3] For example, the ancient Egyptian, Vedic, Buddhist and Hindu traditions.

that science and spirituality are nearing agreement on this issue. The principle implication of this assumption is that we can create our own reality.

ASSUMPTION 2: That we are all interconnected in a cause and effect soup that some have referred to as the Field, the Totality, Allness, among others. Again, many modern scientists are beginning to describe theories that are in accord with very old spiritual beliefs that emphasize the interconnectedness of all things. This is my assumption in *The Intuitive Investor*. The primary implication of this assumption is that our experience of life is not separate from the experiences of others.

ASSUMPTION 3: That there is an interconnected consciousness that is referred to in terms such as the collective consciousness, the field, or group mind.

ASSUMPTION 4: That, as individuals, you can choose to access this collective consciousness anytime you want, or need to.

The preceding two assumptions are also increasingly in accord with both science and spirituality as they converge. The primary implication of these two assumptions is that you are able to feel and experience what others are feeling and experiencing even when separated at a distance.

ASSUMPTION 5: That your experiences, not someone else's, are the ground for what you believe.

It is my assumption that at the ultimate core, science and spirituality have the same purpose, which is to provide meaning and explanation for our experiences. Put another way, both science and spirituality are a pursuit of the truth, and thus not at odds with one another. For most of us, our ultimate truth is that our experiences are real. So when provided with an experience, your experience serves as the basis for your belief, rather than faith alone.

ASSUMPTION 6: That new experiences are the ground for change, growth, and empowerment.

ASSUMPTION 7: That you are open-minded about and want new experiences, change, growth, and empowerment.

The Four Principles of the Intuitive Investor

Unique to this book are the Four Principles of the Intuitive Investor. The Four Principles are:

stages of consciousness that underlie the functioning of the mind.

An understanding of them will allow you to instantly access your creativity, intuition, and manifestation abilities and then to merge the fruits of those processes with your left brain and its knowledge. It's important to know that the tools throughout the book can be used without fully understanding or accepting the principles behind them. After all, you can use a screwdriver without understanding the principles of torque and leverage, right? However, if you understand the principles then you have the overarching knowledge needed to create your own tools. Because of their importance I will be spending a lot of time explaining the meaning and use of the four principles, especially as applied to investing, but here is a brief summary:

PRINCIPLE I: INFINITY Unlike the left brain, which helps us to solve linear problems where there is a definite answer, the right brain helps us to solve non-linear problems where there are infinite possibilities. Before you evaluate anything as an investor you begin with infinite possibilities. You and I didn't make it this way; it's just the way things are—

So the Infinity Principle is firmly grounded in reality.

Because Principle I, Infinity, means infinite possibilities, it also means that the universe itself is infinite; and that means that you and I, and everyone else, is a part of It. If you were not a part of It, then the universe would not be infinite. So Principle I means that you are not separate from the universe. And *that* provides the natural bridge into the other large part of the essence of Principle I, Infinity, which is that everything is *interconnected*. In conclusion then, you are part of an infinite, interconnected universe full of undifferentiated possibilities.

PRINCIPLE II: PARADOX The very nature of being an investor requires us to discern from an infinite sea of possibility that information and those possibilities that are worth our interest and energy. In short, investing is about separating great investment *probabilities* from investment *possibilities*. So

Principle II, Paradox, is about distinguishing the probable from the infinitely possible. The key words associated with the Paradox Principle are "probability" and "distinctions."

Paradox arises when your consciousness tries to resolve the left brain's need for distinctions with the right brain's perception of vast interconnection. A part of the essence of the second principle is captured by this statement: it is all relative.

PRINCIPLE III: HARMONIZING Once you have narrowed down infinite investment possibilities to limited investment probabilities, you must be able to understand the investments you are considering. You do this by harmonizing with each aspect of an investment. This harmonization leads to understanding. The key word for Principle III is "understanding."

PRINCIPLE IV: ACTION The essence of the Fourth Principle is *choice*. This is because choices lead inexorably to action. Once you understand the investment choices before you then you must decide in which ones you want to invest.

The process described by the four principles can be summarized as follows:

> Beginning with infinite investment possibilities, investors narrow these down to investment ideas that are probably worth exploring. Then investors try to understand those investment ideas before deciding whether or to buy or sell the investment.

An Expanded Definition of Investing

Because the heart of investing is making beneficial choices, an investment book must help you to make those kinds of choices. Yet a set of tools that help you to make beneficial choices should not be limited in their use to just investing. Therefore a new definition of investing is useful in order to increase the potency of the methods to becoming an "Intuitive Investor." I think that you will find that the tools that I share with you can affect every aspect of your life.

There are several traditional definitions of investing.

The following is from the American Heritage Dictionary:[4]

in•vest [(in-věst')]; verb.

1. To commit (money or capital) in order to gain a financial return: "invested their savings in stocks and bonds."

2. a. To spend or devote for future advantage or benefit: "invested much time and energy in getting a good education."

   b. To devote morally or psychologically, as to a purpose; commit: "Men of your generation are invested in what they do, women in what you are" (Shana Alexander).

Alternatively you have from the Investopedia[5] the following:

Investing: The act of committing money or capital to an endeavor (a business, project, real estate, etc.) with the expectation of obtaining an additional income or profit. Investing also can include the amount of time you put into the study of a prospective company, especially since time is money.

These definitions are fine. But they assume a context that makes them too limiting. And that just does not serve the purpose of unlocking your whole brain for greater investment success. Theses definitions assume that investing is solely about money and capital. This is the understanding that most people have about investing. But let's explore a different definition that reveals the full power of investing as both a science and an art.

Investing is:

1. Making a decision

2. Consciously making choices so that the benefits of those choices exceed the costs of those choices

3. Consciously expending energy (i.e., resources) so that the benefits of the expended energy exceed the costs of the expended energy

The definition of "investing" is expanded beyond the realms of money and capital because the skills you are exploring are used in all of your life.

---

[4] *American Heritage Dictionary of the English Dictionary, Fourth Edition;* (New York: Houghton-Mifflin Company, 2006).

[5] Investopedia, http://www.investopedia.com/terms/i/investing.asp.

This is because life is a continuous flow of decisions. And decisions are subject to analysis and scrutiny, as well as your creativity and intuition. In short, decisions/investments are best when you are fully conscious, and that means that you are utilizing your mind's full powers. You constantly make investment decisions even if you are not conscious that you are. Please have this new definition of investing in mind as we proceed.

2

Why Intuition is Essential for Investing Success

"A ... reason why science cannot replace judgment is the behavior of financial markets."

—MARTIN FELDSTEIN
Professor of Economics at Harvard University,
president emeritus of the National Bureau of
Economic Research, and American conservative

IN CHAPTER TWO I discuss the very most important skill of an investor—understanding information. Next I go into detail about why intuition, not factual analysis, is the real source of investment success. Additionally I review the two primary sources of information that investors use when evaluating investments: numbers and words. Both numbers and words have strengths and weaknesses as limited approximations of investment information. Because of these limitations investors need an alternative source of information. In this case, the right brain and its powers of creativity and intuition robustly help to fill in the gaps left by numbers and words. The chapter concludes with self-assessments and exercises designed to give you real world experience.

The Most Important Investment Skill

The most important investment skill is understanding information.

This is because information is the basis for investment evaluation and investment decisions. Understanding information well equips investors to recognize when they don't have enough information; to rapidly sift through unimportant information; to see what other investors miss; to more artfully respond to crisis or panic as it affects investments; to properly evaluate the management team of a business to know when it is time to either buy or sell an investment; to uncover hidden risks; to avoid herd mentality. It's quite simple really:

> ➤ Having bad information ≠ bad investment choices.
> ➤ Having good information ≠ good investment choices.
> ➤ Understanding bad information = avoiding bad investment choices.
> ➤ Understanding good information = good investment choices.

Just because you have bad information does not necessarily mean that you make a bad investment choice, because you may get lucky. Likewise, having good information does not necessarily result in good investment choices either. If you don't understand that the investment information you have is good, you may fail to act on the information. However, understanding bad investment information does result in the avoidance of a bad investment choice. The preservation of investment capital is a positive outcome. Likewise, understanding good investment information does lead to good investment choices. The appreciation of investment capital is also a positive outcome. The basis for successful investment is that *investors must understand information.* This interconnection of the investor (i.e., understanding) with the information landscape (i.e., information) is critical and the subject of the remainder of this book.

Investing Is As Much About Intuition As It Is Analysis

Understanding information is the most important investment skill. But unfortunately, most investors suffer from the opposite situation: a misunderstanding of information. Specifically, one of the most important of all investing secrets is that:

There is no such thing as a future fact.

In the future, events will occur that will become new facts, but there is no such thing as a future fact. Facts only absolutely answer questions about the past—they only pertain to the past. And the future is unknowable. Thus, which future facts will be important is also unknowable. Yet, investing is an activity whose results unfold in the future. You try to capture future benefit, traditionally income and/or capital gains, from your investments. But whether or not the fruits of investing are available for you to harvest is unknowable ahead of time. Future benefits realized from an investment are contingent on investment performance and the facts of that performance are unknowable ahead of time. Facts are unknowable ahead of time. What are the consequences of this fact?

Your choices, such as purchasing an investment, are always *emotional* acts, even if facts are involved in assessing your choices. This is because it is your choice to *trust* that past facts are likely to repeat themselves as the future unfolds.

Therefore, the act of making an investment is actually an emotional act.

What all of this means is that investing is as much a soft, emotional, subjective, creative, feeling, substantive, organic, right-brained process, as it is a hard, factual, objective, analytical, thinking, structured, linear, left-brained process.

Yet the left brain is massively over-emphasized as the source for excellent investment returns. This is important because the world of investing is a vast, non-linear experience, yet the tool that we primarily use to analyze investments is the limited, linear left brain. It is likely you have spent most of your life educating and training the left brain to make effective decisions. I am assuming you went to school to learn how to think; not to learn how to *feel*. So cultivating your right brain so that it is equal in its capacities with the left brain is one of the secrets of investment success.

Like anything, the left brain has both strengths and limitations. Our analytical brains are excellent when dealing with questions where there is a definitive answer. In investing it answers very well questions such as last year's profitability, company A's return on invested capital relative to company B's, the percentage of a firm's sales that are international, etc. The left brain is also good at helping to understand linear problems. For example, mathematically calculating the compound annual growth rate of a stock over the course of five years is a problem answered well by the left brain.

Most of what is considered *information* is conveyed in a linear fashion and the two primary tools used to convey experiences are numbers and words. Importantly, there are other means of conveying experiences, including expressing feelings through music, painting, sculpture, architecture, use of color, dance, etc. But for now the focus is on the two most conventional descriptions of experience.

"You may learn all about the sun,
all about the atmosphere, all about the rotation of the earth,
and still miss the radiance of the sunset."

—ALFRED NORTH WHITEHEAD,
English mathematician and philosopher

Moving Beyond Conventional Descriptions of Our World

As mentioned previously, the two most common tools for describing and expressing the world around you are numbers and words. Numbers are made understandable and powerful by mathematics, whereas words are made understandable and powerful by language. Mathematics and language provide the structure and ordering principles for numbers and words so that your left brain can make sense of the information that numbers and words are trying to describe. Notice the use of the word *structure*. Structure is essential if you want to "speak the language" of your left brain. These two elegant descriptions of the world, numbers with mathematics, and words with language, are analogous to one another.

Advantages of Numbers

Naming
Sometimes numbers are used to name things, such as in their use as Social Security numbers, the chapters of a book, and patent numbers.

Measuring
Investors are interested in numbers mostly in their measuring role because this is their primary role in conveying investment information to you, the investor. Examples of this information include revenues, profits, interest rates, currency exchange rates, units sold and people hired. More specifically, when you look at a company's income statement (aka profit and loss statement) you will see entries such as "net sales" or "net income." Those numbers are absolute. The number is either $213.7 million or it isn't. Numbers are less ambiguous than words when measurement is called for. The only mathematics involved in recording and reporting $213.7 million is counting.

Comparisons

Because of their unambiguous ability to quantify, numbers are very effective for making comparisons between disparate pieces of information. For example, you can easily compare the total profits of a business with the total profits of its competitors. This is a task that is very difficult to do with words. Without numbers you are forced to say something like, "The profits of the ABC Company are larger than those of the XYZ Company." What if you want more depth to the answer and you ask of your words a follow-up question: "What makes you so certain of that?" Without numbers the answer is ambiguous: "Well I just have a feeling that the profits are better, because the ABC Company is able to afford a better office space and its office furniture is better and its employees seem happier." Without numbers you are forced to look for indirect or circumstantial evidence that the ABC Company's profits are superior to its competitor, the XYZ Company.

Mathematics: The Machinery

By contrast to the measuring and comparing function of numbers, the growth rate of a company's sales over the past five years is not pure, raw data. Instead an artificial mechanism, mathematics, is used to generate this piece of information. The machinery in this case is a calculation that makes use of the mathematics of calculus (don't be scared, this is *not* a math book).

As previously stated, mathematics, its calculations and its mechanisms are ways of describing the world around you. However, mathematics is NOT reality. Instead, it is a method, way, or philosophy for describing reality. The same is true for words, isn't it? The words that describe the love you feel for someone are NOT the same as the feeling, are they? Your descriptions of things are ALWAYS going to be an approximation of reality and not the reality itself. This is important to know because often decisions that are mathematically derived have the imprimatur/smell/taste/feel/look/sound of fact, when in fact the answers of mathematics are at best theories that approximate reality. In particular, despite the fact that mathematicians study *non-linear* mathematics, most people know only about the mathematics where the answers are certain, such as geometry, algebra, trigonometry and calculus. But even non-linear mathematics has a difficult time describing particular aspects of life that everyone probably considers to be essential to life experience.

Disadvantages of Numbers

Qualitative Assessment

Numbers are not good at describing feelings or sensations or preferences. Imagine if you asked someone, "How much do you care for me?" and they responded, "17!" OK, whatever that means. True, they could have more effectively answered, "On a scale of 1 to 10, I would rate my caring for you a 7.5." Here they are conveying a greater amount of information than before because they are invoking the comparative power of numbers. However, the person that you are talking with still did not give you a sense of what makes them care for you. At best they gave you a sense of *how much* they care for you. Furthermore, for this comparison to work then both parties must agree on the meaning of the scale, or on the point of comparison. In other words, 7.5 relates to what consensual understanding of a 10 on an overall scale? If the two people have a different understanding of 10 or 0 then the information conveyed is still ambiguous and words are likely needed to lend greater meaning to the comparison. Numbers are bad at this kind of thing.

Advantages of Words

Distillation of Experiences

Most peoples' lives are filled with many complex, multi-dimensional experiences that often overwhelm them. One of the tools used to make sense of these experiences is the distillation of experience into words. This puts experiences into a form that the linear, left brain can more easily examine. Additionally, words put experiences into a form that can be shared with other people. For most people, without words, the communication of experiences is very difficult.

Greater Qualitative Precision

Words, when organized by language, allow you to get very complex in your understanding of, and communicating about, qualitative experiences. That is, words allow you to focus your thought energy very specifically. So, one of the primary strengths of words is greater precision than numbers when describing a qualitative event, such as the nature of the CEO of a business. Words also aid in your understanding of an experience and in your sharing of experiences with someone else. Because the understanding of individual words is often very different, words are combined together into sentences so that there is greater assurance that there is a shared understanding. This, however, is also why learning that focuses on words takes so long. Everyone tries to get on the "same page" as to the meaning of all of the words so that there is a mutual understanding about ideas and experiences.

Evocation

When you understand the true meaning of words then you can direct your consciousness toward those words, recall them from memory, and re-experience their profundity all over again. For example, if I say the word "mother," even without context, it is evocative. Words also allow different people to focus energy in a similar fashion so that understanding is possible without having had direct experience of the same thing.

Disadvantages of Words

Interpretation

Even when experiences are described well, words leave the understanding of information open to nearly infinite interpretation; whereas numbers are more absolute—5 is 5 no matter where you are on Earth. This interpretation problem adds noise to an investor's understanding of information. Not coincidentally, obscuring the understanding of information (for example, by lying) is easier with words than it is with numbers.

Linear

Sentences are linear and word order is important. Yes, sentences can be written in many different ways to convey the same information. However, once you start expanding on a topic and sentence builds upon sentence the order of the information becomes increasingly important. Can you read a novel backwards? And I don't mean simply looking at the last chapter to know whodunit. I mean can you read each and every word, starting with the last word of a novel, backwards? Obviously that's absurd and all of the meaning would be lost. In this way, words are just as limited as numbers in describing experiences. This is because they rely upon linearity for understanding information from what is a non-linear, organic, multi dimensional world.

Approximations of Experience

Even though most of us can be moved emotionally more by words than numbers, words are still just an approximation of experience. Words are used to describe experiences, but they are not the experience. Have you ever felt something so difficult to describe that you say, "There just aren't words for it?" Your experience of the world is greater than the ability of words to describe it. Alternatively, have you ever spoken with someone whose native tongue is not English and she says something like, "There is no word for it in English?" Just because there is not a word to describe something does not mean that it does not exist. Likewise, just because there is not a scientific theory to describe something does not mean that it does not exist.

LIMITED TO FAILURE

Numbers and words are both limited in the same critical way: they are narrow, linear approximations of the vast, non-linear reality. Investment opportunities are also vast and non-linear. So can you imagine evaluating a prospective investment based solely on information described by words? While this may seem more imaginable to you than making an investment decision using just numbers, using only words provides an equally incomplete picture of a prospective investment. Yes, combining numbers with words results in a fuller understanding of investments; but this combination still results in a limited understanding of the information of a prospective investment. This is because the combination still predominately utilizes only one-half of your brain's capabilities—the left brain. Ultimately, use of just numbers and words is too limited for investment success. What is needed is a way of experiencing the world that is more in harmony with the actual vast, non-linear world. Such a tool would lead to greater understanding of information and greater investment success.

Your Natural Intuitive Tool, the Right Brain

YOUR SOURCE FOR SUCCESS: THE RIGHT BRAIN

Given that your experience of the world is beyond the descriptive power of numbers and words, it is also beyond your left brain's ability to fully comprehend it. Yet the human mind is in fact well-equipped to deal with the organic, multi-dimensional, non-linear, and unseen aspects of reality. In my years of successful experience as a professional investor it is the use of the right brain where most of the *real* money is to be made. This isn't because the right brain is superior to the left brain. It is because most investors overlook the power of their right brain to solve investment problems and to provide them with actionable information. So shouldn't you as an intelligent investor explore the very real possibilities, and sometime limitations, of your right brain? Who doesn't want additional and

✦ This Is Not Behavioral Finance ✦

There is a branch of economics and finance that has gained tremendous notoriety since the early 1980s called Behavioral Finance. These subjects will not be explored in this book. For those familiar with Behavioral Finance it may seem on the surface as if I am discussing the same subjects, but I am not. Behavioral Finance has as its purpose highlighting the limitations of the right brain, in order to refine the left brain. I will be talking about the exact opposite problem: the limitations of the left brain with the goal of higher refinement of the right brain. Behavioral finance is a subject well worth exploring, but its many axioms and prescriptions have largely been developed to answer questions in which an exact and quantifiable answer is possible. But as previously discussed: there is no such thing as a future fact. Behavioral finance cannot answer the truly important questions confronting you as an investor. An example of such a question is: Why is this business worth my money? Because you are dealing with the future when you make investment decisions, behavioral finance cannot help you entirely because of its limitations.

powerful tools for improving investment returns? Best of all, these natural tools already reside in your right brain; you just need to learn how to access them more regularly.

WHAT IS THE RIGHT BRAIN?

The right brain is a resource for understanding the organic, interconnected, multi-dimensional world that you live in. It is also a part of everyone's natural abilities, even if hardly ever used consciously by most. The right brain excels at connecting into and experiencing the vast, interconnected universe. It also does a nice job of creating the linkages between knowledge and fresh intuition to develop new solutions to problems. The right brain also does a good job of serving as a bridge between intuitive insight and the analytical structuring that turns intuition into money. If numbers and words are the currency of the left brain, then *feelings* are the currency of the right brain.

FEELINGS, NOT EMOTIONAL RESPONSES, ARE THE KEY TO THE RIGHT BRAIN

The key to tapping your right brain and its creative, intuitive, and wealth-manifesting powers is to understand its currency, which are feelings. Feelings are the actual physical sensations you receive as information when you use your five senses. But feelings also are the sensations you receive as information from your intuition. Each person has, what I will call, a *feeling-self* that allows one to attune to extremely subtle, non-sensory information. People are in tune with this aspect of themselves when they are walking down the street and encounter someone that "just does not feel right," or when you get a sudden inspiration about what to do next in your life that "feels right."

Some would call the feeling-self an empathetic state. In an empathetic state you literally take on the same condition of that with which you are empathizing. Thus, when the feeling-self is predominant you can be easily hurt by emotional situations. In my opinion, the ego bodyguards the feeling-self by creating behavioral defenses that are designed to be on the look out for potentially hurtful situations that can easily damage this sensitive core. In other words, the ego is the part of the psychic apparatus that *reacts* to experiences. So the ego is useful.[6] However, if the ego is in operation *unconsciously* it cuts us off from our feeling-selves with emotional barriers.

It is the feeling-self that receives intuitive information: In investing this could be the character of the management team in charge of a business, the essential timing of an investment purchase or sale, or the future prospects for a company's products.

Emotional responses are the same feeling-sensations received earlier but with the added content of prejudice. In other words, feelings are clear signals perceived, but are complicated by distorted signals because of the added static of prejudice. Feelings are clear, but the emotions or emotional response become cloudy. Prejudice happens when we take the extra step of assigning preference to our experience of something. An example will help to illustrate the *critically important* distinction between clear feeling-sensations and clouded emotional response.

> Say the weather outside is cloudy and temperatures are lower than normal. Your senses provide you with all sorts of infor-

---

[6] Note: this contravenes most standard meditative and/or spiritual practice. But to deny the ego's existence is to set oneself apart from it, which simply results in additional duality and, more egoic constructs.

mation about the weather. Your eyes see diminished amounts of sunlight due to the clouds. Sound travels differently on lower temperature, cloudy days. Your skin communicates information about the temperature to you. The moisture in the air due to the clouds leads to a different taste and smell for the oxygen you breathe. Your intuition suggests that you will be fine if you go out for a hike. All of this, however, is just information. But what happens if you have a negative thought about the day's weather and think or say, "I hate hiking on dreary days?" You turn the feeling-sensations which were simple, clear, pure information into an emotional response by adding your preference for warmer days. Isn't it also possible that another person having the identical feeling-sensations actually likes, and is excited by lower temperature and cloudy days?

Importantly, both people, even the one who prefers cloudy days, turn the information conveyed by their feeling-senses, including intuition, into an emotional response. This occurs because both people *choose* to respond in a prejudiced way to a feeling received, in a pure and authentic form, via their feeling natures.[7] For isn't it possible that the person who hates hiking on dreary days will actually have a fantastic time? Isn't it also possible that the person who likes hiking on dreary days will have a miserable time?

Most significant was that the most important piece of data that either prospective hiker received was the information from their intuition: you will be fine if you go out for a hike. This is because the right brain excels at analysis of the multi-dimensional world. The right-brain's intuition gives a clear signal, in the form of feelings, of likely outcome.

Here is an example of intuition as applied (or not) from my career as an investor. This was the situation circa 2003:

> The legendary and largest insurance company in the world, AIG, is headed up by the more legendary and larger, Maurice "Hank" Greenberg. Hank has been the CEO of AIG for decades and runs it as an independent nation state. I am very impressed with its continued ability to underwrite insurance policies resulting in an excellent "combined ratio." This ratio is basically an insurance company's cost of providing insurance.

---

7 Tom Kenyon and Virginia Essene, "Feeling and Human Evolution," in *The Hathor Material: Messages from an Ascended Civilzation: 7th Printing* (Orca, Washington: ORB Communications, 2006), 45–6.

So to make money in the long-run your "combined ratio" needs to be less than 100% of revenues. All of the analytical measures of AIG look, and always look, wonderful. Not only that but also the stock is trading at a discount. But what about management? Hank Greenberg is a management legend; albeit very gruff. My intuition tells me that something is fishy with AIG. In fact, my co-manager Andrew Davis and I have several conversations about Greenberg's gruffness and arrogance. AIG's CEO reminds me of a little, constantly agitated, Napoleon. However, the annual business performance is always outstanding.

Unfortunately, for my shareholders I don't act on my intuition. Investors began selling off AIG due to mounting suspicions of deep malfeasance as it becomes public knowledge that Hank Greenberg and other executives have created a secret compensation club within the company that defied regulatory scrutiny and deified upper management.

I didn't honor the clear and potent information provided to me by my feeling-self/intuition because I *thought* I must be wrong. After all, who was I to question Hank Greenberg who was THE scion of the insurance industry? In other words, I let my thought-based prejudices of the situation get in the way of my intuitive insight and unfortunately my decision lost a lot of money for my shareholders.

Pure feelings are delivered to you by your senses, including intuition, and only become emotional responses and part of your ego when you add judgments and preferences. I believed the extant analysis about Hank Greenberg that he was a management legend above reproach and preferred to believe everybody else about him and AIG, rather than my own intuition—this was not a real assessment, but was my buying into prejudice. Consequently, my ego got in the way of my feeling-self and prevented me from making the correct decision for my shareholders.

So the secret to tapping into your intuition is to strip away the noise of our emotions to get at the clear, true signal of the feeling-sense that intuition provides. This subject is covered in detail in chapter twelve, but along the way I will be laying the essential groundwork to help you become an Intuitive Investor.

BALANCE

In truth, the right brain and the left brain are equal in importance. The goal is to strive to make your right brain the *equal* of your left brain: to let it become a critically important part of your *complete* investment repertoire. The sum of the two distinct aspects of your brain is greater than the sum of its parts. When the two halves are functioning in concert it results in a synergistic display of intelligent and prudent investment decisions whose results can be fantastic. Yet if you use a grand cosmic scale to weigh the amount of literature dedicated to the analytical aspects of your mind relative to the creative/intuitive aspects of your mind, I am certain a gross imbalance will occur in favor of the analytical. After all, most of you have heard of "financial analysts," but how many of you have heard of "financial intuitionists?" So there is some catching up to do.

The Intuitive Investor and You: Self-Assessment

Here are some questions to ask yourself to engage your mind and to help you reflect on how you approach investing.

Consider how your understanding of information affects your investment decisions. Have you lost money by not understanding a critical piece of information? Are you overwhelmed by information and uncertain of how to make sense of it all? When has understanding information worked to your advantage? What are your primary sources of investment information? How do you interact with this information—do you take it as gospel, or do you have a questioning attitude about it?

What proportion of your investment decision making relies upon facts? Have facts ever definitively answered an investment question for you? If so, what led to you trusting those facts? Have you ever lost money on an investment because facts you trusted didn't repeat themselves in the future?

Beyond numbers and words how do you describe your world? What are the advantages of these other descriptions of your life? What are the disadvantages? Do you find that numbers and words capture most of your experience of the world? If not, what critical information is left out by numbers and words? When you have examined investments in the past, what proportion of your research relied upon numbers and words?

Have you ever had the experience of another person having an entirely different experience of an event than you did? What were some of the sources of those differences? What proportion of your daily experience do you have no opinion about? Where do your preferences come from?

Your right brain and its creativity, intuition and wealth manifestation can be developed more easily than you believed. Experiment with the simple exercises that follow to nurture and grow the effectiveness of your right brain.

Exercises

GAINING CONSCIOUSNESS OF THE LEFT BRAIN'S TENDENCY TO IGNORE THE RIGHT BRAIN

THE *FEELING* OF TEMPERATURE Start taking deep, full-bodied breaths until you feel relaxed. Tune your senses into the temperature of the space that you are in. Take a moment to reflect on your experience of the temperature.

How did you reflect upon your experience of temperature? Did you translate your sensory experience into numbers, such as degrees Fahrenheit or Celsius? Perhaps you translated it into words? If you translated the sensation of temperature into either numbers or words, did this happen without you noticing it?

Repeat the exercise, but in this go-around make a conscious effort to not translate your sensation of temperature into either numbers or words. Just experience the temperature for what it is. Did you still have a conscious feeling of the temperature even without the use of numbers and words?

Write down your experience in your notebook. For the rest of the day, make an effort to notice your experience of the world and how much of it you automatically translate. Try to gain the capacity to interrupt the automatic translation.

THE LIMITATIONS OF NUMBERS AND WORDS Remember the most beautiful sunset you have ever experienced. This may be the sunset on the night of your honeymoon. It may be the sunset that included a gorgeous double rainbow after a depressing day of rain. The sunset may be the one you witnessed the day that you retired. Whatever the specifics of your sunset, put it into your mind now. Re-experience it fully. Now, in your notebook, write down the number that describes all of the wonderfulness of that sunset. If you showed your number to a stranger would they be able to share your experience of your greatest sunset?

Now return to the image of your sunset and all of the feelings associated with that gorgeous play of light and clouds and countryside. In your notebook begin to describe with words your experience of the sunset. How does relating your experience in words differ from that of numbers? Now share your description with another person, someone not present during the real sunset experience. Ask the person to reflect back to you their experience of the sunset based solely on your words. Don't cheat by filling in gaps in your friends' understanding by talking with them. How close is their re-telling of the sunset to your actual experience of the sunset? Were they able to convey the powerful sensations and emotional content that you specifically experienced that evening? What parts of your experience did they leave out or not understand?

If you haven't done so already, write down the emotions associated with your sunset. This may be the temperature, the light, the smell of flowers, or the sounds. Most importantly, write down any non-sensory emotions you experienced; perhaps relief, love or awe. What part of your sunset experience do you most directly relate to? In what ways are sunsets and businesses similar in their complexity? Can you imagine evaluating a prospective investment based solely on information contained in numbers? How about solely in words?

REVIEW

In this chapter we learned the following information:

➤ The most important investment skill is *understanding information.*

➤ Because *there is no such thing as a future fact,* investing is as much a soft, emotional, subjective, right-brained, creative, feeling, substantive, organic process, as it is a hard, factual, objective, left-brained, analytical, thinking, structured, linear process.

➤ While germane to the left brain, *numbers and words are both limited and linear* approximations of an unlimited and non-linear experience of reality.

➤ In order to understand information better we need the right brain to connect with the unlimited, non-linear reality.

3

The Infinite Possibilities of the Information Landscape

"...Many Worlds in One, describes a new cosmological
theory that says that every possible chain of events,
no matter how bizarre or improbable, has actually
happened somewhere in the universe—and not
only once, but an infinite number of times!"[8]

THIS CHAPTER BEGINS WITH a discussion of Principle I, Infinity. This initial principle helps you to recognize that the information landscape is vast and interconnected, an environment that the right brain thrives within. Being in accord with Principle I requires that you be as free of personal boundaries as possible so that you may also be connected to the vastness of the information landscape. Tools for identifying your personal boundaries will be shared. Specifically, feelings of ignorance and fear will be a focus because—emotions relating to them often obscure reason and access to the right brain's creative and intuitive functions. The goal is to make both ignorance and fear your investment allies. The chapter concludes with self-assessments and exercises to aid you in accomplishing this goal.

Investing induces, even in the most seasoned investors, moments of chaos, panic, and disorder. The fact is that few things in life are more difficult than investing. There is obtuse and impenetrable jargon. There is a constant news flow about the world and about your investments. There is a continual need to reevaluate. There are difficult decisions to be made. Investing is often disorienting and spawns many intense moments that are utterly mystifying. This is especially true when you tackle new investment problems whose prospective solutions do not respond to your old ways of doing things. But how do you transform your emotions of chaos, panic, and disorder into potent tools? Where do you begin in your understanding of information?

---

[8] Alex Vilenkin, Ph.D. *Many Worlds in One: The Search for Other Universes* (New York: Hill & Wang, 2006), 3.

✦ Overwhelming Ignorance and Fear ✦

I finished the Bank of America Technology Conference on Monday, September 10, 2001 in San Francisco by listening to Michael Dell speak to a standing room only audience about how the recent Hewlett-Packard-Compaq merger would not result in a stronger competitor for Dell, Inc. Mr. Dell was particularly direct about what he felt were the shortcomings of the strategy of HP's chairwoman, Carly Fiorina. The next morning I walked up the hill from my hotel, the Renaissance Stanford, to the Palace Hotel where the Conference was to reconvene. As I neared the crest of the hotel's hill I saw two taxi-cabs parked in the middle of the street. They had obviously come to an abrupt and awkward stop. The doors of both cabs were flung wide open and were surrounded by many Wall Street financial managers intently listening to the news report blasting from one of the taxi's radios: "That's right, I repeat, a second plane has crashed into the World Trade Center!" The normally cool, calm and collected money managers flew into a panic. Most screamed into their cell phones checking on co-workers and loved ones. Some burst into tears. Others were put into an immediate catatonic state.

My thoughts were panicked as well. "My God! I was supposed to be in that building today!" As of February, 2001 our third quarter Davis Selected Advisers board meeting was scheduled to take place on September 11, 2001, on the 92nd Floor of Tower Two of the World Trade Center. But due to a twist of fate, our firm's board members, executives, and portfolio managers are all in Chicago for our board meeting instead. This recurring thought was my obsession as I hoofed it back to my hotel. I needed to get to a television to see what the hell was happening. I needed access to news!

I turned on the TV and saw an unimaginable sight. One of the WTC towers collapsed in front of my eyes. I thought to myself: "Those buildings have 100,000 workers!" "This had to be an intentional attack!" "Last week Vornado almost won a bid against Larry Levine for the World Trade Center." "Did anyone I know die in that?" "The other tower is on fire!" "Will they attack the Golden Gate Bridge?" "What the hell is going on?" Composure was almost impossible.

As hours vanish in front of the television I eventually made many phone calls into the late evening. I confirmed with tear-filled friends that they had lost old friends and associates in the attack. Mercifully, I confirmed that my co-workers were all fine. My most important call was with my fellow Portfolio Manager, Andrew Davis. Neither of us has ever dealt with a situation like this in our portfolio management careers and we were both overwhelmed with feelings of ignorance and fear as we tried to understand the infinite possibilities. Given a choice on this day, both Andrew and I would have preferred not to be the custodians of our shareholders' dreams and responsible for their money. But the deep responsibility was ours and was inescapable. The question was: What are we going to do?

Introducing Principle One: Infinity

Considered from a secular perspective this principle is:

The universe is infinite.

In terms of the most important investment skill, that of "understanding information," you must begin at the beginning with the undifferentiated landscape of infinite possibilities of available information. Principle I, Infinity, addresses the "information" half of "understanding information." This could be the most recent Gross Domestic Product report; it could be the bringing in of a new Chief Executive Officer at a prospective, or current, investment; or it could be a cold snap in Chile. The possibilities are endless. Acknowledgment of this Principle insists that you consider the full information landscape to ensure that you do not leave anything important out in your evaluation of an investment.

Principle I, Infinity, is the first fact underlying the functioning of the right brain. This is because the right brain is designed for the organic, multi-dimensional possibilities of the universe, and less so for the linear, two-dimensional structures of the abstract world. A part of the essence of the principle of Infinity is that all things are *possible*. If all things are not possible then the universe is not infinite.

Because the universe is infinite, it also means that you are a part of It. If you are not a part of It, then the universe is not infinite. Principle I means that you are not separate from the universe. And *that* provides the natural bridge leading to the other large part of the essence of the first principle—everything is *interconnected*. You are a part of the universe. This means that while the concepts of you and me exist, they are both a part of the **whole** universe. Principle I insists that you seek out these interconnections to best understand the world and thus make better investment decisions.

The vast details of infinite possibilities are the very material that investors are confronted with on a daily basis as they try and understand information. In order to make sense of all of this detail you need to be able to separate out signal from noise, the probable from the improbable, decision from indecision, gain from loss, relevant from irrelevant, knowledge from ignorance, fear from anxiety, and so on. You must be able to see the landscape. The principle of Infinity, tells you the nature of that landscape: vast and interconnected. With that knowledge it is possible to have understanding.

At first, Principle I may seem unnecessarily generalized or obtuse, but it serves as the basis for the rest of the Principles and the rest of the book. It may seem like a philosophical concept, but the Infinity Principle is not. Many scientists across many disciplines believe that the universe is infinite and interconnected.[9] In fact, quantum physics' clearly established nonlocality principle is evidence of Principle I's rootedness in reality. Nonlocality simply suggests that everything is interconnected.

Because the universe is infinite you need tools that help you to be in alignment with that vast and bewildering landscape, namely boundary identification and exploration. Principle I, Infinity, asks you to be as free of boundaries as possible. For example, in order to wrap the mind around a bewildering event like September 11, 2001, an understanding of personal strengths and limitations is needed. What is more, an understanding of the interconnections of the daunting flow of information is needed—otherwise there is paralysis and an inability to make critical, timely decisions.

> *"Only as you do know yourself can your brain serve you*
> *as a sharp and efficient tool. Know your own failings,*

---

[9] Alex Vilenkin, Ph.D., *Many Worlds in One*, a physicist; Dean Radin, Ph.D., *The Conscious Universe*, electrical engineer and psychologist; has an extensive summary of scientific opinion about the topic; Amit Goswami, Ph.D., *The Self-Aware Universe*, quantum physicist; has an extensive summary of scientific opinion about the topic; and Michael Talbot, *The Holographic Universe*, author; has an extensive summary of scientific opinion about the topic.

passions, and prejudices so you can separate them
from what you see."

—BERNARD BARUCH, American Financier, Investor (1870–1965)

For intuition to work fully-fledged, emotions have to be consciously controlled. Otherwise emotions introduce projected prejudice into the signal we receive from our intuitive sense. While emotions do obscure the valuable information that comes to us via our intuition, unlike the typical thinking in the investment world, we do not want to be free of our emotions.

Emotions serve to identify personal boundaries, and consequently opportunities for expansion of ourselves and of investment expertise. The right brain likes vast, unfettered possibilities. This is the basis of Principle I, Infinity. So to be more in accord with the first principle of the Intuitive Investor, personal boundaries need to be identified, considered and allowed to either expand or be eliminated. Two of the strongest emotions encountered as investors are those surrounding ignorance and those surrounding fear.

The Gift of Ignorance: Separating the Unknown from the Known

What is the typical and instinctive emotional response to feeling "in over your head?" For most, the response is to mentally seize up and to avoid the situation that led to emotions surrounding ignorance. Most want these difficult emotions to immediately desist. Feeling ignorant is most often very uncomfortable and surrounded with tremendous emotion. This is especially true when answers to a problem are desperately needed, or when the costs of a bad, or delayed decision cannot be afforded. For me, on September 11, 2001, in addition to the fear I felt as a citizen of a country under attack, I wanted desperately to run away from my emotions of feeling ignorant. I did not want to be the one responsible for having the answers about the likely future state of the world and the affect the attacks would have on my shareholders' investments. Yet, still after many years as a successful investor I am presented with problems for which I do not know the immediate and obvious answer. I also know that my reflex is still to duck, turn, and run for cover in these moments—this is a natural, reflexive response. Yet investors do not have the option of turning away from these moments. So what can be done?

Moments of general investment ignorance are *always* large money-making opportunities. This is because many other investors confronted with the same situation are also experiencing the same strong emotions caused by feeling ignorance that you are, and they are running from those emotions. Their choice to punt is your potential gold mine if you can overcome your emotions surrounding ignorance and turn your emotions into advantage.

That moment where you recognize you feel ignorant is an extraordinarily valuable gift because you have an unambiguous sense of the limitations of what you know. Furthermore, if you have consciousness in that moment then you also have an unambiguous sense of your limitations in how to apply what you know to solve the investment problem at hand. Noticing the limits of your knowledge then allows you to place yourself on a mental map that includes all of **what you know** and all of **what you do not know**. Best of all, ignorance has an obvious and simple remedy: increase your knowledge.

The steps to turning your feeling of ignorance into a powerful investment tool:

1. *Conscious recognition* of when you feel ignorant.

2. *Overcome* your emotional response

3. *Expand* yourself by ending the ignorance; if necessary repeat steps 1-3

4. *Move forward*

CONSCIOUS RECOGNITION

The essential key is to notice when you feel ignorant. When you notice that you feel ignorant, incapable, overwhelmed, dense, illiterate, inexperienced, moronic, obtuse and thick, you are well on the way to transforming the crippling emotions associated with ignorance into an invaluable tool. I have given you this long list of synonyms, because words are lenses for focusing thought-energy, and it can help you to recognize the many hues of feeling ignorant.

Daily you must invest in yourself by increasing your conscious awareness of your emotions surrounding feelings of ignorance. Often the emotions that need focusing on are so much a part of yourself that you cannot easily divorce yourself from them. Earlier you consciously separated your words from your experience of the temperature of a room. That was a *conscious* act of interrupting your normal reflexive program of assigning words to sensory stimuli. The goal here is very similar: interrupt your reflexive response to emotions around ignorance and gain consciousness of the moment when you experience these emotions.

OVERCOME

You must begin to treat emotions about ignorance in a conscious and objective fashion. Thus, in the future when you have these emotions, rather than choosing to identify with the ignorance, you treat the emotions about ignorance as an object, or as a specimen to be studied and not felt. It helps to actually picture the emotions relating to ignorance as some *thing*. Then you can begin to divorce yourself from your emotions.

For example, you might choose to picture your feelings about being ignorant as a dark room that you cannot peer into. The dimensions of the room are unknown and its contents are never seen in full light. Confronted with the dark room you instinctively rush past it. You do not have to use my example here. Instead, if you can put the brakes on your emotions by another method then feel free to do so. The idea is to objectify the emotions so that you can disrupt the connection between your emotions surrounding your state of ignorance and your automatic defensive responses. You move from having the *experience* of your emotions to being the *observer* of your emotions.

To be clear, the goal *is* to feel the emotions caused by your state of ignorance, not to dismantle them. This is because your emotions powerfully indicate that you have hit a personal boundary. So the goal is to avoid responding to your emotions with unconscious aversion. Instead, you want to have that conscious queasy-feeling moment wherein you know definitively that you have arrived at the edge of your knowledge boundary, as communicated to you by your feelings of ignorance. Once you have experienced this moment you should take a deep breath and wait for the (possibly) overwhelming defensive response to your emotions about your state of ignorance to dissipate. You must be kind and forgiving of yourself since no one person knows everything. In terms of the "dark room" analogy, you have seen that dark, spooky room that represents ignorance, but instead of shuffling rapidly past for the safety of a more comfortable space you choose to peer into the darkness. That is, you choose to interrupt your normal defensive response mechanism.

EXPAND

Now create a new association with your emotions about having ignorance so that the same old aversion is irrevocably short-circuited. One technique is to change the association from a negative emotion to a positive one. You do this by celebrating that wonderful moment when you feel ignorant because emotions surrounding that moment have graciously revealed the limits of your knowledge.

MOVE FORWARD

Now you are peering into the dark room and now you want to see what lies beyond the threshold; so you turn on the light! Turning on the light is analogous to seeking out information to end the ignorance about a problem you are confronted with. That is, you seek answers to your questions. Among the questions (sources of ignorance) that Andrew and I discussed on the evening of September 11, 2001 were these: Were more attacks planned? When would the financial markets re-open? How much of our shareholders' money were we going to lose? Which industries would be shaken the most? Which of our companies had been directly affected? How would all of our companies be indirectly affected? What would be the economic impact of the attacks? How could we raise some cash, in the face of what was likely to be many fund redemptions, to take advantage of any potential buying situation? The two of us decided to assess the likely effects of the attack on each of the companies in the Davis Appreciation and Income Fund. We then decided we would compare notes once our individual evaluations were done. Even after our discussion, we still were ignorant of the answers. But we had short-circuited the strong emotional response to ignorance—running away from our massive problem of a lack of understanding of the pertinent information—and we began to place ourselves on a mental map. Our ignorance pointed us in a natural direction in order to get our questions answered and to expand our ability to understand the information of September 11, 2001.

By following the steps outlined you automatically become a better investor by making productive use of your emotions surrounding ignorance instead of letting them limit you. Now many previously impossible things are now, newly possible.

INVESTMENT APPLICATIONS

1. Consciously feeling the emotions about being ignorant gives you an intellectual compass that tells you that you need more infor-

mation in order to make a better decision. As long as you are conscious of when you feel ignorant, and are dogged about overcoming your ignorance, then your investment decisions are automatically better informed. On September 11, 2001, both Andrew Davis and I felt ignorant. Our ignorance dictated the direction of our fact-finding so that we could answer our many important questions. Let the gift of ignorance guide your understanding of investment information.

2. With a better sense of your own emotional response to feelings of ignorance you now notice emotions about ignorance in others. Now you notice the compensatory things that people do. This clues you in to the veracity of, and quality of, the information that others provide. The information could be a company's annual report, a company's quarterly earnings conference call, a story in a newspaper, an article published on the Internet, or a brokerage firm's analyst report.

The Gift of Fear:[10] How Fear Limits You and Distorts Your Intuition

I guarantee investing triggers fear. When it does you thank your lucky stars for the invaluable gift of recognition of your personal boundaries and limitations. In this moment you learn more about who you are and can elect to change and grow as an investor. Additionally, another layer of the onion that obscures the proper functioning of your intuition can be peeled away.

Fear-expert, Gavin De Becker, a three-time presidential appointee whose pioneering work changed the way the U.S. government evaluates threats to its highest officials states the following:

> "[R]eal fear [is] not like when we are startled, not like the fear we feel at a movie, or the fear of public speaking. [Real] fear is the powerful ally that says, 'Do what I tell you to do.'"[11]

---

[10] Gavin De Becker, "In the Presence of Danger," *The Gift of Fear: and Other Survival Signals that Protect Us from Violence: 10th Printing* (New York: Dell Publishing, 1998).

[11] Gavin De Becker, *The Gift of Fear: and Other Survival Signals that Protect Us from Violence: 10th Printing* (New York: Dell Publishing, 1998), 5.

✦ Not Letting Fear Get in the Way of Making a Decision ✦

In the early days of my investment management career I was a lowly research analyst—a position that granted me the power of buying and selling suggestion, but not discretion. My boss, a Portfolio Manager, was on a bicycling vacation in Morocco. So when a dramatic piece of news regarding one of our Fund's businesses, U.S. Restaurant Properties, hit the newswires I could only pass along the information, not decide what to do. In response to the news, the price of the company's stock proceeded to drop precipitously.

My co-worker, who was the analyst for the Davis Real Estate Fund, and my de facto superior while my boss was incommunicado, intuitively feels that the right thing to do is buy more shares of stock in U.S. Restaurant Properties. However, he is *terrified* that he might make the wrong decision. He wants to confirm that it's ok with our boss to buy additional shares. So my co-worker, in this era before global cellular phone coverage, tries fruitlessly to reach our boss in Morocco. Unfortunately, the financial markets do not wait for an investor's fear to subside and there was a strong chance that this unique buying opportunity would quickly fade. What to do? I overcame my fear, honored my intuition that buying then was the correct decision, and called my institutional salesperson at Cantor Fitzgerald to place a buy order on behalf of our boss and our shareholders. My fearful co-worker was imploring me to stop, saying, "He will be very angry that you did this. Are you sure you want to do this?" I did.

Eventually our boss called to check in and he asked to speak with my co-worker who enumerates what has happened since the last check in. Among the things he mentioned was U.S. Restaurant Properties' bad news and my commensurate purchase of additional shares in the business. My boss said absolutely nothing. In fact, I talked with him to give him the news about the Fund for which I work and I specifically brought up the purchase and asked if it was ok. He said, "Sure," and immediately moved on to something else that he felt was more important. Eventually the purchase of these additional shares turned out to be a good decision for Davis shareholders. My co-worker never moved past his overall investing anxiety and left the investment business shortly thereafter.

In Mr. De Becker's quote he is making a distinction between anxieties and fears. Anxiety is an unconscious manifestation of old emotional traumas, whereas fear is a *natural* and essential intuitive feeling from deep within yourself that serves as a warning of an impending threat that could potentially be harmful to you.

The emotion of anxiety is among the most self-destructive in investing. Anxiety can paralyze and lead to catatonic indecision. Yet investing demands that timely, lucid decisions are made even in the presence of discomfort. Worst of all, anxiety is one of the most powerful obstructions to a healthy intuition.

Symptoms of the anxiety disease are: convincing yourself you are not good at math; that you need someone else's help in making important decisions; that you *don't* need someone else's help in making important decisions for yourself; that your financial situation is adequate; that your financial situation is inadequate; and that you have already achieved all that you are capable of achieving.

Imagine that you are placing a buy order for a stock with your broker and you begin shaking and start sweating before you can place the call. You feel as if you are feeling genuine fear and you hesitate to buy, shelving the decision for later. This example of "fear" is most likely an example of "anxiety" as indicated by the physical response of nervousness (the shaking and sweating) and the hesitation to act (shelving the decision for later), as opposed to the definitive action suggested by Mr. De Becker.

Genuine fear is a deeply intuitive sense that let's you know that your investment interests are in danger. For example, imagine you are about to purchase shares of stock in a business that your friend recommended to you. On the very day you intend to purchase your shares you have a feeling of crystalline clarity and are fearful of a purchase—you don't think twice about it and do not purchase the stock. In this case, your fear is likely rational and serving you because you feel there a genuine chance of losing your money. Fear, in this instance, is demonstrable because your experience is associated with feelings of clarity and definitive, immediate action.

These examples highlight a critical distinction, the difference between the *emotion of anxiety* and the *feeling of real fear*. You can neither afford to be paralyzed by anxiety nor let anxiety obstruct your intuition. You also cannot afford to ignore intuitive feelings of fear that may save you tremendous amounts of money. Being a good investor means learning to make both anxiety and fear your allies. Both, like ignorance, are important gifts for recognizing your arrival at a personal boundary. In the case of anxiety, you will want to overcome the personal boundary that your anxiety erects and that manifests in investing as confusion, indecision and hesitation. In the case of fear, you will want to honor its intuitive message and stay well within your personal boundaries.

Here are the essential steps for turning anxiety and fear into powerful investment tools:

1. *Recognize* when you feel fear/anxiety; if it is fear, stop; if it is anxiety, then you can continue.

2. *Transform* your emotion of anxiety from an emotion to a thought.

3. *Examine* the source of your emotion of anxiety.

4. *Evaluate* whether or not your defensive mechanisms are still serving you.

5. *Dismantle* the defensive mechanism if it is not serving you.

6. *Recondition* yourself by making a decision in the presence of the anxiety.

7. *Expand* beyond your current, self-imposed limitations.

RECOGNIZE

The essential key is to learn how to tell the difference between the emotion of anxiety and the feeling of fear. To tell the difference between anxiety and fear you need to understand how these responses arise.

Responses of anxiety and fear are experienced when there is first a stimulus, or a cause. Then there is usually an automatic and unconscious response, an effect. This sequence of the initial stimulus to the automatic, unconscious response must be interrupted. In these moments it's likely that you feel you have no control over yourself. Fight and flight! Bystanders beware. You may wonder to yourself: Was I born this way? Am I hard-wired to respond this way? In general, the answer is "no." There are reasons for the unconscious response.

It is likely that in your emotional past there was once a "new-to-you-at-the-moment" situation in which you felt threatened and vulnerable. In short, in this moment you had no appropriate tool to combat or overcome the threat. Hence, in this seed-moment you experienced *real* fear. These high stress moments are survived and whatever solution *seemed* to work at the time becomes the "way of dealing with" this particular type of problem.

It's as if the brain long ago created a mini-computer program taking the form of an "if-then" statement. If stimulus x then response y. So, in Pavlovian-like fashion, the brain continues to respond to similar situations in the present with the same old feelings of vulnerability and anxiety. The problem with this is that if the original, fear-inducing stimulus happened to a person aged 5, then the solution-routine to that fear stimulus still in use represents a 5-year-old child's emotional technology.

So a primary difference between anxiety and fear is that new difficult situations, for which you have no natural learned response, usually trigger actual fear. Whereas, if you have dealt with a similar fearful situation in the past for which you have an automatic, conditioned response, then this is most likely anxiety. But the reason that the brain constructed these defensive mechanisms, experienced as anxiety, is that the source of our intuition is deeply sensitive and is easily wounded. We all have experienced emotional trauma. These past events wounded our feeling selves so defenses were purposely and usefully erected to prevent further damage. The trick is to gain conscious control over when these defenses are up and when they are down and also to evaluate whether or not they are still necessary.

Unconscious anxiety does not serve you. Anxiety is the blur of emotion that makes your thinking hazy and prevents you from dismantling old, reflexive, restrictive emotional responses. Anxiety prevents you from growing as a person and as an investor. Fear serves you. It lets you know that you need to pay attention—that the fish is out of its water.

So when you are experiencing what feels like fear, you must stop and ask yourself if this is in response to a new, difficult, and threatening situation. Or is your response similar to many other similar situations in your past? If this is a new situation, you have to honor your feeling of fear. If you find your response to the situation to be the result of an old pattern, then proceed to the next step.

TRANSFORM

Next, it is essential to short-circuit your unconscious anxiety mechanism. Ideally, you still want to experience your anxiety so that you are conscious of approaching and bumping up against your personal boundary. You do not need to experience the stress of your emotions to recognize and deal with them. Instead you choose to transform your emotions into thoughts. When you do this you accomplish two things: you protect your sensitive feeling mechanism, and you gain mental awareness of your emotions. This mental awareness allows you to change them (a hallmark of the left brain).

So when you experience anxiety, calm down by assuring yourself that you are safe and that you are not in immediate harm. With this breathing room, you now change your anxiety from an emotion into a thought. This may take some practice, but it *is* possible.

If you have trouble with this practice, try to picture your emotion of anxiety as a rare, elusive and endangered leopard whose appearance is always unexpected and fleeting, yet scary. Further, you are an experienced naturalist looking to understand and preserve this rare and wondrous predator. For many years you have been looking forward to a sighting of this rare beast so you persevere through your anxiety and go out in search of this beastie. Ideally this exercise helps you to objectify your anxiety so that you can separate it from your reflexive response. This allows you to switch from the *experiencer* of your emotions to the *observer* of your emotions.

This practice of transforming emotion into thought will likely be ongoing, but it will be rewarding. For those of you who take pride in being "sensitive" this may be a difficult tool to integrate into your repertoire. This is because you may feel this tool is in direct violation of your identity. I promise that this tool does not make you less sensitive. Instead, it makes you healthier because it gives you options with regard to your emotions. By gaining conscious awareness of your feelings then you can **choose** to be affected by them or not. Ultimately, this makes you more effective as a person and more effective as an investor.

EXAMINE

After you transform your *emotions* of anxiety to *thoughts* by objectifying them, your next step is to examine the source of your anxiety. Remember, it may be that your feelings of fear are entirely appropriate given your situation. But the overwhelming majority of the time what masquerades as fear is anxiety. Additionally, those anxieties are an emotional response created in the past when you felt vulnerable and incapable in a situation.

Now, if you can, go back to the original event where you created your anxiety response. It is usually the case that when you examine the original event that led you to feel anxiety you discover that your anxiety and fear **was entirely justified** in the original moment. In the original moment you were probably very young or inexperienced and you lacked the emotional or intellectual tools necessary to deal with the situation. This realization is your "get out of jail free card" for any continued feelings of guilt, shame or inadequacy associated with the original event. That is, your original feelings were entirely warranted given the circumstances. Forgive yourself for not being perfect and invulnerable—no one is either of those things. But: CHOOSE TO MOVE ON.

Now that you have identified the source of your emotions of anxiety, ask yourself: Is your defense mechanism still serving you? In all likelihood the answer is that your continued emotions of anxiety in response to current situations that are similar to your original frightening event are **not** serving you. This is because you likely now have many years of life experience and have solved many other more complicated and difficult situations than the original one. This means you no longer need to feel anxiety in these situations.

Alternatively, instead of evaluating whether your defense mechanism is still serving you, you can evaluate the ways that this anxiety is limiting you from embodying your full personal power.

DISMANTLE

Now, to the best of your ability, you dismantle anxieties no longer serving you. Then you recondition yourself so that you do not respond to certain situations with unconscious and, often, uncontrollable anxiety. One method is to imagine yourself as two separate people: the original, fearful you that created the anxiety defense mechanism, and the new, more capable, less vulnerable you. The new, more capable you reassures the old, fearful you that you are now all right and that the original source of your fear can no longer bother you. This technique is one that I have personally used to dismantle anxieties.

INVESTMENT APPLICATIONS

1. Because you now recognize your anxiety you can move past it and make more decisive investment decisions. This peace of mind makes investing more comfortable and something you are more willing to consciously participate in. In the Morocco example my co-worker's anxiety led to indecisiveness, and ultimately greater emotional turmoil. This meant that his job was always uncomfortable for him and he ended up leaving the business.

2. Eliminating anxiety means your investment decisions are timely. Good timing is one of the essential ingredients to investment success as real opportunities disappear quickly. My former co-worker's anxiety almost led to our firm missing out on a timely and rare investment opportunity.

3. Being aware of your anxiety means you can recognize it in others. As you analyze the world around you this gives you actionable investment information. For example, imagine you see the executive of a business you are interested in investing on television and she answers a question about the upcoming year's revenue outlook but the answer has a hint of anxiety. This lets you know that the investment is more risky than previously believed.

4. Recognizing your anxiety clearly tells you when have reached a personal boundary. That lets you stop and evaluate your boundary. Ultimately, that helps you to become a more decisive investor. In the Moroccan example my co-worker's anxiety boundary prevented him from acting and that would have unnecessarily cost our shareholders' money. I had a similar anxiety boundary but the difference was that after evaluating myself, and the situation, I chose to move past my boundary. That decision made me a better investor and to make money for my shareholders.

5. Recognizing genuine fear (versus anxiety) gives you an unambiguous alert that you need to not invest. On September 11, 2001, I experienced lots of anxiety, but also genuine fear. The genuine fear led Andrew Davis and me to thoroughly evaluate the world. Much of the money I made for shareholders was earned in the subsequent years based on decisions made in the aftermath of September 11, 2001.

6. Gaining control over anxiety removes one of the principal obstacles allowing you to move your intuition from serendipity to a tool.

The Intuitive Investor and You: Self-Assessment

Reflect on some of the following questions to become better acquainted with the infinite possibilities of the information landscape.

Do you ever feel awed by the vastness of information in your life? How do you process through this information to get to the information that is important to you? Is it sometimes difficult to tell the difference between one piece of information and other pieces of information? What emotions are associated with the vastness of information?

Have you ever traced the interconnections between an important event in your life and all of the elements of it as they unfolded? If so, when you were tracing the various causes that led to your experience, at what point did you stop? What emotions did you experience when you traced the causes of your experience?

What investment situations make you feel ignorant? When you feel this way, what is your usual response? In what ways does your usual response benefit you, or place an artificial boundary around your capabilities? Can you imagine responding in a different way? Have you ever been grateful for having your ignorance pointed out to you? If so, what made you feel grateful?

What investment situations make you feel anxious? How do you usually respond to these situations? How has your anxiousness either benefitted, or limited you? Does your anxiety place a boundary around your abilities as an investor? Is it possible for you to respond differently next time? Have you ever confronted your investment anxiety? If so, how did you confront it? What were the results?

Have you ever experienced the type of fear that led to stark clarity and immediate action? If so, how much did you have to *think* about your response to the situation? What led to you feeling real fear? If you have experienced real fear, but rationalized your experience, what led you to make this choice? If this deeply intuitive signal occurs in your life again, what will your response be?

Write your reflections down in your notebook. The following exercises will help you to gain greater comfort with the infinite possibilities of the information landscape. Specifically they will help you to better understand Principle I, Infinity, and help you to make ignorance and fear your investment allies.

Exercises

DEVELOPING COMFORT WITH VAST INFORMATION Becoming a more intuitive investor requires that you begin to both perceive the investment landscape, as well as how you personally relate to that landscape. What do you know and what do you not know? What do you understand and what do you not understand? What are you capable of deciding, and what are you not capable of deciding?

Choose an investment situation that feels overwhelming to you. This could be because of the vast amounts of information available, including differing opinions; it could be because of the many undifferentiated choices available to you; it could be because the current investment climate is chaotic, or some other reason.

In your notebook write down each of the pieces of information you know about this investment situation. Record each piece of information as separate islands floating on the page.

Now record how you relate to each of these pieces of information. For example, do you understand a given piece of information? Do you know where to get an answer to any question that you may have? How did you come by the information that you recorded? Are you comfortable with the information that you have put in your notebook? What parts of your record make you feel good, and why so? What parts of the investment information make you feel ill at ease, and why so?

Imagine the following: What are your limits in understanding the investment? Where do the boundaries of your comfort with the investment lie? What do you wish you knew, but don't know about the investment? Are you comfortable enough to make a decision?

RECOGNIZING VAST INTERCONNECTIONS The goal of this exercise is to begin to understand the myriad things that affect the quality of an investment. When doing this exercise use very small writing to ensure that you don't run out of room.

Select an investment that you would like to understand better. In the center of a page in your notebook in small writing, put the name of the investment; then circle it. Around this center begin writing the major things that interest you in this investment. This could be: a low P/E ratio; a quality management team; your satisfaction with their products; its success at competing in the marketplace; the overall level of the stock market; someone you trust's recommendation; the point of the economic cycle; or a high dividend. Circle each of these nodes. Now draw lines from these nodes to the center where you wrote the name of the company.

Now consider the major things that affect each of the nodes you wrote down above. Start placing these "causes" on the page around each of the relevant nodes. Then connect these newly encircled pieces of information to the nodes you recorded above.

Take it one step further. Identify causes of the causes you wrote down above and place these along with the others. Connect these new causes to the previous ones.

What patterns in the interconnections do you see, if any? Do any of these causes repeat themselves? If so, these are likely major issues to be aware of. Do any of these causes seem like root causes? That is, causes that begin the cascade of falling dominoes that might affect your investment. Highlight any chain of events that **feels** important to you.

For example, you might have a sequence like this: Apple Computer ← my daughter loves her iPod ← my daughter isn't the only one ← consumers are buying expensive gadgets ← consumers are buying ← salaries are rising. Here you would start with Apple Computer and then proceed with the other nodes until you got to a root cause; in this case: consumers are buying. Another node, also starting at the center with Apple Computer, might be: Apple Computer ← my friend owns Apple stock ← my friend has made money in Apple ← my friend got a raise. This node terminates at a similar point to the previous node. In this case, your interconnections analysis may have identified a root cause for considering an investment in Apple: consumer incomes are rising.

OVERCOMING IGNORANCE Write down the following responses in your notebook. In which investment situations do you feel ignorant? Perhaps it is some investment jargon or the difference between a Treasury bill and a Treasury bond; it doesn't matter. For how long have these situations made you feel ignorant? What is your response when these investment situations arise? In what ways do your responses limit you and limit your improvement as an investor? What has prevented you from getting more knowledge to help end your feelings of ignorance? In what ways can you objectify these emotions so that you can overcome them? What concrete things are you going to do to overcome these feelings of ignorance?

ANXIETY REVIEW Toward the end of the day when things are slowing down review the events of the past week. Write down in your notebook any moments in which you felt anxiety. These could have been about global issues, political issues, relationship issues, work-related issues, health issues, or even finance issues. The more anxiety issues you can think of the greater the benefit this exercise will have for you (you can include in the list any anxiety you feel about doing the exercise).

Record your response to these anxious moments. In what ways did your anxiety limit you? Be honest with yourself and feel free to take the time necessary to understand those limits.

Aim to describe when you feel your anxiety, where in your body you feel it, when it gets worse, when it gets better, when it first started, and what are the effects in your life of this particular anxiety? Do any of these moments seem to be part of a pattern? If so, try and name the pattern and describe it in your notes.

In the forthcoming week make a promise to yourself to monitor the situations that make you anxious. As you begin to gain consciousness over these moments you will be able to interrupt the painful feelings of anxiety that you experience. The important thing is to simply recognize when feelings of anxiety rise within you.

If you feel like it, repeat this exercise until you gain consciousness over when you feel anxiety. This exercise, the daily review of your feelings, will lead to you having a greater ability to recognize your daily flow of emotions. Greater consciousness of your emotions will allow you to transform your fears and anxieties into powerful investment tools.

Now that you have your anxiety survey, when you are thinking about your investments try and recognize when your anxieties arise. As you recognize these anxieties describe them in your notebook using the same approach described earlier.

INVESTMENT SKILL INVENTORY It is important to understand your strengths and weaknesses as an investor. Your goal is to understand your boundaries with regard to the investment information landscape. However, in this exercise I am going to have you begin somewhere else.

Consider some of the best decisions that you have made in your life. Write down the factors that led you to making these choices. What aspects of the decision were you comfortable with at the time you made your decision? Record these factors. What things were you uncomfortable with? Record these, too.

Which personal strengths have continually helped you to make good decisions? This could be an ability to comprehend analytical information. It could be an unflappable quality that makes you cool under fire. It could be a willingness to try new things. Whatever your strengths, write those down.

Now repeat the exercise, but instead write down some of the worst decisions that you have made in your life. Which personal weaknesses, if any, led to you making a bad decision? It could be that you didn't have enough information. It could be that you trusted someone that you shouldn't have trusted. It could be that you entered a decision with too much bravado. Write down your weaknesses as you perceive them. Try and have fun with this exercise; after all, these events are in the past now.

Your catalog of strengths and weaknesses are a reflection of how you make choices. Since investing is simply consciously making choices so that the benefits of those choices exceed the costs of those choices, your catalog will also reveal your strengths and weaknesses as an investor.

Knowing who you are allows you to develop tools to more fully exploit your strengths. For example, if you have an excellent capacity for understanding numbers, then the pursuit of numerical financial analysis is likely to improve your investment returns. Alternatively, you may have an excellent capacity for creative thinking. Therefore, you can focus on uncovering seismic changes to the business landscape.

Knowing your emotional and knowledge-based weaknesses allows you to avoid the pitfalls associated with these limitations that would hurt your investments. For example, you suffer from unnecessary bravado that causes you to choose overly aggressive investments relative to your financial situation. Consequently, in making future investment choices, you consciously evaluate prospective choices to ensure that your bravado is in check.

EMOTIONAL INVENTORY Increasing your knowledge about your personal emotional boundaries is an essential starting point for becoming a more intuitive investor. Because emotions distort the clear signals communicated by the intuitive feeling self, it is important that you gain consciousness about your emotions. This allows you to short circuit their operation.

Begin by writing a brief autobiography in your notebook. You know this story already. These are the events of your life that you choose to share with new acquaintances, your friends, your children, and your spouse. This is the story of yourself you relate at cocktail parties and with strangers with whom you strike up a conversation. Go ahead and write down those events now; feel free to write these stories down in the manner that feels best.

Record answers to the following questions in your notebook. Why are these the events you chose to write down? Why do they hold importance for you? What emotions are tied up with each of these events? What did you learn from these events? How did these events shape you?

Pay particularly close attention to strong emotions surrounding an event, such as anxiety, pride, elation, shame, regret, revulsion, or awe. Are these strong emotions still serving you? In what way do these aspects of your personality limit you? Can you imagine yourself without these limitations?

Record your experience with this exercise with an eye toward being conscious of your emotions and how they limit your ability to change and grow.

PERMISSION TO CHANGE Consider the following question: What is the most important relationship in your life? After you have spent a little while considering the question, write down your answer in your personal notebook.

Normally the answer to any investment question is: it depends. However, there is a right answer to this exercise's question. The answer may surprise you. The most important relationship in your life is with *yourself*.

The beautiful thing about this is that you are the only one who gets a choice in the quality of that relationship. No one else gets a vote. You can be loving and forgiving with yourself, or you can be hateful and unforgiving.[12]

Now in your notebook, consider the following question: In what ways are the choices you have made in your relationship with yourself still serving you? Because you are the only one who gets a vote in how your relationship with yourself is, you are the only one who can grant permission to change yourself.

Return now to the answers you wrote down in the Emotional Inventory exercise. Are you able to push past the emotional boundaries you identified earlier as limiting you? These two exercises, taken in conjunction, make you a better investor because you now have an honest assessment of your capabilities and limitations. And this always suggests a clear pathway for getting better: cross your boundaries.

The principal benefits of taking the emotional inventory and giving oneself permission to change is to gain consciousness of oneself. With this self-knowledge in hand you automatically will be making better investments. Additionally, you will also end up with a topographical map of who you are relative to all of the other myriad possibilities out there.

---

12 John Selby, *Seven Masters, One Path: Meditation Secrets from the World's Greatest Teachers* (New York: HarperSanFrancisco, 2004), 109.

REVIEW

This chapter saw the introduction of Principle I: Infinity. This first principle of *Intuitive Investing* teaches that the universe is full of infinite possibilities and interconnections. Adherence to Principle I means that you extend your boundaries outward from yourself to encompass as much as you can, and ideally, everything. This wide view of the investment information landscape ensures that you do not leave out any important information, any possibility with regard to that information, or any interconnections with regard to that information. This ensures that you begin without prejudices. A lack of prejudice allows access to the right brain and ensures new and now assessment of investment possibilities.

Now you also have tools to recognize your personal boundaries: awareness of when you experience emotions from ignorance and anxiety. You also have a topographical map of who you are relative to everything else. Thus, you now have improved your perception of the investment landscape. Thinking in terms of infinite possibilities, you can now seek the interconnections between events taking place in the vast information landscape.

Activation of your intuition necessitates accord with Principle I, Infinity, which, in turn, necessitates the erasing of the left brain's/ego's unnecessary emotional distortions to restore the ability to experience the universe as it really is, not how the ego would like it to be. It's likely that you now better recognize your boundaries and see a clearer path to move beyond them.

If you elected to confront both your emotions from ignorance and emotions of anxiety via this chapter's exercises you are likely to now possess valuable tools for identifying your personal boundaries. In the case of ignorance you now have a tool that automatically tells you what you need to learn to be a better investor. In the case of anxiety you have a tool that allows you to strip away old emotional architectures that prevent unfettered access to your right brain. Finally, your recognition of fear let's you know when you are safe within your personal boundaries and that you should definitively not act or change a thing.

4

The Narrow Probabilities of the Information Landscape

"But because of remarkable recent developments in cosmology, we now have answers to the ultimate cosmic questions that we have some reason to believe... The worldview that has emerged from the new developments is nothing short of astonishing... That worldview combines, in surprising ways, some seemingly contradictory features: the universe is both infinite and finite, evolving and stationary, eternal and yet with a beginning." [13]

IN TERMS OF THE MOST IMPORTANT investment skill, understanding information, you now have right-brain tools to place yourself on the topographical map of infinite investment and information possibilities. This was accomplished by erasing the boundaries erected by ignorance and anxiety. In short, we have dealt with the "information" half of understanding information. But now you need tools to begin to narrow down those possibilities; you need to move toward the "understanding" half. You need to grasp which pieces of information are directly interconnected with a prospective investment and how probable it is this information is important to you. Your right brain is a powerful tool to assist you in discernment.

Principle II, Paradox, is about separating out which information is important. In effect, it is about beginning to **see** the noteworthy features on the topographical map of the information landscape. To accomplish this, three skills are introduced: contexts, continuums, and scale. All three skills are in accord with the second principle. Contexts help to make sure you are

13 Alex Vinlenkin, Ph.D., *Many Worlds in One: The Search for Other Universes* (New York: Hill & Wang, 2006), 5-6.

looking at the right map. Scale helps you to fine tune your vision of the map with its features. Continuums help you to zero in on the specific features of the information landscape's topography.

The chapter concludes with self-assessments and exercises designed to help you fully absorb the information. The goal is for you to exit the chapter with tools that help you to begin to zero-in on relevant information using your right brain's intuitive powers.

✦ The Importance of Discernment ✦

In the late 1990s there was a vast convergence of technologies happening. People were buying cellular telephones in increasing numbers. They were also buying Personal Digital Assistants (PDAs) to replace their old personal organizers. Manufacturers of both phones and PDAs were planning devices that combined both technologies to maximize consumer convenience. A Battle Royale was about to ensue between the cell phone companies and the PDA manufacturers for dominance of this "converged" industry. But there was an additional wrinkle.

Simultaneously, communications companies were beginning to roll out broadband Internet service that was likely to make dial-up modem access of the Internet a thing of the past. The executives of both cellular companies and PDA companies were promising a new technology that would combine all three products in one: a cellular phone and a PDA with high-speed Internet access. Both industries referred to this technology as 3G, which is short for Third Generation cell phone technology.

In turn, the cellular tower industry used the sexy story of 3G to attract billions of dollars in investor capital. Yet, there were not currently enough cell phone users to justify the premature $ billions that had been invested in vast cellular networks. Dependant upon more cell towers being built out, the cell phone industry was on the hunt for the "killer app" (the cell phone application) that would be sexy enough to attract the millions of new cell phone users that will make the economics of 3G cellular networks possible.

As a research analyst focusing on cellular communications I knew that the network of cell phone towers and their electronics was not nearly fast enough to accommodate functional Internet access on a cell phone. I also knew from my understanding of the cell phone industry that microchip manufacturers didn't quite have the semiconductor technology needed to put all of this gadgetry into a single, small pocket-sized device. Yet, to hear the cellular industry's phone manufacturers and tower owners talk about it, the convergence miracle of 3G was around the corner.

I was a user of all three technologies and loved all of them. Yet, I could not wrap my mind around who would win the battle for consumer supremacy: the cell phone makers, or the PDA makers. I also could not grasp whether or not such a unified technology was even possible. If so, would the convergence happen quickly enough to justify the $ billions invested in these businesses? I was also uncertain if, and when, 3G would ever happen. And the question that the cell phone manufacturers were obsessing about was also intractable: what is the "killer app" for the cell phone industry?

Unfortunately for my shareholders, I improperly assessed a number of the critical issues. In particular, I overestimated the value of the cellular tower companies and the amount of time it would take for subscriber numbers to grow to numbers that justify the $ billions invested. However, I properly assessed the eventual existence of a converged 3G technology, which firms would succeed as the primary providers of 3G and the "killer app."

Introducing Principle II: Paradox

This principle can be secularly described as the following:

The secret to understanding the universe is accepting paradox.[14]

Principle II, Paradox, is all about *distinctions*. It is a fancy way of saying that there are many sides to every story; every investment issue has many ways of looking at it.

Principle I, Infinity, is about focusing on the whole picture, whereas Principle II, Paradox, is about focusing on the parts of the picture.

The first principle of Infinity is about accepting *all* possibilities, whereas the second principle of Paradox is about assessing the *probabilities* of those possibilities occurring.

The Principle of Infinity gives powerful insight to help you see that everything is inextricably interconnected. It is about the blurring of bound-

---

14 Received via meditation on March 6, 2005 in Santa Fe, New Mexico, USA.

aries and it is about indistinctness and the indefinable, whereas the Principle of Paradox is all about separating information from its infinite source to define it. But the nature of all definitions is that they are paradoxical.

Definitions are paradoxical because when we single out something and treat it as distinct from everything else we get the idea of its opposite. For example, when we think about something being hot, it automatically suggests its opposite, cold. Ultimately, all distinctions naturally appear as opposites and yet get their meaning from each other. This is how most people perceive the world. That is, things are seen as being distinct from one another. I am not my father or my mother, I am me. My toothpaste is not my career. A business's product is either good or bad. An investment is either a buy or a sell. A business is either growing or it is not. A management team is either good or bad.

Take for example a fundamental investment concept: the appropriate price to pay for a business. The business is either over-priced or underpriced. Yet, the only way to recognize if a business is under-priced is to also have an idea of what over-priced is. So the two ends of the price spectrum are not separable from one-another. If you remove the idea of over-priced, then under-priced loses its meaning.

Principle II, Paradox, is the second fact underlying the functioning of the right brain. Paradox arises when the linear left brain tries to make sense of the infinite, probabilistic nature of the universe. The left brain short circuits in these situations because its currency, logic, needs absolutely true answers, not relatively true answers. The left brain thinks of opposite concepts as opposed to one another, whereas the right brain feels opposite concepts as in harmony with one another. Rejection of paradoxes and emphasis on absolute answers is a sure sign of being too left-brain centric and results in poor decision making. The mental frustration felt when confronted with paradoxes is resolved when absolute answers are not pursued, but when answers with probabilities are allowed for instead. In other words, answers are found only when the mind is allowed to jump out of narrow, deterministic thinking.

Adherence to Principle II means you are in accord with the probabilistic nature of the universe. It means that you are in a position to access your right brain and its creativity and intuition. The Paradox Principle pushes you to continually seek out answers. It forces you to shed the notion of impossible and focus instead on the probable vs. the improbable. Accepting paradox also allows greater utilization of the right brain because the absurd is no longer rejected because of the need of the linear left brain for logic.

This is **not** license to let the patients run the asylum. The universe is simultaneously objective and subjective; analytical and intuitive; linear and non-linear, and so forth. That is, it is paradoxical.

In the natural world light simultaneously exists as both a wave and a particle. This paradox is known as a wavicle. Until scientists accepted this paradox they were stuck in an endless debate about the true nature of something as fundamental as light. This single-minded attempt to reconcile the opposites resulted in a distorted understanding of the universe until the paradox was accepted. The Principle of Paradox allows for the fact that two contradictory ideas can simultaneously be true. Therefore, it is also ideal for helping you to understand information. In fact, this second principle begins to address the "understanding" half of "understanding information."

Here are some very common investment paradoxes/opposites to become familiar with:

➤ Relative and Absolute—as in business valuation (P/E vs. Discounted Cash Flow based)

➤ Quality and Quantity—as in evaluating information

➤ Risk and Return—as in evaluating investment opportunity

➤ Future and Past—as in determining the value of a business now

➤ Destruction and Creation—as in the innovation cycles of a business

➤ Breadth and depth—as in seeking knowledge about an investment

RELATIVE AND ABSOLUTE

When valuing a prospective investment there are two opposite, yet complementary methods: relative valuation and absolute valuation. Relative valuation is the method that most investors use and its forms are more familiar to most. Relative valuation is seen in the familiar "comparables" analysis in real estate appraisals and in the price to earnings ratio (P/E) of stock investments.

Among its merits, relative valuation is grounded in reality because it relies upon prices that actually exist in the marketplace and avoids the shortcomings of any one analyst's, perhaps delusional, assessment of a business. Additionally, relative valuations are typically very easy to come by as they are published by any number of statistical sources. However, relative valuation is incomplete because it assumes that there is a rational basis for the valuing of an entire market. For example, in the dot.com bubble of the late 1990s and the real-estate bubble of the early 2000s, continued rising prices of individual investments were justified because a given investment was "cheap" relative to alternative investments. However, what was not questioned was whether or not the entire market was over-valued, including its lowest-priced investment.

Absolute value is important because it is less susceptible to the madness of investment bubbles. This is because the unique characteristics of an investment are built into a singular assessment that stands alone and apart from relative valuation. Unfortunately, absolute valuation, most typically in some form of "discounted cash flow" analysis, is susceptible to prejudice and preference on the part of the analyst. Here the analyst adjusts modeled variables to conform to a preconceived and preferred investment outcome. So there is no "reality check" with an actual market. Additionally, absolute analysis requires a more sophisticated understanding of a business, investment jargon, and financial analysis.

Fortunately there is an elegant solution: embrace paradox. This means using both relative and absolute valuation techniques; resulting in a robust valuation of an investment. Using both methods results in an overcoming of the shortcomings of both methods. What's more, if both relative and absolute methods are in agreement as to the value of an investment then you can have great confidence as to the real price of a business.

QUALITY AND QUANTITY

In effect, this paradox is the same argument for The Intuitive Investor. Typically investments are evaluated quantitatively, but with little effort put into qualitative assessment. But quality and quantity may also be applied to the analysis of any piece of investment information. For example, if an important retailer reports its same-store sales growth for the holiday season, it is possible to qualitatively and quantitatively evaluate the information. The same store sales figure may be suggestive of a change in direction of a trend as the retailer loses its traditional middle-class customer—a qualitative distinction. Simultaneously, you may conclude that while the retailer has lost some of its middle-class customer base, that this was a one-time occurrence. Therefore, you assign an "importance grade" to the data of 3 on a scale of 1 to 10. This helps you to assess not just the quality of a statistic, but also the magnitude of its importance.

RISK AND RETURN

In investing greater returns are often associated with greater risks. Unfortunately, there are many times when these two opposites are not combined into a more complete, complementary analysis. For example, in investment bubbles investors focus to a much greater degree on returns than on risks. Typically this drives up the prices of investments. Unfortunately, any purchase is riskier when purchased more expensively. One does not covet the same hamburger to a greater degree when it is offered at triple its normal price. In fact, most people would probably respond, "That had better be a damned good hamburger," thus recognizing the risk of a bad outcome because the price is higher. So an acute awareness on your part that the financial markets' perceived returns ≥ actual risks = a selling opportunity for an investment because those perceived returns are likely delusional.

Conversely, there are times when investors are too obsessed with risks and they anticipate economic apocalypse. In these instances where your awareness that the financial markets' perceived risks ≥ actual returns = a buying opportunity because investors' anxieties are likely overblown. So awareness of congruence between risk and return is essential for investment success.

FUTURE AND PAST

In the discussion of "there is no such thing as a future fact" this distinction was discussed at length. In short, investors must be aware that their fact gathering is complementary to actual investment decisions made about the future. Ideally, analysis has an equal amount of emphasis on factual analysis with future judgment. If either one feels too heavily weighted then the investment process needs to be adjusted to re-establish greater equilibrium

Additionally, too much of an emphasis on the past is likely to be an indication of too much of an emphasis on the left brain and its anal retention—there are always more facts to analyze. Obsession with the past is also a very strong indication of either or both the emotions of ignorance and fear being present; nothing that occurred in the past will definitively answer what will happen in the future.

Conversely, too much of an emphasis on the future is likely an indication of too much emphasis on the right brain and its susceptibility to outright fantasy. Obsession with the future is a very strong indication of too much emotion in your analysis—most likely too much enthusiasm.

DESTRUCTION AND CREATION

The nature of capitalism was described brilliantly by Joseph Schumpeter in his book, *Capitalism, Socialism and Democracy*. In short, he described it as a process of creative destruction. In a well-functioning capitalist system entrepreneurs create new ideas, new products and new businesses in a quest for profits. If these ideas are bad and do not succeed, they communicate to other prospective entrepreneurs that those ideas will not work right now and to not invest further capital in these bad ideas. If the ideas succeed then they lead to additional investment and to competition and to the destruction of old ideas and the businesses making use of those ideas. Eventually the competition is so fierce that any excess profits earned by the entrepreneurs are whittled away.

As an investor, knowing that destruction is essential for the proper functioning of a healthy capitalist system, allows you to take a deep breath in the midst of financial market downturns. Additionally, it suggests that the creative cycle is typically followed by a cycle of destruction. Both aspects of capitalism, though opposites, are essential for economic health and complementary.

BREADTH AND DEPTH

In attempting to understand information, investors need to constantly adjust back and forth between the opposites of a breadth and a depth of understanding. Principle I, Infinity, suggests that a breadth of information is important. Here you keep your mind open to any investment possibility, no matter how strange, counter-intuitive, or out of fashion. This suggests that you read and consume and process as much information as you can, yet at a shallow level. So breadth is about the information half of the "understanding information" equation.

Once something emerges topographically from the vast information landscape then you analyze that feature in-depth. That is, you shift from information to understanding. A deep understanding of information leads to a robust topographical map that leads to intelligent and intuitive assessment of investments.

What follows are three very powerful tools for making distinctions amongst the information landscape. Ultimately those distinctions lead to an understanding of information.

Contexts: Choosing a More Sensible Information Map

In the last chapter your initial map of the investment information landscape was infinite in size, but now distinctions need to be made. Possibilities need to be narrowed down to that which is interesting and investible. The first distinction is determining whether or not you are looking at the right map. That is, do you have the right *context*?

Con•text [(kon'tĕkst')]; noun. The circumstance in which an event occurs; a setting.[15]

This definition of context is perfect, so I want to spend a moment with it. "Circumstance" is the first word we'll focus on. "Circum" comes from the Latin word for circle. In the word circumstance it suggests encircling, surrounding, demarcating, etc. This entire chapter is about establishing accurate, proportionate and meaningful boundaries around information. So "circum" suggests a boundary.

"Stance," the second portion of circumstance, refers to the location of a thing, a person, an idea, an opinion, etc. In investing a thing can be virtually anything, including a business, the products of a business, the competition of a business, or the marketing of business products. A person could be the CEO of a business. Ideas represent the strategy and tactics of business execution as well as an investment thesis, such as "renewable energy" will ultimately trump "fossil fuels." Lastly, investment opinions could be your financial adviser's, a financial analyst's, a television pundit's, or yours. Thus, for our purposes, the combination of "circum" and "stance" results in a word that means establishing a boundary around investment information.

The last word in the definition of "context" is setting, meaning the environment or arena in which something takes place. In investing, setting might mean the economy, the financial markets, economic policies, the airline industry, and so forth. Setting is thus any actionable information that might result in the purchase or sale of an investment.

Taken together, the words that make up the definition of "context" mean identifying the important, investible information from everything else. Or stated another way, it means defining the circumstances of a prospective

---

15 *American Heritage Dictionary of the English Dictionary, Fourth Edition* (New York: Houghton-Mifflin Company, 2006.

investment. Proper context ensures that you are looking at the right map regarding an investment.

In the cellular telephone example at the beginning of the chapter there were many possible contexts, but several felt important: the future of the cell phone industry; the future of the PDA manufacturers; the future of the convergence of cellular and PDA technologies; and the "killer app" that would attract millions of new cell phone subscribers. Each context narrowed down the vast possibilities to questions that seemed relevant. However, each context required additional research of the information in order to lead to understanding.

The total of investment contexts is infinite; but a single investment context is finite. How does context switch from the infinite to the finite? The answer is that **you choose the context** from many others. You choose which mini-map you want to examine. This means that facts must have relevancy to you personally. This means that you are the most important part of the investment equation; not your broker, or your parents, or a Wall Street analyst, or an investment newsletter writer, or a financial magazine article.

When you choose a context you place yourself in relation to information and this is when you can begin to seek understanding. For example, it may be that you feel technology investments will do well over the next ten years. Because of your feeling you might choose the context/map of technology investments. That then becomes the point of focus for your research. It may be that you feel the stock market is overvalued. In this case your context can become one of looking for evidence on the information landscape that either supports or refutes your feeling.

Here are a few examples of investment contexts: the current economic climate; the future state of the financial markets; the current political environment; historical interest rates; a time in the middle of a war; a period after a 35% rise in stock markets; a period after you have lost your job; a time of hiring a new investment advisor; a period before purchasing a subscription to an investment newsletter; and most importantly, your interest in any of these topics.

There are two types of investment information: original data and filtered data. The best source of data as investors is original data; information with a minimal amount of analysis, manipulation and shaping by another person. This is because anytime someone analyzes data they are altering the purity of it with their own personal contexts, preferences and prejudices. Examples of high-quality, original data include (see the Appendix for where to access this information):

➤ Information submitted by a company to a financial regulator, such as the U.S. Securities and Exchange Commission

➤ Information published directly by a company, such as its press releases and quarterly and annual reports

➤ Information published by a governmental regulatory agency, such as data regarding a nation's gross domestic product

While this data has some filtering, it is minimal and therefore mostly free of prejudice. This simplifies your job as an investor. However, it may require wading through jargon. It is mostly because of jargon that investors rely upon other people's filtered data. There is nothing wrong with this as long as you are able to sort through the data and identify its prejudices so that you can make your own conclusions. Mostly the prejudices come from analysts having determined a context. Thus, a fuller understanding of the importance of context is necessary if you are to identify bias, and hence how the information has been distorted.

Context is always important because facts alone have no meaning. Facts, in and of themselves exist without context, yet it is context that gives them meaning and turns them into actual, actionable information. Facts, without context, lie undifferentiated on the investment landscape. For example, consider the following statistic:

"Real Gross Domestic Product (GDP) increased 4.9 percent."

What does this mean? You may think you know, but many assumptions must be made to believe this fact has relevancy. Maybe the assumption is that the statistic pertains to your home country. But without the country in question being named there is no context and no understanding/no real information conveyed. How does the analysis shift if, in fact, the country is Mozambique? Next, what time frame is being considered above? Knowing that it is the third quarter of 2007 for the United States provides more context, but not much.

Even with this information, the context of a *question* is needed to understand the statistic's importance. What if the question is, "How did third quarter 2007 United States GDP compare to the same quarter in 2006?" Compare that question with: "What gives you confidence that U.S. consumers felt well about the economy in the third quarter of 2007?" Very importantly, the question (i.e., the context) changes the understanding and relevancy of facts.

Many investors treat facts as answers to questions, yet they never consider what question the facts are supposedly answering. Investors also rarely check to see if there is congruency between the answer and the question.

Answers can exist by themselves but it is the question that gives them meaning. The opposite is also true, questions really only have meaning depending on the answer.

As an example, imagine the absurdity of relying upon the following answer to a question, without a question being present to give it meaning:

"Yes!"

When questions and answers are *in accord* with one another then confusion is minimized and real information is conveyed. Understanding follows. When this occurs it is safe to make decisions with the information you have. Accord is a feeling of harmony that must be sensed by you intuitively. See the exercise at the end of the chapter for help with this.

Context can also mean "point of view." To illustrate this, let's use a classic example from the movie *Annie Hall* when Alvy Singer and Annie Hall are both visiting their therapists:[16]

Alvy Singer's Therapist: "How often do you sleep together?"
Annie Hall's Therapist: "Do you have sex often?"

Alvy Singer: [lamenting] "Hardly ever. Maybe three times a week."
Annie Hall: [annoyed] "Constantly. I'd say three times a week."

Who is right in the above example? The facts are the same for both Alvy Singer and Annie Hall however, the context/point of view is radically different and consequently, the meaning is totally different. So when confronted with facts, and especially the opinions that they support, you must ask yourself: *Is the context correct?* If the context is not correct then it usually means there is bias or an attempt to mislead in the information. Yikes!

Here is an example of how improper context can mislead. Classically, in surveys, almost all people describe themselves as "above average drivers." Clearly this is impossible because averages are composed of those who are above average and those who are below average. This confusion about averages is frequently quoted as an example of the irrationality of most people. But it really is an example of a poor question asked without context.

---

[16] Internet Movie Database, http://www.imdb.com/title/tt0075686/quotes.

The question, "Do you consider yourself to be an above average driver?" is a terrible question. First, it assumes that everyone has the same criteria/context for what qualifies as above average driving. What if some drivers believe above average driving is about always obeying traffic laws? What if for others the definition is that they have never had an accident? What if some drivers consider getting to work, and back home again, in a timely (that is, fast) fashion as the appropriate criteria? Some people consider themselves to be above average drivers because they drive a low carbon emissions vehicle.

The question, "Do you consider yourself to be an above average driver?" is a context-less question; thus it is meaningless. For real data to be gathered from this question, the context must be included. Drivers should first be asked, "What criteria are appropriate to judge whether someone is an above average driver?" And then follow up that question with, "Do you consider yourself to be an above average driver by those criteria?" This gets around the fact that everyone considers themselves to be an above average driver based on *their own specific criteria*. Beware of facts conveyed without a clear context!

In the cellular phone/PDA example at the beginning of the chapter there was a lot of bluster coming out of both industries. However, the fantastical statements of 3G were incongruent with the reality that there were not enough cell phone subscribers to justify additional $billions of investments. The lack of congruency suggested that the critical issue was how each industry hoped to get more subscribers to justify the investments. In turn, that meant that the key issue that I needed to examine was: what will be the "killer app" that would attract all of the new subscribers. So my focus shifted to that singular context.

In summary, context must be understood before accepting a fact as useful and worthy of your attention in the investment decision making process. Remember too that questions and their factual answers must be in accord with one another. Context distortion is the source of much of the manipulation of statistics and facts, especially in the world of investing.

The first tool for understanding the information world outside of your personal boundaries is context. A definition of investment context is: the part of the information landscape you *feel* needs examining.

INVESTMENT APPLICATIONS

1. Knowing that you have to establish context to begin understanding information suggests the permanent first step for analysis: choosing what feels important to you.

2. Understanding the importance of congruency between questions and answers, and contexts and analysis, means that you avoid situations when the feeling of accord is not present. In turn, you are less fooled by data that has been manipulated.

Scale: How Far Above the Information Landscape to Fly

As an investor, once you have determined the information that interests you then you need to establish a relationship between your understanding and the information. Now that you know what portion of the information map you want to look at, you need to determine how you want to examine it. That is, you need to decide your preference for the map's scale.

The use of proper scale is a tremendously overlooked secret to investing success. Let me illustrate this with a question: What is the proper scale for watching a football game? Say you are seated in outer space hovering around the earth. Would that be a great seat for seeing the action? Probably not, you are way too far up from the action for anything on the playing field to be meaningful to you. Likewise, what if your eyeballs are right on top of the ball itself? You also miss most of the action, despite being in the absolute heart of the game. Clearly, you are too close for anything to be meaningful.

So what's the ideal scale to see a football game? That's a question of judgment that each of you must answer yourself. Your preference for scale should be the scale, or scales, that provide you with the most actionable investment information. However, a natural starting point for examining scale is to ask: what is the fundamental value driver of a business? It might be the amount of research and development dollars spent, the revenue per (railroad) track mile, number of website hits, quality of service, quality of products, or the customer experience.

Scale can be adjusted by numbers when the fundamental value driver of a business can be measured by quantity. Words can also be used as a scale when quality is the value driver of a business. When the value driver is how the business, its products, or its management makes you feel, then the proper scale is how you feel about these things. However, your right brain is the source of an assessment of what the fundamental value driver is in the first place.

One of my investment secrets is that I identify the fundamental operating units of a business beyond dollars and then rescale information for greater clarity. In the cell phone/PDA example the most critical scale was total market capitalization of cell phone tower companies per subscriber. This number was huge and suggested a massive over-investment in cellular network technology, especially when this number was compared with total profits per cell phone subscriber. That is, investors were paying too much money per subscriber relative to the profits generated by each subscriber.

There are numerous examples of industries that think in terms of units other than dollars, such as in the oil business, barrels of oil are the fundamental unit. So, if you know an oil company produces $100 million in profit in a quarter and you know that they also produce 5 million barrels of oil, it's useful to calculate profit per barrel of oil. You can then compare that figure to the company's competitors. This is a change of the scale from dollars to barrels of oil. In the airline industry they quote a number called "revenue per passenger mile," where miles are the fundamental unit. In the hotel business they quote the "occupancy rate," where how many hotel rooms are filled each night is the fundamental unit. In a business that is people driven, such as consulting, numerical data scaled to employee head-count is often revealing; such as sales per employee. These are all examples of changing the scale and they are designed to illuminate the fundamental quality of a business.

Can you see how adjusting the scale changes your perception, and therefore your understanding, of things? This is a critical concept for you to understand and to add to your repertoire. Anything that can be measured can have its scale changed to help illuminate valuable information.

Here are some more examples of scale in the realm of investing: number of products sold; dollars of revenue; local vs. regional vs. national vs. international opportunity for a new business idea; number of employees whose tenure is greater than five years; percentage of employees that are executives; number of machines that need to be replaced; GDP per capita; and percentage of the population over age sixty-five.

Here's one of my favorite demonstrations of how changing scale radically changes your perception of information. Say you have a million

✦ Adjusting Scale to Evaluate the Quality of a Business ✦

Imagine you have two technology companies that produce widgets. One is absolutely gigantic and, in terms of revenues and profits, dwarfs its nearest competitor. Most investors purchase the larger company because it is overwhelmingly the dominate player in the space. However, you read an article in a major business publication about the industry in which the leaders of both firms are quoted. You are impressed by the business acumen of the smaller competitor. Consequently you begin to dig into the second company's financials more deeply. Using the traditional measures that everyone else is using you can only conclude the larger company is the better investment.

However, you decide to use some alternative scales to weigh the strength of both businesses. Technology firms rely upon the creative and intuitive ideas of its employees. You conclude that people are the fundamental driver of these two companies. So you research a little and discover the headcount of each firm. You use this number to calculate profits per employee and see that the profit per employee at the smaller firm is more than double that of the dominate company.

Given that these are both technology businesses you also want to evaluate the quality of each firm's "research and development" (R&D) expenses by creating a new measurement:

$$\frac{\text{Revenues This Year} - \text{Revenues Base Year}}{\substack{\text{Total R\&D Investment} \\ \text{in Lead Time}}} = \frac{\text{Incremental Revenues}}{\substack{\text{Total R\&D Investment in} \\ \text{in Base Year}}}$$

$$= \text{Return on R\&D}$$

That is, you want to see how much revenues increased due to each firm's investment in research and development.

You know from your research of each company's annual reports that the lead time on new products moving from idea to retail product is, on average, two years. That means research done two years ago results in a new product this year. Consequently, you go back to two years' worth of annual reports and calculate the difference between this year's revenues and revenues from two years ago. This is a measurement of revenue growth. Now you want to scale that figure to the amount spent on R&D two years ago.

You then divide your two numbers. This rough estimate gives you a new way of looking at both businesses using a new scale. In calculating this number you discover that the smaller technology company has nearly 3x the return! You complete your analysis of both businesses and buy shares in the smaller competitor. In part, you buy because your use of new scales leads you to believe the smaller firm is the stronger long-term competitor.

---

dollars and spend one dollar every second. How long does it take to spend your money? The answer is 11.6 days. How long does it take to spend a billion dollars if you spend a dollar a second? The answer, in this case, is 31.7 *years*! That's pretty shocking isn't it? And what if you spend a trillion dollars, one each second? The answer is 1,000 times as long as the time for spending a billion dollars, or 31,688 years—or longer than the length of surviving written history! By making your scale "spending a dollar every second" you clearly see the magnitudes of difference between a million, billion and a trillion. By changing the context/scale from a string of zeroes on a page to cash coming out of your pocket changes the entire understanding of the data.

Finding the proper context and/or scale turns data into information. Realizing this fact engages your right brain and liberates your creativity from the shackles of mundane thought. The best part is that there are no rules in scale changing! The only rule in investing is to make conscious investment decisions whose benefits exceed costs.

Arguably, the scale most overlooked is time. Changing the time scale drastically alters understanding. Take for example, a marriage. If you evaluate the quality of a marriage by the seconds that pass then most marriages will always look like a success. That's because during most of the seconds of a marriage both spouses are content with the state of things; whether this state is absolute bliss, or mostly indifferent. In other words, a high percentage of the moments, as measured by seconds, are moments where the state of the marriage is stable. The problem of course is that you are absolutely shocked to hear that the marriage that looked so stable at the scale of seconds actually results in divorce. The "seconds" scale is far too sharp for you to get a view of the importance of change in relationships.

Another way to measure the marriage is a scale whose sole data point is the exact length of the marriage, such as forty-three years. In this case, the marriage is either as long as "until death do you part" or "until lawyers help you part." Either way you do not have a way of really knowing or comparing the quality of this marriage to other marriages until it's over. In a search for meaning, the only thing you can say is "marriage *a* lasted longer than marriage *b*."

So what's the proper time scale for measuring the success of a marriage? Or maybe you think marriage shouldn't be evaluated based on time but instead by some other criteria. Again, it's up to you to decide.

Getting the time scale right when you analyze a business is critically important. Do you evaluate future prospects over ten minutes, ten hours, ten days, ten months, or ten years? It *does* change the answer of whether to buy, or not buy. A primary difference between so-called value investors and so-called growth investors is a differing appreciation for time. Growth investors typically have a shorter time horizon (i.e., scale) than value investors. After all, growth investors are looking for companies' earnings to increase 100% over one year, not over the course of sixty years.

In the 3G convergence anecdote the proper time scale was essential for understanding the information of the cellular and PDA industries. If cellular subscriber penetration reached 70% of the population (as driven by the "killer app") within five years it was a much better answer than if that same 70% penetration occurred in fifty years. Because of the huge amounts of money invested, getting the proper time scale was actually the most important issue for evaluation, and not the "killer app."

Alter your scales many times to maximize your insight when evaluating investments. Very frequently new information is revealed by changing the scale. Think of this process as learning to know when to utilize your eyes only, a microscope, a pair of binoculars, or a telescope, when looking at information. Sometimes you want to use a scanning electron microscope when examining an issue and at other times you want to use one of the huge-mirrored telescopes of an astronomical observatory when trying to understand something. Beware that many information providers change scale to manipulate information. Just as you need congruency in your questions and answers, you also need it in information where scale is important.

An example of considerations of scale would occur if a company you are examining bumps up against an obscure international trade law. The regulator in charge of enforcing the law then begins a formal investigation.

What is the appropriate scale for making sense of the likely outcome of the investigation? Because you need a high degree of understanding of the legal details then most likely the proper scale for your evaluation most closely resembles an electron microscope.

Alternatively, the global economy is in the midst of a deep recession that some are saying is borderline apocalyptic. What is the appropriate scale? It's likely the proper scale is more like a big astronomical telescope. The economy will recover. It's more a matter of when, not if.

Until you are more in tune with your creativity and intuition be guided by a thorough process: examine information that feels important with varying scales. If you feel your creativity and intuition has been waiting to be unleashed, begin adjusting the scale of data any time it feels right.

INVESTMENT APPLICATION: Anything needing measurement or evaluation can be re-measured or re-evaluated using a different scale. Changing scale is like changing the filter on a camera lens to keep out a specific frequency of light so the remaining frequencies create a different image on the film.

Continuums—Zeroing in on Relevant Information

"When we bring energy to conscious awareness through
the act of perception, we create separate objects that exist in space
through a measured continuum. By creating time and space,
we create our own separateness."[17]

Once you have chosen your map (context) and how you want to view the map (scale) then you have to be able to zero in on the relevant features of the information landscape to create distinctions, or separateness. This is a job handled very well by continuums.

Defining, bounding and framing (DBF) information are the essential elements of creating *continuums*—a powerful tool for comprehending investment information. This is because DBF empowers you to actually grasp the information on the landscape. Defining, bounding and framing

---

17 Lynne McTaggart, *The Field: the Quest for the Secret Force of the Universe*, updated edition (New York: Harper Collins Publishers, 2008), 174.

may sound like similar concepts, but they are not the same thing, though they are complementary to one another.

"Defining" is the act of broadly naming an issue that becomes your continuum. It is important to choose the proper scale for the continuum during the "defining" stage. "Bounding" is the act of limiting the extremes of your continuum; the idea is to place bounds around the issue to a probable range, or band, of possibilities. The last step in creating a continuum is "framing" the issue. In other words, once the bounds are established you gradually pull them in from the bounds' extreme ends and ever closer to the beating heart of an issue.

To make the process of creating a continuum clearer let's answer one of the questions from the cellular phone story from above: Will 3G technology ever exist? This was a critical question to have a good answer to, because in the late 1990s billions of dollars were being invested in hopes that 3G would become a reality. If the answer to the question was "no," you would absolutely not have invested your monies in the cellular industry at that time. If the answer was "maybe," you needed to know how probable the existence of 3G was so that you could invest accordingly. Here's how I did it.

My first job was to "define" the continuum. This was easy to do as the continuum was defined by my question: "will 3G technology ever exist?" My scale was a qualitative scale, an existential scale: to be, or not to be. It looked like this:

Defining

Will 3G Technology Ever Exist?

Because of the nature of this question, a "yes or no" question, it automatically suggested the answer to the next step in my DBF-analysis: bounding. One extreme on my continuum was thus labeled "yes, 3G technology will exist." The other extreme of the continuum was labeled, "no, 3G technology will never exist."

Bounding

Even though it appears that "yes or no" questions have only two possible answers, the fact is that "yes or no" questions are bounded by probabilities and probabilities range from 0% to 100%. So on one extreme end of my continuum I had "no" that translated as "a 0% chance that 3G technology ever exists." On the other end I had "yes" which translated as "a 100% chance that 3G technology exists."

The last step in DBF is "framing." Where on this continuum was 3G technology in the late 1990s? This is where investing switches from fact-based, left-brained analysis into artful, right-brained analysis. What is your *feeling* about this issue?

For me, the relevant facts *felt* like this: consumers love all of these technologies and want them in one device, and billions of dollars are behind the development of 3G. Consequently, despite the infinite range of probabilities, from 0% to 42.1348% to 100%, I felt there was a 100% probability, as indicated by the dot below.

Framing

Framing usually will not result in a 100% probability. Instead a range is more likely. In fact, I could have answered the 3G question with: there is a better than 50% chance of 3G technology existing; or there is between a 60-75% chance of it existing. This range is determined by intuition.

While answering this question may seem as if it was unimportant, it was actually quite significant because it allowed me to move from the existential question/context "will 3G exist?" to a new context for my analysis: "when will 3G exist?" This, in turn, altered my scale. No longer was there the qualitative question: will 3G exist? Instead there was the quantitative question of "when will 3G exist?" This suggested the need for a new continuum, with time as the scale.

Back in 1999 I felt qualitatively that it was nearly impossible for 3G technology to exist within one year's time. So I brought in the frame from the left-bounded end of the continuum (the left vertical dotted line above). I also felt that within fifteen years 3G would be fully implemented. So I brought the frame in from the right bounded end (the right vertical dotted line above). Really I felt there was a five-year range when it might all unfold, but the earliest I felt it would unfold was around 2009, or ten years into the future. This frame is your "most likely" scenario based on your intuitive assessment of the probabilities.

My assessment of "when will 3G technology exist?" was actually the most important part of my investment analysis of the technology. The reason was that if my "most likely" scenario was ten years into the future, then the economics of 3G were not going to generate high enough returns to justify an investment. Unfortunately, I was more concerned with the "killer app" than I was with the time it would take to unfold. In part, this was because I brought a prejudice to my analysis: I liked the idea of 3G technologies unfolding and wanted to be a part of it. This, by the way, is why the Intuitive Investor technologies of chapter three are so important to address first. Prejudices lead to preferences which lead to an emotional evaluation, as opposed to an intuitive evaluation. Ironically, I did do my analyses correctly, but in looking at the investment topography, I put greater emphasis on the little topographical hill of "the killer app," instead of on the taller (more important) topographical hill of "when will 3G technology exist."

DBF is like forging a sword where you have two essential elements to consider: sharpness and flexibility. You may be tempted to insist your sword is as sharp as possible so that you have maximum lethality. However, a real sword that is too sharp actually shatters like glass on impact with any hard obstacle, like armor. Thus, real swords also need flexibility so the shock wave sent through the blade upon impact is able to be absorbed. Likewise, you also want sharpness *and* flexibility in your DBF. You don't want your DBF to be so broad/flexible that absolutely anything could be true; but you also don't want your DBF to be so narrow/sharp that you miss the truth of an issue either.

Another helpful analogy for understanding continuums and their defining, bounding, and framing issues, is that of a grasping hand. The Paradox Principle is about opposites being in harmony with one another to grasp information. One bounded end of a continuum is like a thumb, whereas the other bounded end is like the rest of the fingers—it takes opposing forces to be able to grasp and pick up an object. It takes opposing ideas to be able to grasp and pick up an idea.

Let's go into more detail about DBF. The first step is to list the major factors affecting either a business or the business environment, these are the contexts. Business examples are: the innovative nature of a business's products; the cost of producing those products; the cost of hiring new employees; the relationship with employee unions; the tax structure; the financing; the cash flow; the dividend policy; the quality of patents; the competition's strength, and so forth. Business environment examples are: the regulatory environment; general relevancy of a business; political environment; and taxation environment. Then you place each of the relevant factors on their own unique continuum. This is the act of "defining" the continuum. Don't forget to choose the scale by which you want to assess the information.

To illustrate, let's use the "innovative nature of a business's products." You define the continuum as: Product Innovation Advantage. With "Product Innovation Advantage" you choose to use "years of advantage" as your scale. You can use any units that make sense though, such as "dollars" or "market share gained." It all depends on the question that you are trying to answer. You would use "years of advantage" if your question is: "For how many years will XYZ Company have a product innovation advantage?" Can you imagine the questions to ask about product innovation if the answers are measured in "dollars" or "market share gained?" Try it.

Once the continuum is defined then you bound the extremes of the continuum. One end is "What's the maximum time of XYZ Company's product innovation advantage?" The other end is bound by the opposite "What is the minimum time of XYZ Company's product innovation advantage?"

Last is the critical art of framing the issue properly: Where does the business actually lie on the continuum? By definition, it lies somewhere between your bounded extremes. In the example "product innovation advantage" you want to avoid being too precise in your framing.

If you frame your issue "product innovation advantage" as 3.7 years, the frame is most certainly going to be wrong. Can you really say with confidence that the product innovation advantage will be exactly 3.7 years? No, probably not; your sword is too sharp and will shatter upon impact with hard reality. What if your frame is "between 0 and 1000 years?" While you are confident the real answer lies within this frame, the frame is also not very useful. In this case your sword is too flexible.

Ideally, your framing is a killer combination of both sharpness and flexibility. For example, your frame is "product innovation advantage is between 2-4 years." You have confidence in your answer because it is neither too precisely, nor too broadly, defined.

The next important point about using continuums is that all things in the universe *change*. Thus, you constantly revisit the investment issues you apply DBF to. This way your process is a living, breathing, organic thing that is robust and capable. Next you must revisit your DBF analyses to evaluate where your process might have become FUBAR (Fouled Up Beyond All Recognition). That is, if you make a mistake you want to understand where the mistake occurs in your judgment.

The DBF technique is ideal for analysis of decisions where factual information is not available and is very robust due to its adaptability to any situation. DBF awakens the right brain in a systematic fashion because it relies upon creativity and intuition for best success. Additionally, DBF is in accord with the right brain and the second Principle of Paradox because it allows for non-absolute answers and probabilities.

DBF is the melting pot for fact-gathering analysis and intuitive judgment. I use the DBF technique in almost every single investment moment. Investors' days are filled with information, processing of information (defining, bounding, and framing), and deciding what to do with information (buy, sell). With practice you learn to use DBF to process information in a few moments.

Here is one of the most powerful "defining" tools for evaluating difficult technology issues:

> Can you imagine a world existing in fifty years without this product? Can you imagine a world existing in fifty years that still needs this product?

This technique is useful for defining questions about the long-term prospects of many technologies and technology firms. In the cellular telephone example ask of 3G: can I imagine a world fifty years from now without 3G? The obvious answer is "no." That's because it's nearly impossible to imagine a future world without the ability to communicate and network wherever you happen to be. What about the long-term viability of video games? What about books? What about automobiles? If you answer these questions affirmatively then the question shifts from viability, to the pervasiveness of the technology in your lives? This is a truly invaluable shift in your thinking. Because of the Principle of Infinity's interconnections, once something is viable then you know its ultimate success can be analyzed and now available for evaluating the distinctions and probabilities of the second Principle of Paradox. This is the very definition of an investment opportunity.

INVESTMENT APPLICATION Defining, bounding, and framing gives you a powerful tool for assessing non-linear, vast, confusing, overwhelming, multi-dimensional, organic information. This tool engages the powers of your right brain and helps you to make more whole-brained decisions. It seamlessly combines left-brain organization of facts with right-brain decision making.

The goal is to accept that both ends of these continuums are harmonious, complementary, operating and valid—the difference is in their probability of importance right now. The sum of these distinct, paradoxical probabilities is 100%, or infinity.

The Intuitive Investor and You: Self-Assessment

To integrate yourself with the information of the chapter, consider the following questions. Write down any observations you may have.

When do you encounter paradox in your life? When you encounter it, perhaps you feel elated, curious, confused, or frustrated. How does paradox make you feel? Do you experience opposites (hot and cold, right and wrong, beautiful and ugly) as opposed to one another, or in harmony with one another? Why do you experience them in this way?

Can you remember a time when you felt very strongly about a situation, but once you saw a different point of view your opinion changed entirely? In situations in your life, how often do you consider different points of view before deciding on a course of action? If you consider many options first, do you have difficulty with decisions? If you do not consider different points of view, can you identify ways in which this may limit you?

Recall a moment in your life when a change in scale caught you off guard and changed your understanding of something. Maybe it was seeing the earth from an airplane for the first time. Perhaps it was seeing a spectacular sight in nature, such as the Redwoods or the Grand Canyon or the Himalayas. It could be that you saw something remarkably small like a leaf under a microscope. How did changing the scale of your everyday life in this moment, change you?

How do you normally think about information and decisions that typically escape left-brained analysis? For example, what to do with your life when you leave college, or whether or not to move to a new city, or whether or not to end an important relationship? What emotions do you experience in these situations? Do you have a process? If so, what is it?

Exercises

EXPERIENCING PARADOX Spend several moments evaluating the truth of the following sentence: "This sentence is false."[18]

Now spend several moments recording in your notebook how this process makes you feel.

The moment you are looking for is the moment where a part of you says, "This is impossible!!" It's in this moment that the left brain short circuits. Remember this feeling by describing it in your notebook.

Now re-read the sentence but don't evaluate the truth of it this time. See if you can arrive at a point where you laugh at the absurdity of the sentence. Can you imagine feeling acceptance of both of the opposite points captured in the single sentence? This is more of the right brain at work—it is not interested in certainty, but probability. It allows for paradoxes. Remember this feeling by describing it in your notebook, too.

Write down the differences in feeling between how the left brain operates vs. how the right brain operates.

CONTEXT EVALUATION Choose an investment situation that seems very puzzling to you. Perhaps this is an investment that you made that you ended up losing a lot of money in. Perhaps it is an investment decision that you just can't seem to have conviction about. Write about this situation in your notebook.

---

18 William Poundstone, *Labyrinths of Reason: Paradoxes, Puzzles and the Frailty of Knowledge* (New York: Doubleday, 1988), 18. After a classical paradox first described by Eubulides in the 4th Century B.C.E.

Next, write down the context that you have been using to evaluate the situation. Maybe you are evaluating an investment loss within the context of having wanted to make a lot of money. Maybe you are feeling hesitation with an investment decision because your context is: wanting to make a perfect choice. Whatever the specifics of your context record them now.

Now take the exact opposite context from the one you have been using. Really embody this opposite context with no hesitation. Perhaps rather than evaluating a previous investment outcome as bad, now you take the context that the investment outcome was good. Maybe, rather than wanting to make a perfect choice, your context instead is: not wanting to make an imperfect choice. Return to the puzzling investment situation and evaluate it from your new contextual perspective. Has anything shifted in your understanding? If so, record these changes in your notebook.

CHANGING THE SCALE TO SEE SOMETHING MORE CLEARLY Select an investment situation from which you want greater clarity. Record the details of this situation in your notebook. Now change the time frame that you were using to evaluate the investment situation. Evaluate the situation with both a shorter and longer time horizon. Try to make the differences in time extreme. Maybe you were evaluating something with a six-month time horizon in mind. Therefore, now evaluate the investment with a one-hour time horizon and a ten-year time horizon.

How does shifting the time horizon change your feelings about the investment? Does changing the time scale reveal new information about the investment? Does the time shift reveal anything about you as an investor? Record these observations in your notebook.

CREATING A CONTINUUM Choose an investment question that has escaped your ability to quantitatively evaluate it. That is, a non-factual question. Maybe this is a question about how the stock market will perform over the next five years, or how an investment's new products will do in the marketplace, or whether or not the company you work for will be engaging in any new hiring.

In your notebook you are going to create a continuum. First give a title to your continuum. This is the "defining" stage of the analysis. For example, the title might be "Stock Market Performance over the Next Five Years." Next, about halfway down the piece of paper, draw a horizontal line—this is your continuum. Now carefully consider the scale you want to use to evaluate your investment question. Is it the scale years, the ultimate viability of a product, or the likelihood that a technology is created?

On the right hand side, label/bound that end with your maximum value for the continuum's scale. On the left hand side, do the opposite. Now you must frame the possibilities by narrowing your bounded extremes. Do this using your intuitive feeling about the issue at hand. Because you are working with the future, and not the past, your intuitive sense (that is, feelings) serves you best in this situation. Now write down in words how you have framed the issue. For example: "between 5-10%," or "yes, the technology will succeed."

In your notebook now answer the following questions: What sources were you using to help you in creating your continuum? Did you incorporate facts? Did you incorporate the opinions of others? Did you solely use your intuition? Did you entertain any prejudices or preferences in your analysis? All of these approaches are valid. The important thing is to know the sources used in your process. What parts of this analysis felt like a guess? How comfortable were you with the guessing? At any point when you were considering the information that contributed to your DBF analysis was there a sense of "knowing," or of "yes, that's the answer?" If so, this is a very important feeling to acknowledge and to honor.

REVIEW

Principle II, Paradox was the guiding force of this chapter with its emphasis on making distinctions from amongst infinite investment possibilities. To aid in this process three skills were taught. The first was *contexts*. Contexts help you to step down the infinite map into more digestible, smaller maps. Stepping down from everything to something can be as specific as the performance of a business through the Holiday season. The second skill was *scale*. Just like on a geographical map, having the proper scale helps you to understand information by helping you to see it in many different ways and from many different angles. The final skill was *continuums*, which in effect is how you begin to discern details on the information landscape. Specifically, you learned how to define, bound, and frame issues that are otherwise difficult to assess quantitatively.

5

A Map for the Investor

"The intellectual takes as a starting point his self and relates the world to his own sensibilities; the scientist accepts an existing field of knowledge and seeks to map out the unexplored terrain."

—DANIEL BELL
Sociologist and a professor emeritus
at Harvard University

IN THE LAST CHAPTER I said that context is the first step in making distinctions amongst the features of the information landscape. There was particular emphasis on information needing to have relevancy to the investor. This is the most important context. How and why is this investment opportunity before me personally important? How and why does this investment opportunity before me *feel* personally important? This chapter deals very specifically with you, the investor, and provides an internal map for investing. This internal map addresses the what, why, who, where, and when of the investor. The internal map then allows you to connect directly to your external investment landscape. Without this relationship between you and the investment there can be no understanding of information. At the end of the chapter are self-assessments and exercises. Completion of them is strongly encouraged to ensure your ability to fully use the chapter's information.

What Is Investing?

To answer the question, "what is investing?" requires a good definition of investing. This is essential for success because it provides the *permanent* personal orientation for you to understand investment information.

✦ An Investment Decision Where I Got in My Own Way ✦

In the spring of 2000 I am told that my Board of Directors intends to promote me from Research Analyst to Portfolio Manager. Simultaneously, I am working on an investment thesis that sees a future explosion of worldwide energy use and I want to invest in companies poised to capture the benefits of this massive demographic shift. During the summer and autumn I spend tremendous time investigating the investments I want to make upon my promotion.

My promotion comes on September 22, 2000. International Rectifier (stock ticker: IRF) is the first purchase I make as a Portfolio Manager. While its stock is trading at $45 per share, my analyses have led me to estimate that IRF is worth $60 per share. This is a 33% discount from fair value. The company is poised to benefit from what I believe will be heightened concerns about energy use and its affect on the environment. IRF's computer chips reduce the amount of energy used by hundreds of electronic devices. Most important, I feel that IRF is an excellent company in terms of fitting into my investment thesis.

I excitedly purchase shares in IRF for my shareholders and its stock almost immediately trades down to $35 per share. How did I mess this up after so much diligent research?

Investing:

1. Making a decision

2. Consciously making choices so that the benefits of those choices exceed the costs of those choices

3. Consciously expending energy (i.e., resources) so that the benefits of the expended energy exceed the costs of the expended energy

The core of each of these definitions is that every time you make a decision you make an investment and in every decision resources are expended for a desired outcome.

What Is Investing?

To consciously expend energy (i.e., resources) so that the benefits of the expended energy exceed the costs of the expended energy.

Investing requires making decisions with consciousness. While a decision made without consciousness does not necessarily result in a bad decision, it frequently does. Lack of awareness of the reasons underlying an investment decision makes identifying the source of mistakes nearly impossible. This makes learning from mistakes impossible. Another reason to emphasize consciousness is that if you are cognizant of your reasoning it is more likely that you make sound decisions from the outset. It's important to know that the reasons for a decision can boil down to something like: "I feel good about this." There is nothing wrong with that as long as you make your decision consciously. So investing requires consciousness.

Despite marshalling many facts, fully valuing the business, and talking with the management of International Rectifier, my purchase of International Rectifier was unconscious. At the time I did not know this. If asked if my decision was conscious I would have vehemently argued that it was. But it was not. Among the unconscious "benefits" of purchasing IRF was a deep-seated desire to have an immediate impact on my Fund's returns (ironically that's exactly what happened). Purchasing IRF was done in part because I felt it would satisfy my desire for immediate impact. That means I overestimated the benefits of purchasing IRF. To reiterate: investing requires consciousness.

The next portion of the investing definition is "expending energy." You let go of something when you make a decision. Even when you stand up out of bed when getting up in the morning you give up lying down. When you invest in a financial asset you likely *expend* your intellectual pride, your faith in your decision making ability, your time, and your money. In real life, though, it isn't much different as you make everyday decisions. Each decision requires that you expend resources. The resources spent could be your effort at work, your time, your money, your opinions, your emotions, your thoughts, your cars, or even your relationships.

Importantly, if you do not have control over a resource then no decision about it is necessary. For example, probably no one has the resources at her disposal to control the weather. Instead, the weather dictates how energy is expended. Therefore decisions always take place *within* the bounds of personal power. This is in accord with both the first Principle of Infinity and the second Principle of Paradox. Among all of the resources possible (Principle I) you make the distinction between what you can control and what you cannot (Principle II).

With International Rectifier the expenses included my shareholders' money, the time it took me to conduct my analysis, my burgeoning reputation, the trust engendered in me by my board, and my pride. Including *all* expenses in investment decisions makes choices more conscious. This results in more careful and better decisions about energy/resources and hopefully better returns!

Why Do You Invest?

The last part of the investing definition is its essence and answers the question "Why do you invest?"

Why do you invest?
To have the benefits of an investment that exceeds its costs.

Formally this is called "benefits vs. costs analysis." The anticipated benefits of a course of action are identified then they are compared with an action's anticipated costs. If the benefits exceed the costs then the action is undertaken.

Sometimes in investing the benefits and costs of a decision are easily quantified because your decisions are based on numerical data. However, this is not usually the case. The difficulty in "benefits vs. costs analysis" is trying to quantify that which is difficult to quantify. For example, how do you assign a monetary value to a human life, or to a patent, or to an excellent management team, or to a slickly designed cell phone in fuchsia, or to having clean drinking water, or to breathing clean air? For the intangible, difficult-to-quantify things, creativity and intuition must be relied upon.

Life's decisions must be made so that benefits exceed costs. When you do this something magical happens. You get *more* from the same set of resources. Or you get the same from a *smaller* set of resources. Conscious decisions result in the literal creation of something that did not exist before!

The creation coming from an investment can look like just about anything. It might be:

➤ A new process to speed up your work; here you create more time for yourself.

➤ A new route to get to work that covers a shorter distance; here you use less fuel which leaves more fuel for something else.

➤ A good investment decision resulting in income or capital gains; here you create more money for yourself.

From nothing much to a lot of something. This is the exciting "why" of investing.

Let's look at a mundane decision and the thought process behind that decision. It's very sunny outside and you are at the beach for a long time. Do you put on sunscreen? There really is a lot of analysis behind the decision.

The primary perceived benefit of sunscreen is avoiding sunburn; that is, you avoid the high cost of sunburns. This comes in the form of pain and the embarrassment of bright pink and peeling skin. In severe cases there are medical costs and lost time on the job.

The perceived costs of using sunscreen include the time and money it takes to procure sunscreen, the time it takes to put the sunscreen on, not wanting to appear like a wimp in needing sunscreen, not wanting to share your sunscreen with your friends (some people think this way), and not liking the feeling of something greasy on your skin; etc.

Depending on the value placed on the benefits and costs of sunscreen determines whether you wear sunscreen or not. Some do, some don't, but this is how the mundane decision of wearing sunscreen is made.

When all of the factors leading to a decision are accounted for it's hard to think of any decision where the decision maker's *perceived* benefits do not exceed costs. But you might be thinking: "Many people make irrational decisions." Let's explore this criticism with another example.

Many people go shopping when feeling depressed. They end up spending money even though what led to their depression in the first place was not having much money. Admittedly, this choice seems irrational. However the choice becomes rational if the feelings of power and satisfaction some shoppers experience when commanding resources (in this case the credit card company's resources) are included in the benefits vs. costs analysis. If the shopper places a high value on such feelings, they might decide to shop even though shopping is a part of what contributed to the initial depression. For the shopper *perceived* benefits exceed *perceived* costs. When objectively analyzing the shopper's choice, it's not that they make an irrational decision; it's that they make an unconscious decision. This is because the long-term costs of shopping more and becoming more indebted are not accounted for in the benefits vs. costs choice.

More generally, as investors, if a business's decision seems irrational, you must dive back into the analytical process and seek the benefits of the decision from the perspective of the business that made the decision. This is because only the insane make decisions to intentionally hurt themselves (where costs > benefits). An unswerving belief that all decisions are made subject to *perceived* benefits exceeding *perceived* costs results in greater analytical rigor on your part as you uncover more of the strengths and (more commonly) weaknesses of a business. The natural consequence is better investment choices on your part. So the definition of investing is not just a definition it's a state of mind ...

> Consciously expending energy so that the benefits of the
> expended energy exceed the costs of the expended energy.

In buying International Rectifier I made the wrong decision. Because of the distortions of my ego and my preference for immediate success as a portfolio manager, I overestimated the benefits of the purchase relative to its costs. If my board of directors wanted to understand my purchase of IRF they would need to factor in my desire to immediately affect the Davis Appreciation and Income Fund in their analysis. Otherwise, it's entirely possible that they might conclude my choice was irrational.

INVESTMENT APPLICATIONS

1. Knowing how important consciousness is in investment decision making, you now seek to understand each aspect of an investment decision. This includes the hard data, the soft data of your intuitive feelings, and (hopefully not) your emotional yearnings.

2. Knowing what investing is, conscious decision making where benefits exceed costs, gives you a powerful framework for trying to understand an investment. In your research you look to codify as many of the benefits of the investment as you can. You then do the same for the investment's costs. Attendant rigor to this process results in a thorough investment analysis discipline.

3. Having a powerful definition of investing allows you to analyze the decision-making ability of the management of a potential investment. If they don't seem to be conscious, or seem to have an understanding of weighting benefits versus costs, this should make you leery.

4. If a business makes what seems like an "irrational" decision you now have an unambiguous signal to increase your analytical rigor, because most people do not make decisions to intentionally hurt themselves. In doing this you likely uncover new, actionable information about the prospective investment and make a better decision.

Who Is the Investor? The Investor Identity

SPECULATORS VERSUS INVESTORS

There are a million ways to make money by investing. And the results of investing are measured objectively, not subjectively. It doesn't matter if you are nice to other people or if you go to church on Sundays. What matters is whether you make money or not. That said, there is a huge difference between speculators and investors.

Speculators are similar to gamblers. Gamblers rush to make money. Their time scale is often extraordinarily short, extending out only to the point where they no longer have any money, or have lost enough money to scare them into stopping their gambling. Gamblers obsess about big money and care little about risks. In fact, many gamblers are attracted to gambles with the highest risks. Gamblers often convince themselves they are different from everyone else. Gamblers often do not have a plan when they gamble because they are in it for the visceral and immediate rush. Gamblers are subject to their emotions.

Unfortunately, many people who purchase interests in investments behave the way gamblers behave. People frequently make investments based on rumor, momentum, and speculation hoping to ride the wave to extreme fortune. With the fortune in hand the speculator believes that he will be happier. There is nothing wrong with any of this, as long as the speculation is serving the speculator. However, a speculator is not an investor.

An investor is a careful investigator looking to uncover opportunities, account for risks, and purchase business interests where returns exceed risks over a preferred investment time horizon. The primary difference between investors and speculators is consciousness. Investors are more cognizant of their choices than speculators are and they take full responsibility for their choices. Additionally, investors bring to bear all of their personal power and capabilities to find that rarest of things: the excellent investment opportunity.

INVESTING IS LIKE DETECTIVE WORK

Having the right analogy is crucial to putting yourself into the identity of an investor. The ultimate analogy for investing is: Investing is like detective work.

Who is the investor?
The investor is the detective.

Think of the great detectives of literature: Sherlock Holmes, Hercule Poirot, Philip Marlowe, Sam Spade, Spenser, and Miss Marple. Think about the process that each went through to uncover clues, piece them together and to catch criminals. All were studies in diligence, creativity, intuition, and analysis.

Let's explore the connection between investing and detective work. Imagine a crime scene, a bank robbery, or a murder. The crime scene is overflowing with evidence. Now imagine inviting five detectives to the crime scene. Who is the detective that solves the crime?

There is something to be said for the detective who is diligent in collecting evidence carefully and precisely. However, the evidence on its own does not solve the crime. The detective who solves the crime is the detective who imagines the story that ties the crucial pieces of evidence together correctly. She is also the detective that follows her intuition to identify critical information, the crucial witness, and the likely suspects.

Detective work is simultaneously an analytical process (gathering and analyzing evidence) and a creative/intuitive process (piecing it together correctly). All the facts gathered by a Crime Scene Investigation unit are useless without the creativity to imagine how the facts re-tell the story of the crime.

Investing is also like detective work because it is sometimes filled with stress. The stakes in catching criminals and in investing money are high. Both investing and detective work are full of people (criminals and business executives) who have a vested interest in obscuring facts for their own gain. Both professions also depend strongly on good timing. That is, detectives are more likely to catch criminals closer to the time the crime was committed than later. Investors are more likely to make money the sooner they act on current information or on a temporary shift in a businesses' price.

Detectives spend most of their time gathering evidence, interviewing witnesses, and talking with experts before making an arrest. Investors spend most of their time gathering evidence, interviewing company management, and talking with experts before making an investment.

In order to catch a criminal it's important that detectives are discreet in their investigative process. In order to buy a business well it is important that investors are discreet in their investigative process.

To view evidence well detectives must keep their personal biases out of the investigative process. Otherwise they overlook important evidence or obvious suspects. To understand information well investors must keep their personal biases out of the analytical process. Otherwise they overlook important information or obvious investment candidates.

The proper investor identity is that of a detective. Now that you know you are the detective, where do you deploy your detective skills?

INVESTMENT APPLICATION Detectives are more familiar to you than investors. So if you identify yourself as the detective then you have the proper investors' mindset. This means you are: earnest in gathering information/evidence; aware of the pitfalls of an investment; creative in trying to understand an investment; careful in your investment choices; and more successful in reaping the benefits of your investment choices.

Where Is Investment Information?

SEEING YOUR WORLD DIFFERENTLY

Actionable information is all around you and it is important to start to see it. This is what I mean in the anecdote "Expanding My Vision" on the next page by the fact that I was always working. I experienced the information landscape with a personal context of An Investor.

Where Is Investment Information?
Investment information is everywhere.

To demonstrate how pervasive investment information is, let's discuss some facts that you could encounter everyday on the information landscape

✦ Expanding My Vision ✦

I am leaving for my first business trip as a Research Analyst, traveling with Andrew Davis, the man who hired me at the Davis Funds last spring. We are en route to the Oklahoma Independents Forum (an oil and natural gas conference) in Oklahoma City. The most valuable part of my trip is the 60 mile drive from Santa Fe, where we work, to Albuquerque's International Sunport. Because I am new to New Mexico I spend the first 25 minutes of the drive enjoying all of the new scenery along the way.

Then Andrew and I pass an exit sign for a town called Budaghers (yes, it's really called that). He proceeds to tell me about the Budaghers family and their ownership of numerous cellular telephone towers. I soon realize that every billboard we pass, every semi-truck trailer with a company name on the side of it, triggers a story from Andrew about the business in question.

I suddenly realize that I have to radically change the way I perceive the world if I hope to be an investor. Andrew views the entire world as an investor and almost everything he experiences he relates back to investing. In my career it eventually gets to the point that when people ask me how many hours a week I work, I answer, "All. I am always working."

(Principle I). Then we will pair that data with powerful questions so that you have context and so that the data becomes information (Principle II).

Look at the new shoes people are buying this year; what does it mean? Look at the mix of products catalogs are selling; are they changing? What about the prices charged for those goods? Are there a large number of Sport Utility Vehicles on the used car lot you pass each day on the way to work? If so, what does this say about the affect of increased fuel prices on the average consumer's budget? Are your children spending more or less time watching television? Are your children spending more or less time playing video games? Has the number of local vs. national ads on pay television increased recently, and what does that say about the state of the economy? At the grocery store, is the number of potato chip brands vs. tortilla chip brands increasing or decreasing; what does that say about consumer tastes? How many people do you know who lost their jobs recently?

Are taxi drivers talking to you about the stock market, and if so, what does that say about the overall price level of stocks? When you go to the movies Friday night, how long are the lines; how long were they the last several times; and what does this say about the health of Hollywood? You were disappointed each of the last three times you shopped at your favorite store. Why is this? What does it mean for the health of the company going forward?

From my own career, here are some examples of the sorts of invaluable information that was ripe for the picking for someone seeing the world as an investor:

> ➤ In 2003, as a shareholder of Continental Airlines, I was on a flight sitting next to a senior Continental Airlines flight attendant asking her about the possibility of Continental declaring bankruptcy if it couldn't renegotiate its union contracts. This was the big fear in the summer of 2003. The attendant responded, "We've already been in bankruptcy several times, and we will NOT re-enter it again. As a company, we will do whatever it takes to avoid it." At the time of this writing, Continental remains a viable business.

> ➤ I was at the grocery store and my intuition indicates that I should pay attention to the mix of tortilla chips on the shelves. It is very different from just five years ago. I begin thinking of the many potential implications. This could be evidence of U.S. food companies paying more attention to the shifting consumer demographics of the U.S. from Caucasian to Hispanic. If so, it would be confirmation that a *long-term* shift has occurred on the information landscape. I also wonder what the affect of this shift is on both potato farmers and corn farmers.

> ➤ I was in New York City traveling in a taxi in 1999 to my investment conference's hotel. In Santa Fe, long interactions with strangers are infrequent. But on this long cab ride, the cabby cannot stop talking about his favorite technology stocks. My previous experience with cabbies is that they don't talk much about investments. So my intuition tells me that the last several years of stock market success have probably resulted in a bubble.

> ➤ In 2000 I was at a cocktail party in Santa Fe and struck up a conversation with a man in his mid-40s. It turns out that he was

previously a lawyer for a high-powered investment bank in San Francisco. My right brain assesses that he seems exhausted, so I estimate that he was recently fired. I ask him how long he has lived in Santa Fe and he answers: "several months." This is an indication to me that the dot.com bubble is about to burst, even though the market has not "corrected." My creativity allows me to piece together that a lack of capital flowing to this dot.com investment bank led to this lawyer being fired. That lack of capital is in stark contrast to the previous three years worth of capital flows. Clearly, businesses and investors are getting nervous.

Investible information is everywhere if you can begin to see your world differently. This is the primary difference between good investors and not-so-good investors. Good investors see everything in the world as a source of investment information.

This may sound like a big shift in mindset and identity, but it isn't. After all, when you start a new, enjoyable job you quickly identify yourself with the new job. How long did it take to identify yourself as a college student once you started college? How long did it take to identify yourself as monogamous after you began a new relationship? How long did it take to identify yourself as a parent when your children were born? All of these changes cause you to see the world differently.

I would argue that investment skills are useful in every decision we make, so shifting how you see the world to the perspective of an Investor is a valuable investment in yourself.

INVESTMENT APPLICATION: Viewing daily life as a source of invaluable investment information makes you much better informed than most investors. Further, being aware of and gathering more information leads to better investment decisions, leading to more money.

When Do You Invest?
The Relationship of Time to Investing

Of the classic questions this is the easiest to answer with regard to investing.

When do you invest?
When you feel that you understand the information about an

investment and when you feel confident that benefits of your choice are greater than the costs of your choice.

The timing of an investment decision, the "when" to buy or sell, is your choice.

The Intuitive Investor and You: Self-Assessment

Consider the following questions; write down in your notebook those personal observations that feel important.

When you have invested in the past, how conscious of the factors leading up to your investment decisions have you been? In what ways did this benefit you? In what ways was this detrimental to you?

Can you remember any investment decision you have made where you didn't feel the perceived benefits were greater than the costs? Was a "benefits vs. costs analysis" a natural part of your investment decision-making process?

Are there any parts of your detective tool kit that seem weaker than others? If so, are you able to do anything to change these weaknesses into strengths?

Do you feel you are missing valuable investment information around you? If so, how can you shift your personal context to that of an investor?

Exercises

ANALYSIS OF A ROUTINE

We each make hundreds of minor, and some major, decisions each day. Right now imagine one of your daily routines. For example, consider such routines as the route you drive to work, making coffee each morning, or watching a particular TV show. In your notebook, simply describe the routine.

How did this become your routine? What led you to go about your routine this way?

What purpose does the routine serve? Record the answers to these questions in your notebook.

Now list the benefits gained, not just the quantifiable ones, of the routine. This might include something as simple as: personal satisfaction. In turn, list the costs that are not just the quantifiable ones, of the routine in your notebook. Are there any hidden benefits to the routine that you have previously overlooked? Do the benefits of the routine outweigh the costs?

Can you imagine another, perhaps better, way of doing your routine? Are there any aspects of your routine of which you were unconscious? How close to "benefits vs. costs" analysis was the development of your routine? Did you discover any hidden benefits to your routine that were previously missing? Do these hidden benefits account for why you engage in the routine? Write down the important discoveries in your notebook.

BENEFITS VERSUS COSTS ANALYSIS Think of an investment opportunity that you would like to either analyze or understand better. In your notebook write down the name of the investment you are considering.

Now begin listing on the left side of your page all of the perceived costs associated with the possible investment. This could include your money, your time, your pride, a violation of your sense of safety if the investment feels risky, offending someone in your life, and other costs.

Now on the right side of the page begin to list the perceived benefits of the investment. Make sure to include anticipated feelings, such as financial security.

For both costs and benefits think deeply about any non-quantifiable, emotional, or feeling aspects that are involved in your decision making.

Now review both your list of costs and benefits, which is greater?

Were there any parts of your analysis that were harder to uncover than others? If so, what made these difficult to uncover? Show your list to someone that knows you well and have them evaluate the list for any gaps in your costs and benefits.

NOTICING INVESTMENT INFORMATION Take a moment to review the events of your day. Was there any investment information around you that you missed? (Hint: Pay attention to your roles as a customer of many businesses, as a watcher of media, or as a co-worker, friend and relative of someone.) In your notebook record the information you missed. How valuable is this information?

Can you agree to shift your perspective to become more conscious of this information? If you missed important investment information, then tomorrow absorb as much of it as you can.

REVIEW

In this chapter I described a personal map for the investor. This internal map helps you to better place yourself in relation to the external map of the information landscape. Knowing what investing is creates a personal context for evaluating information—information is either pertinent to your personal investment process, or it is not. Knowing who an investor is, a detective, allows you to approach the investment landscape with the proper mindset and thus, understand information better. Additionally, knowing that you live within a sea of investment information changes your life and empowers you to approach and explore your world as an investor.

Section Review

In Part One, "Preparing the Ground for Your Creativity, Intuition, and Wealth Manifestation," I first shared with you the most important investment skill: understanding information. You learned that there is no such thing as a future fact, yet investing is an act whose results unfold in the future. Additionally, you discovered the limitations of the primary modern world tools, numbers and words, in fully describing the real world. The limitations of facts, numbers and words all argue for an investment in the right brain. The right brain is your source for creativity, intuition and wealth manifestation. What's more, the right brain nicely compensates for the gaps in an exclusively left brain investment analysis. The currency of the right brain is feelings, not emotions. The difference is that emotions are feelings distorted by personal prejudices, leading to poor investment decision-making.

The first Principle of Infinity was introduced and addresses the "information" half of "understanding information." It acknowledges the vastness and interconnectedness of information. In order to be in accord with the first Principle an investor must be as free of boundary as possible. To this end, two primary sources of investor limitations were discussed: the emotions surrounding feelings of ignorance and fear. Techniques for expanding past the boundaries created by both were shared as well as techniques for turning both of these limiters into investor strengths.

The second Principle of Paradox was next introduced to address the "understanding" half of "understanding information." This principle acknowledges the need for investors to begin to narrow down infinite investment possibilities to narrow investment probabilities by making distinctions. Three tools were shared for doing just this: contexts, scales, and continuums. Contexts allow the investor to switch from the infinite information map down to a smaller, more digestible map. Adjusting scales helps the investor in revealing prominent features of the information map. Finally, continuums allow you to really zero-in on relevant information and detail.

Each of the preceding mapping tools addressed the external, rather than the internal, environment. Thus, a Map for the Investor was necessary to connect the investor with his landscape. Knowing what investing is, and who the investor is, allows you to place yourself in relation to the information landscape in a more effective manner.

Activating Your Creativy and Intuition for Wealth Manifestation

IN PART ONE WE BEGAN to do the ground work for greater activation of your right brain. In part two, the goal is to take the clean slate created in part one and begin to fill it with new right brain possibilities.

We begin with Principle III, Harmonizing. It addresses both halves of "understanding information." This third principle is about being in accord with the parts of the information landscape that are distinct and interesting to you. To this end the Seven Essential Investor Attitudes are introduced. Each Attitude suggests how the investor should adapt his or her mind to investing in order to understand information better and to ultimately make better decisions.

Principle IV, Action, is the next principle and it addresses what to do once you understand information. Essentially you must take action to either buy or sell the investment, or gather more information. Behavior is about choice in motion, which is action. To this end the Seven Essential Investor Behaviors are introduced. Adherence to these Behaviors provides a ready-made, potent structure for the investor's right brain.

Next the Intuitive Investor Tool Kit is given. The three tools are Your Cousin Vinny, the Investment Thesis, and the Lessons Learned List. Each tool uniquely addresses each moment of the life of an investment: before buying, while holding, and after selling. Additionally, each tool fully utilizes all of the four principles and enables your right brain to help you make better investment decisions.

6

Seven Essential Investor Attitudes

"When we observe the world ... we do so on a much deeper level than the sticks and stones world 'out there.' Our brain primarily talks to itself and the rest of the body not with words or images, or even bits or chemical impulses, but in the language of wave interference: the language of phase, amplitude and frequency—the 'spectral domain.' We perceive an object by 'resonating' with it, getting 'in synch' with it. To know the world is literally to be on its wavelength."[19]

IN PART ONE YOU LEARNED the tools to identify and remove personal boundaries, to make distinctions amongst a sea of information, and to bridge the internal and external investment worlds. In this chapter you begin to take advantage of the changes to your mind explored earlier. For this purpose, Principle III, Harmonizing, is introduced. The third principle addresses both aspects of "understanding information" by putting you in accord with information—leading to understanding. Additionally, the Seven Essential Investor Attitudes are introduced. They are like subconscious mental programs that are always in place to help you more easily access your right brain. The chapter concludes with self-assessments and exercises designed to help you integrate the information within yourself.

Introducing Principle III: Harmonizing

The secular meaning of this principle is

The secret to increasing your personal power is to harmonize with what you want to understand or embody and then you become it.[20]

---

[20] Received via a dream on June 29, 2006 in Dayton, Ohio, USA.

✦ Harmonizing with What I Want ✦

I was an intern at Portfolio Management Consultants in Denver while still in graduate school. My dream was to become a Portfolio Manager at a mutual fund. I had dedicated my life to this goal for the previous four years, yet I had never met an actual portfolio manager. Finally I meet several portfolio managers from Delaware Investment Advisors who visited our offices. I am transfixed by the way they dress, the way they answer questions, and their overall demeanor. I want to be just like them and I want what they have, too.

✦✦✦✦✦

The essence of the third Principle, Harmonizing, is *understanding*.

This chapter is about the next step in "understanding information" once distinctions have been made among the vast sea of large amounts of investment information, you now need to "understand the information." That is, you need to harmonize with it. Now, you need to "get it."

The third principle of Harmonizing provides you with a shortcut to understand anything. You do not need to reinvent the wheel, only harmonize with something you want to understand, want to be, or want to accomplish until it becomes a part of you. Once there is close accord (and discord is minimized) between you and what you want to harmonize with then it's as if you become that thing. Then you understand that thing from every possible direction.

Think back to anything you have ever learned in life. There is all of the time invested learning the details of something new. But then there is that singular moment when "everything just clicks." That moment is the moment when you have harmonized with the thing you wanted to understand and you have become it. Specific to investing, by trusting an established professional, me, you harmonize with information that works and avoid much of the "trial by error" that I had to go through to master this information myself.

Having observed the Delaware Investment Advisors' portfolio managers, I adopted their way of being, their frequency/vibration, during my post-

✦ The Benefits of My Skill at Harmonizing ✦

On March 9, 2009 there is a panicked selling of U.S. equities. The selloff is the culmination of a rapid decline in the health of both the U.S. financial system and its economy. The real estate bubble has, finally, definitively burst. I want to know if this selloff represents the bottom of the market so I tune into the mood of the market. It feels to me that the panic that has been palpable in the air has finally dissipated. Consequently, I call the market bottom on March 12, 2009 and publicly publish my prediction on my blog: jasonapollovoss.blogspot.com. Not only that, but I suggest to my readers that same day that they buy U.S. equities. In fact, March 9 was the market low during the deep 2008-2009 recession and the S&P 500 rose 48.5% from my March 12, 2009 post.

✦✦✦✦✦

graduate school job interviews in order to land my dream job at Davis Selected Advisers. Because I had harmonized with the portfolio managers my presentation was as if I was already a professional research analyst.

Think about comedic impersonators and what they do to embody the essence of someone or something else. They allow themselves to harmonize with the personality of someone else and take on their mannerisms, cadence, accent, and other qualities so that you are convinced you are really looking at someone else. This demonstrates the Principle of Harmonizing.

The third principle is not just about emulating a persona; it is applicable to all learning. It is about getting in synch with what you want to understand.

My prediction explained above was made based on my *harmonization* with the "mood" of the market. To me it felt as if the panic energy that had been present since the collapse of Bear Stearns had finally abated. Not only that, but investors felt genuinely exhausted. I then combined this intuitive insight with my knowledge (a left brain function) of what happens when valuations are ridiculously low, to come up with my creative suggestion (a right-brain function) that my readers buy U.S. equities. Once you are able to harmonize with something in its clear, pure state then understanding follows. This is the essence of the Principle of Harmonization.

The Seven Essential Investor Attitudes

In "A Map for the Investor," I described the: who, what, where, when, and why of investing. But I did not discuss the "how" of investing. How you invest depends on your attitude. Adapting the mind to include The Seven Essential Investor Attitudes is like creating subconscious mental programs that are always present and help you to access the right brain with ease. These beneficial Attitudes are also germane to improving your investment returns.

Here is what I mean by an attitude:

at•ti•tude [(ăt'ĭ-tōōd', -tyōōd')]; noun.[21]

1. A position of the body or manner of carrying oneself: stood in a graceful attitude.

2. a. A state of mind or a feeling; disposition: had a positive attitude about work.

   b. An arrogant or hostile state of mind or disposition.

3. The orientation of an aircraft's axes relative to a reference line or plane, such as the horizon.

4. The orientation of a spacecraft relative to its direction of motion.

5. A position similar to an arabesque in which a ballet dancer stands on one leg with the other raised either in front or in back and bent at the knee.

Though it may seem otherwise, definition 4 is the most useful. I am going to rewrite its definition to make this more obvious:

Attitude is the orientation of a mind relative to its direction of motion.

The Seven Essential Investor Attitudes that follow help you orient your right brain to your direction of motion: understanding information.

---

[21]*American Heritage Dictionary of the English Dictionary, Fourth Edition* (New York: Houghton-Mifflin Company, 2006).

Attitude 1: Focus on Risks Before Opportunities

It's natural to focus on opportunities when you invest; after all, you invest to grow your resources. But it is much more valuable and actually easier to focus on an investment's risks than its opportunities. This is because, by definition, opportunity unfolds in the future and the future is unknowable—there is no such thing as a future fact. Additionally, sources for opportunity are unlimited and largely unknowable, too. Risks, by contrast are very consistent and more predictable.

Executives of major corporations hesitate to publicly project their sales and profits farther than one year into the future. Consider that these are the very people on the "frontlines" of business fighting so hard to capitalize on every new business opportunity. They are closer to the "fight" than anyone can be. When high-technology businesses (such as semiconductors and biotechnology) are asked what proportion of their Research and Development (R&D) projects make it to the market they consistently report that the percentage is extraordinarily low. Forget about asking which products will be blockbusters because they do not know. It is virtually impossible to know with precision what opportunities will exist for a business five years from now.

✦ Opportunities Are Elusive ✦

In 2000 a group of my fellow Davis Funds investment professionals are speaking with Bob Wayman, the Chief Financial Officer of Hewlett Packard. We are one of the firm's ten largest shareholders. Our conversation covers a great number of topics and at one point Christopher Davis (Andrew's very accomplished brother) asks Bob a question: "If you had it all to do over, would you do it the same way?" Bob's answer did not address the intended context of Chris's question, but was startling and informative. Bob is a nearly 40-year veteran of Hewlett Packard and says (paraphrased), "I am not sure that I would choose to work in the technology business again because every 18 months you have to invent a brand new multi-billion dollar business just to grow a little bit, and that's very difficult to repeat year after year because the pace of change is so rapid."

The other difficulty with obsessing solely on opportunities is that capitalism is extraordinarily efficient. Most all of the advantages enjoyed by a new product are quickly eroded away as other profiteers/capitalists enter the new market and compete away the advantage. There are some protections for new products, such as patents and copyrights, but they do not protect indefinitely. Money moves very fast, and minds move even faster. Consider the Hewlett-Packard story as a big ole caveat to being carried away by the siren's song of opportunity, growth, and Candy Mountain.

Risk is a very different animal from opportunity. There is a fairly standard laundry list of risks that businesses throughout time, and the world over, have faced and will face. These risks do not change all that often. In fact, a business's risks are some of the easiest things for executives to anticipate. Open up any publicly traded company's Securities and Exchange Commission filed 10K[22] (the annual report) and there is an entire section disclosing the risks faced by the business. By the way, this list is written by paranoid company lawyers trying to avoid investor lawsuits brought on by poor-risk disclosure. Risks are easier to identify ahead of time than opportunity.

Now, on the other hand, what *is* difficult to discern is the timing of specific risks. So how do businesses compensate for the unexpected timing of their risks? They purchase insurance or they self-insure themselves against the risks. That's how *predictable* risk is. There is an entire and huge industry in place to compensate businesses for unexpected loss: the insurance industry.

The insurance industry is based on actuarial/statistical data. In other words, most business risks are so predictable that insurance companies can rely upon past facts to ensure their future results. Not only that, but the insurance industry has been around for several centuries, all the while collecting risk data that just do not fluctuate that much. Assessing risk ahead of time is not "rocket science," or even "new product development science." There is good transparency when you analyze risks. Yes, some risks are difficult to ascertain ahead of time, such as terrorist attacks, major weather related events, earthquakes, and meteor strikes (the notorious "Acts of God" clause). However, these sorts of shocks to a business's system are extraordinarily rare.

The trick for investors is to spot and identify the risks inherent in a type of business or in a specific business *before* investing hard earned money.

---

22 Securities and Exchange Commission, http://www.sec.gov/edgar; or see Appendix I: Resources for Intuitive Investors.

If I am uncomfortable with even one major risk
in a prospective investment, I do not invest.

This is one of my rules as an investor because in my experience any investment risk identified before purchase eventually does rear its ugly head while you own an investment. Please remember, that all rules have exceptions (Principle II, Paradox, at work) so use your wisdom in assessing when to apply this rule: focus on the risks of investing before the opportunities for investing.

INVESTMENT APPLICATIONS

1. Focusing on risks before opportunities dramatically improves your investment results because now you can use a study of investment history to identify potential investment pitfalls *before* making an investment. History is defined, whereas the future is not. The same business risks tend to repeat themselves over and over again predictably resulting in investment losses.

2. Focusing on risk before opportunity helps you to preserve the capital you already have. It has been my experience that investment returns often happen slowly and over many years, whereas investment losses usually happen extraordinarily rapidly. So preservation of your capital is more important than growth of your capital.

3. You are now better able to assess the management of prospective investments. Many entrepreneurial business leaders ride waves of euphoria derived from their perceptions of grand opportunity, only to fall into the water and be eaten by sharks when risks rear themselves. Knowing that business leaders should also focus on risks before opportunities allows you to now recognize an imbalance of euphoric thinking relative to pragmatic thinking and avoid investing in a delusional business leader.

Attitude 2: Comfort with Uncertainty

Let me discuss a dirty little secret ... namely that most of the natural world and its phenomena escape simple linear mathematical description. This is surprising, especially when you consider the high degree of certainty that scientists have about the completeness of their understanding of, and

✦ Uncertainty Is Natural ✦

One of the reasons I move to Santa Fe is the presence of the Santa Fe Institute. I deeply respect its work in non-linear mathematics and chaos theory. In 1999 I have the privilege of hearing one of the founders of the Santa Fe Institute, Murray Gell-Mann, Nobel-prize winning physicist in 1969, speak publicly. His intent is to update the public on his current research obsessions. He says something startling in his discussion: When you describe the universe (that is, creating models/formulas/theories/approximations) it is important to "maximize the ignorance" of any such equation.

descriptions (theories) of, the universe as represented by simple mathematical formulae. There exists a cadre of thinkers who believe that the entire universe from just after the Big Bang to the very moment you are reading this book right now can be described by mathematical equations. It's their feeling that if they have all of the relevant equations and the initial conditions of the universe (that is, the proper inputs into their formulae) they can then tell you what will happen in the very next moment of your life. They feel that even the speed of a fruit fly's wings around your apple next summer is determinable with their formulae and initial conditions! These folks are known as determinists.

I admire determinists for their fortitude in trying to explain Infinity. Perhaps someday they will be proven correct. However, currently a very low percentage of the natural world is describable in the way they desire.

> "Pedagogically speaking, a good share of physics and mathematics was—and is—writing differential [calculus] equations on a blackboard and showing students how to solve them. ... As every science student knows, solving differential equations is hard. But in two and a half centuries, scientists have built up a tremendous body of knowledge about them. It is no exaggeration to say that the vast business of calculus made possible most of the practical triumphs of post-medieval science, or to say that it stands as one of the most ingenious creations of humans trying to model the changeable world around them.

So by the time a scientist masters this way of thinking about nature, becoming comfortable with the theory and the hard, hard practice, he is likely to have lost sight of one fact. Most differential equations cannot be solved at all ...

"The solvable systems are the ones shown in textbooks. They behave. Confronted with a non-linear system, scientists would have to substitute linear approximations or find some other **uncertain** [emphasis mine] backdoor approach ... When people stumbled across such things—and people did—all their training argued for dismissing them as aberrations. Only a few were able to remember that the solvable, orderly, linear systems were the aberrations."[23]

While most people like the idea of reducing the world and investing down to mathematical certainty, the fact is that this can never be done. Determinism is just another variation of that perennial human desire: a need for certainty. Yet the future remains disgustingly uncertain. To be investors (believers in the future) you must become comfortable with uncertainty. Determinists we are not! Investors have the attitude that the future is unknown and you act accordingly. Investors are comfortable with uncertainty.

What the heck did Murray Gell-Mann mean by "maximize the ignorance"? When describing the world it's best to balance descriptive power with simplicity. In other words, a complex description of a phenomenon is worse than a simple one. By maximizing the ignorance you strip down theories to their bare essentials with nothing extraneous and unnecessary included. Maximizing the ignorance is another way of saying: minimize the B.S.

Some may be familiar with this concept in a different form, Occam's Razor. This is a principle that says the explanation of any phenomenon should make as few assumptions as possible, and eliminate those assumptions that make little or no difference in explaining what you are trying to understand.

Investors must recognize "the point" where additional data no longer gives greater comfort in helping to make investment decisions. Yet many investors continue to heap data onto their analytical process hoping that their information mountain makes an investment decision for them.

---

23 James Gleick, *Chaos: Making a New Science* (New York: Penguin Books, 1987), 67–8.

Mountains of data do not stave off anxiety surrounding an uncertain future. The only remedy is to become comfortable with uncertainty by utilizing the right-brain's intuitive powers to identify likely future outcomes—as I did in predicting the market had reached a bottom on March 9, 2009.

INVESTMENT APPLICATIONS

1. Comfort with uncertainty helps to eliminate anxiety so in the long run you make better investment decisions.

2. If you are comfortable with uncertainty then you are more likely to invest. Only by investing can future investment benefits be realized.

3. Being comfortable with uncertainty eliminates the "heaping data" problem. Too much data is a sign of too much left-brained thinking and anxiety. Too much data can confuse rather than illuminate investment analysis. Comfort with uncertainty leads to you being more decisive. Ultimately, decisiveness also helps to eliminate problems associated with poor timing.

Attitude 3: A Good Decision Is Most Often ≥ the "Perfect" Decision

---

To become better investors you must realize that a "good" decision is most often greater than, or equal to (≥), the "perfect" decision. Pursuits of perfection are very expensive and a sign of the left-brain's absolutist thinking. That perfection is expensive is practically a law of nature. Consider the following example from environmental economics.

Imagine you have a polluted river needing to be cleaned up. You have a clean-up budget of $100 million. It takes roughly 10% of the money to get the river 90% clean. It takes the remaining 90% of the money to get the river 99% clean. The costs of cleanup skyrocket rapidly. Perfection is expensive.

Another example: Think of the training needed to become an expert athlete. Most can reach the 90th percentile by investing two years of our lives to get there. However, to get to the level of skilled professionals, the 99th percentile, takes around twenty years, or ten times as much time. Perfection is expensive!

When making a decision to buy or not buy an investment, it is important that your attitude is to focus on making a good decision, and not the perfect decision. This thinking is relativistic in nature and strongly in accord with right-brain thinking.

The "perfect" decision is not knowable ahead of time. Only by looking back can you determine what the best decision was given a certain set of circumstances. Also, what often looks like the perfect decision ahead of time frequently turns out retrospectively, to be a disaster. Change is constant and what is trusted to be true now often alters course in the future.

Since it's impossible to know the perfect decision ahead of time the consistent investment strategy for the Intuitive Investor is to come up with a set of *possible* decisions. Because each of your analyses are likely intelligent, all of your possible decisions are likely good decisions. Thus, a bad decision is unlikely. If you insist on searching for the "perfect" decision you will likely both expend many resources and become paralyzed and unable to make a decision. There is a time and place for the "perfect" decision, but only very rarely.

INVESTMENT APPLICATIONS

1. Mastering this attitude frees you from the left-brain perfectionist's grid-lock that frequently ensues when an investment decision is being made.

2. This attitude gives you a "get out of jail free" card allowing you to actually make a decision, instead of obsessing about one.

3. Free of the "perfect" decision paralysis, you are decisive and have better investment timing.

4. Avoiding the pursuit of the "perfect" decision frees up resources for analysis in other areas of interest.

Attitude 4: Forgive Yourself for Not Being Perfect

Mistakes are inevitable when investing because investing involves countless facts and constantly changing situations. Consequently, the day will eventually arrive when you make an investment mistake. Accept now the inevitability of a future investment mistake. This puts your mind more in accord with the relative nature of the right brain, as the right brain accepts variation. Additionally, this helps to remove the emotional prejudice and pressures associated with perfection. Once a mistake is made you forgive yourself for not being perfect.

Once a mistake is made, rapidly forgiving yourself puts your mind in a healthy space where you can evaluate what went wrong without unnecessary self-criticism. But it's important to not turn forgiving yourself into carte blanche for ignoring your mistakes. That's not the point of forgiving yourself. Think of the compulsive gambler/speculator and how each successive losing hand/bad investment purchase is forgiven with, "I was unlucky. The next time will be different."

You must also thank your lucky stars for mistakes. Mistakes quickly identify gaps in knowledge and understanding and they suggest an immediate and logical direction for learning. In turn, that learning leads to greater information understanding and better investment results. Having the proper attitude toward mistakes means that you can engage errors head-on, correct them, and take advantage of them in the future.

INVESTMENT APPLICATIONS

1. Accepting your mistakes as inevitable removes the left brain's absolutist perfection pressures. This leads to greater decisiveness.

2. Forgiving yourself for not being perfect gives you the ability to exit the emotional space that distorts thinking and intuition. In turn this allows you to learn from your mistakes.

Attitude 5: You Are Holding Investment Interviews

Similar to interviewing a candidate for a job, investors search for excellent candidates to buy while eliminating the unworthy candidates from their search. As an investor, you are the boss of your investment portfolio. Further, you should make investment candidates run the analytical and intuitive gauntlet before purchasing them. Sincerely embodying this attitude minimizes emotional prejudices and distortions where there is a preference for immediate satisfaction and you "buy just to buy." This allows for a better functioning of the right brain.

✦ I Am the One Making the Decision ✦

In 1998 I am speaking with the investor relations' representative of a prospective investment, Tower Automotive. I am on the phone with her for approximately 45 minutes. The myriad of questions I ask are all tough and designed to eliminate Tower Automotive as an investment candidate for the fund for which I am an analyst. So far I am very impressed with Tower and how they run their business. So impressed, in fact, that I ask my final question, "Based on my research and valuation model I feel that Tower ought to be trading around $40/share, yet your stock has consistently traded for around $30/share. Is there a reason for that?" Tower's Investor Relations person responds, "Why don't you send your valuation model to me and I will correct it for you." A mini-argument ensues about responsibility. I feel that it is the investor relations representative's job to provide information about Tower and my job is to understand the business and estimate its value.

Tower Automotive was a very attractive investment candidate. However, when its investor relations person insisted I send my valuation model to her, I knew there was a problem. The problem was her not honoring my role as both a portfolio manager and prospective owner of Tower. On the surface this seems noble of her, but it was a clear disrespect of my responsibility and it did not bode well for my long-term ownership relationship with the company. I did not invest in Tower; in other words, I did not hire the company for my portfolio's job vacancy.

Though there are many complex issues, Tower Automotive ultimately declares bankruptcy on March 28, 2007.

Another way to consider this Attitude is that creating your investment portfolio is similar to sculpting an image out of marble. You first imagine the final image. Then you remove big chunks of marble to get closer to your vision of the final image. You then methodically trim smaller and smaller amounts from the marble until the image is refined. The last step for the sculptor is to polish the marble to an excellent finish so the quintessence of the image shines through. By removal, near-perfection is attained. Consider many companies in the beginning. Then eliminate them one by one, until you are comfortable enough to invest in your final choice or choices.

INVESTMENT APPLICATIONS

1. Investing can be intimidating. It's you, the "Little Guy," vs. "Big Business." So your mindset must be that you are holding investment interviews for an exclusive position in your portfolio. It's your money and when you buy/hire a business its managers legally *work for you*. So this attitude empowers you.

2. Because you have the mindset that there are only a few openings in your portfolio for candidates, you are very picky. This likely results in a more thorough and diligent analysis and a better purchase.

Attitude 6: Why Does It Have to Be This One?

In the United States alone there are approximately 10,000 publicly traded companies, so when considering an investment, ask yourself: why does it have to be this **one**? You look to eliminate investment candidates, not to include them! This mindset allows you to immediately eliminate businesses that do not meet the greater majority of your investment criteria.

During my entire investment career I really liked only around twenty businesses. The Davis Appreciation and Income Fund actually held around thirty-five to forty-five investments, but that's because portfolio managers must be in accord with very strict diversification regulations. Consequently, the fund held more businesses than I wanted it to hold.

Logically, if you truly are 100% confident that an investment is going to perform exceptionally well and with low risk, shouldn't you invest ALL of

---

✦ Choosing One from Many ✦

After my divorce I was dating again and very interested in a woman. I felt that I was in love. Frustratingly, the woman does not share my affection. I talk with my good friend Angela B. who says, "You need to learn the rule of 2.5." Puzzled, I say, "What the heck is the rule of 2.5?" Angela says, "There are 2.5 billion women on the planet, why does it have to be this **one**?" "Hmmm," I say.

✦✦✦✦✦

your capital in it? Of course you should. Diversification (often deworsification) of your portfolio is done because you cannot be 100% confident in your choices.

As you gain greater confidence in your investment abilities you learn that your portfolio is less risky with a few excellent businesses than with many so-so businesses. Adherence with this Attitude creates confidence in your investments. That confidence, in turn, reduces your anxieties about money. Less anxiety allows for a more creative, more intuitive right brain. Look to eliminate candidates from your portfolio! Why does it have to be this one?

INVESTMENT APPLICATIONS

1. This attitude gives you confidence as it puts you in the Drivers Seat.

2. There is no need to invest unless you are perfectly *comfortable* with the investment. You have this luxury because there are 9,999 others to choose from! So this attitude reminds you to be exceptionally picky in searching out prospective investments. This leads to a higher quality, lower-risk investment portfolio.

Attitude 7: Beware False Prophets

By false prophets I am referring to information that is manipulative and distorted. Typically, the false prophets take the form of misuse of analogy, adjectives or archetypes.

THE IMPORTANCE OF ANALOGY

If you want to know if someone has an excellent right brain, look very carefully at how they use analogy. This is because the right brain evaluates information harmonically. So if the structure of new information *is like* (harmonizes with) the structure of information already understood, understanding then takes place immediately. Take for example the following quote from the economist, Aaron Levenstein:

> *"Statistics are like a bikini: What they reveal is suggestive,*
> *but what they conceal is vital."*

Clearly, Mr. Levenstein is someone with such an expert understanding of statistics, that when he sees a woman in a bikini, he also sees how it relates to statistics. This is one of the hallmarks of the right brain. So a clue to someone who has an excellent right brain is someone who uses analogy well. You can use this to evaluate the management of a prospective investment.

Unfortunately analogy is also a source of manipulation of information and consequently, of investors. Two important things to remember about analogy:[24]

1. No analogy is perfect. There is always at least one difference between two things being compared. If they were identical then there wouldn't be two things to compare.

2. There is always some similarity between any two objects, no matter how different.

BEWARE OF THE ADJECTIVES

Our next false prophet takes the form of extreme language used to describe businesses and business opportunities, such as:

"The first company to do x."
"The only company to do x."
"It's revolutionary."
"They are revolutionary."
"They are rewriting the rules."
"They cannot fail."
"It's a no brainer."
"Even an idiot could run this business and make money."
"It's a new world."
"It's an entirely new paradigm."
"There has never been a time like this."
"There has never been a business like this."
"Simply amazing."
"The worst economic downturn since the Great Depression."

It is extraordinarily rare for the landscape of business and for businesses themselves to be truly, greatly changed. There are many reasons for this, but mostly capitalism is highly efficient at quickly competing away any busi-

---

24 Fallacy Files, http://www.fallacyfiles.org/wanalogy.html.

ness advantage. In some cases, it takes less than a year for rivals to form and to organize themselves to begin bleeding the excess profits of the innovator away. Think Facebook versus MySpace. There are very few examples of long-term competitive advantage. Think of professional sports and how difficult it is for any one team to dominate for long. Again, the typical reign of dominance is usually only three years or so. There are reasons for this, including the statistical information available about athletes, the information available about teams' performances (such as game film, former coaches who reveal plays, weight or training methods) and importantly, athletes' free-agency. Free agency is analogous to the free-flow of capital in investing. Free-agency means that valuable team assets leave every season. Having a successful corporation long-term is more difficult than having a successful sports franchise. That which is truly extraordinary *is*. I see very few companies that deserve exceptional monikers and most have difficulty competing over short periods of time, let alone over the course of five years.

Unfortunately, it is the nature of the investment business to attract hucksters and exaggerators, aka snake oil salesmen. Furthermore, the business presses are not in the business of conveying information. They are in the business of selling advertising. That means that they need for you to be glued to the screen/monitor for as long as possible so that they can show you an advertisement. Thus they consistently stretch the truth to the exact point where it is interesting to a mass of people. The primary culprit is the use of superfluous adjectives that do not add to the truth of the reporting, but definitely contribute to the appeal of the reporting. The exaggeration is not just in the woohoo, positive direction either. Negative extremism exists, too.

Beware of the adjectives, as they are the primary culprit in investment hot-air. Adjectives are designed to activate your emotions; and as a side effect they activate the prejudices and distortions of emotions, too. This leaves you vulnerable to manipulation. So ignore adjectives when you are evaluating a prospective investment. Because it's your money, reserve the right to assign your own adjectives to a prospective investment but only after you have carefully evaluated it.

INVESTMENT APPLICATIONS

1. Embodying this attitude gives you the ability to evaluate crucial information with less distortion. This leads to better investment decisions.

2. There is usually a high correlation between risky investments and excessive adjective use. A preponderance of adjectives raises your cautiousness. It is likely that you will avoid buying businesses based solely on hype.

ARCHETYPES ARE NO SUBSTITUTE FOR ANALYSIS

Closely associated with the misuse of analogy and adjectives is the use of investment archetypes. Archetypes are generic, idealized models of persons or of concepts. They are patterns of behavior and appearance that serve as molds for personalities and for understanding.

Let's discuss an example of an archetype. In most action films who is the protagonist? It's the loner hero who is an ex-special forces soldier who is treated badly by his government, but nonetheless remains a patriot and is reliably called upon to do the right thing in a time of crisis. This is a classic archetype and we all recognize him. Importantly, there are many other archetypes.

The benefit of archetypes in life is that they aid in communicating lots of information quickly about a subject without having to do much analysis. The brain seems hard-wired when meeting new people to quickly assess the person and to determine with which archetype the new acquaintance most resonates. For example, when talking about a friend, you might say, "I have a friend Bob who is a Perpetual Bachelor …" As soon as your listener hears you say, "Perpetual Bachelor," he or she pretty much knows Bob. One probably doesn't need to hear any more stories about Bob to determine how he will react in certain situations either. So archetypes aid in the speedy conveyance of information and sometimes they aid in understanding. But the problem is that archetypes are generalities and they obscure as much as they reveal. Archetypes are not a substitute for *real* analysis. For example, what if Bob is not a Perpetual Bachelor but is instead impotent? In this situation the assessment of Bob is obviously incorrect.

Most people identify with an archetype and modify their behavior and appearance to conform to one. Someone might choose to be the guy who buys a Harley Davidson motorcycle in his late 30s or early 40s and now goes riding on the weekends. Or someone might be the suburban yogini who rarely misses a chance to roll out the yoga mat. Someone might now be the straight gal or guy that never does the things that got them into trouble as a sorority sister/fraternity brother. Whatever archetype is chosen, most people adopt the permissible behaviors and appearance of their chosen archetype fully.

Trusting in archetypes is not usually costly when you choose how you present yourself to the world, or assess a new acquaintance or watch a movie. But in investing trusting archetypes is deadly to your investment returns. It's essential to conduct analysis of reality not psychological phantoms. Here are the main investment archetypes to steer clear of:

➤ The Rocket Ship

➤ The Immortal One

➤ Old Ironsides

➤ The Plague Company

➤ A Stranger Comes to Town

➤ The Boy Genius

You probably recognize some of these archetypes from the colorful names I gave them, but let's explore them in depth. Pay close attention to whether or not you personally identify with one of the archetypal businesses and have invested in one.

The Rocket Ship

The Rocket Ship is the hot growth company that has a new product that serves a new and quickly growing market. It is primarily characterized by the word EXCITEMENT. These businesses receive lots of attention from investors in the form of an ever increasing stock price. Price fluctuations are extremely sensitive to news—ANY NEWS; as well as, attention in the form of gossip. You know these companies well, don't you? If there is positive news then there is lift off in the share prices. If there is negative news then there is melt down in the share prices.

Often Rocket Ship businesses occupy a disproportionate share of the evening business shows' news flow. You hear the names of these companies and of their executives, as well as the companies' stories talked up in coffee houses, in taxi cabs, and by your friends and relatives. For a business to be widely gossiped about, it is a good sign that the business is a Rocket Ship. There is a mythic quality to the story of the Rocket Ship that is similar to the fascination people have with this season's "great sports team" or this season's "hot celebrity."

The problem is that rocket ships almost always disintegrate in the atmosphere on their ascent to the heavens or fall back to earth. The excitement surrounding the Rocket Ships causes investors to ignore obvious and pertinent data about the business that otherwise would cause them to not invest. For example, the "hot market" whose product the Rocket Ship manufactures for is not really growing as fast as people anticipated. Or the "hot market" has many new Rockets launching simultaneously. Or the astronaut-executives don't know how to stabilize the flight of the Rocket company and they themselves prepare to abandon the ship and its passengers. Or the Rocket company is not built that well and the higher it flies the more strain is put on it.

The company you are examining may fit the archetype of the Rocket Ship well, but like most generalities, they fail at the margins. That is, archetypes fail to describe issues unique to a business, ones that determine whether the business turns out to be a good investment or not.

The Immortal One

A close corollary to the Rocket Ship business is the Immortal One (also known as the Perfect One). This is the company that walks on water (w.o.w.) and can do no wrong. It is the company that most others, typically the Rocket Ship companies, are compared to. The Immortal One's earnings are said to be "predictable;" or that, "they always make their earnings estimates;" or "they always exceed their earnings estimate by at least $0.02." It's usually the case that extreme adjectives are used to describe the Immortal One, such as phenomenal, spectacular, incredible, once-in-a-lifetime, and so forth. But adjectives are to be handed out like war medals only after an investment has earned your respect after much thorough analysis.

The Immortal One is potentially dangerous for investors because the company that "never fails to deliver" eventually does just that. Because of the unexpected nature of the failure it usually leads to huge declines in the company's stock. The Immortal One is also dangerous because most investors secretly harbor desires of finding the next Immortal One before anyone else. That "find" is the investor's ticket to fame and fortune. I myself have fallen prey to this sort of thinking in my career several times, including my thinking about International Rectifier.

Note: it's possible that the company in question *truly is* extraordinary, so you must be careful to avoid dismissing every company just because it neatly fits the archetype of the Immortal One.

Old Ironsides

Occupying the space directly opposite the Rocket Ship is Old Ironsides. This is the boring old battleship company that refuses to die, yet steadily and reliably executes its missions despite lots of competition and disdain from most investors. These businesses are those founded several generations ago, and have names that are known by multiple generations of folks who either use or know about their products. Old Ironsides companies cannot move very fast, are not sexy, and the perception is that they are to be retired soon along with the other relics of a bygone era. The share prices of these companies are typically more stable and often they pay (gasp!) a dividend. That's how unsexy they are—they actually provide their investors with a cash return.

The danger is that investors might never see the vast potential for return that Old Ironsides can provide because their eyes are firmly fixed on the sky looking for Rocket Ships. Often the real opportunity of Old Ironsides takes the form of its dividends or the financial assets of the company (that is, stock) being purchased inexpensively so that capital gains are a real possibility. The other danger for investors is trusting Old Ironsides' archetypal story to such a degree that they miss that Old Ironsides is, in fact, rusty and about to capsize under its own behemoth weight. Again, you must evaluate and evaluate more, and never rely upon an archetype to do your thinking for you.

The Plague Company

Just as the Rocket Ship has its extreme version, as the Immortal One, there is an extreme case for Old Ironsides, too, as the Plague Company. This company is diseased and about to die. Investors avert their eyes from the Plague Company because it is painful to look at and they don't want to "get any of it on 'em" lest their investment portfolios implode. The Plague Company can do no right and is the butt of investors' jokes and the target of ridicule from most of the investment community, including professional investors, investment news providers, and academics. The academics might talk of using the Plague Company as a case study for business school students of how *not* to run a business.

The danger of course, is the Plague Company may not be terminally ill, but just going through a period of severe illness. There are whole and famous investment careers founded on the identification and pursuit of Plague Companies. You can bet that if the news about a company includes a discussion of "emergency financing," a "white knight," or the firm being on its "last legs," it must be a Plague Company. Like the Immortal Ones, you are careful with the Plague Company. This is because price declines can be sharp, sudden, and frequent until the Plague Company stabilizes its health. Scrutinize, and do not stereotype.

A Stranger Comes to Town

A Stranger-Comes-to-Town company is one whose management fails to satisfy either their customers or their capital owners, so they get on horses and leave town in a real big hurry. Then a stranger comes to town and saves the company from the evils that hound it. New management is of course the Stranger. Frequently they are heroes from a similar company, or heroes from another and sexier industry, or heroes from another business era. The Strangers are brought in to resuscitate the business and to save the day. The thinking usually goes something like, "Well Bobby saved the XYZ Company and that was a tougher situation than this one, therefore company ABC is going to be turned around and be just as successful." The investment battlefield is littered with the corpses of Strangers who have taken the job of sheriff in the new town and that are killed by the same circumstances as the old sheriff. Again, the Stranger might be what the company needs to right itself, but then again, archetypes are no substitute for analysis.

The Boy Genius

The Boy Genius is the human equivalent of the Immortal One. This is the portfolio manager, investment adviser, business news pundit, or investment newsletter writer, who walks on water. The story begins when the boy genius was a young man and he worked very hard selling lemonade or newspapers. He then parlayed this quaint occupation into his first virginal investment, which of course made him an instant millionaire. Now when the Boy Genius isn't living the life-of-luxury he pontificates about currencies or commodities or stocks that are just as sexy as his lifestyle is sexy. The story of the Boy Genius only includes the misfortunes of his mother and father's economic means, but never the misfortunes of his investment choices. A skewing toward perfection in the story of an investor is a sure sign of the Boy Genius archetype attempting to work you over.

Your familiarity with these archetypes allows you to see through the obscuring smoke of news around most businesses. This is because most investment news is of the same character, retelling the same old investment myths involving the same old investment archetypes. Always remember that every investment situation is unique and requires real analysis to be understood well. Once you start paying attention to archetypes you will likely be amazed at just how pervasive they are and just how strongly they affect the perception of a business. Beware and be aware. Take no shortcuts!

INVESTMENT APPLICATIONS

1. Similar to "beware the adjective," this attitude allows you to clearly evaluate potential investments. If you are aware of the archetypes then you likely make better investment choices.

2. Others use archetypes in their thinking. Because of this you are not fooled by investments that are appealing to many others. The opposite is also true. Opportunities hidden to others, because of their obsession with archetypes, are more obvious to you.

The Intuitive Investor and You: Self-Assessment

Remember a moment when you were learning something and everything all of a sudden "just clicked." What did this feel like? Did you feel integrated *with* the information? What was your understanding like before the "click," and after?

Is it your tendency to focus on risks or opportunities when you consider an investment? Where did this preference come from? If you focus on the risks more predominately, are there any emotions associated with that emphasis? If so, what emotions arise for you? If you tend to focus on opportunities to a greater extent, what emotions arise in these moments?

Think about your relationship with uncertainty. Do you deeply prefer certainty? If so, take a few moments to consider why you prefer certainty. How often does your experience of the world match your preference?

Have you ever missed out on an opportunity because you were overly concerned with making a perfect choice? If so, what lessons did you learn from that situation?

When you make a mistake what is your usual attitude toward yourself? Are you intolerant? What do you do to learn from your mistakes?

Have you ever felt a pressure to be invested? If so, from where do you feel this original pressure came? How comfortable are you doing nothing as an investor?

How would you feel speaking with an executive from a prospective stock investment? What is your understanding of the role of a shareholder in a corporation? What happens to your attitude when you imagine yourself as an owner of the business?

Have you ever been obsessed with your investments? What were the signs of that obsession? How often did you check the news or stock price of the business? What led you to feeling that this investment was the One?

Have you ever invested in an investment archetype? If so, what was the result?

Exercises

A LESSON IN RISK ANALYSIS Most investors do not know that each publicly traded corporation in the United States is required to file an audited annual report with the Securities and Exchange Commission. Nor do they know that each annual report, the 10K, is required to list the significant business risks that the company faces. Rectify that right now.

Go to the always free website: www.sec.gov/edgar/searchedgar/companysearch.html. Then enter a stock ticker symbol for a stock in the box labeled "or CIK or Ticker Symbol." If you don't know a ticker symbol then enter the ticker symbol for Wal-Mart: WMT.

This brings up a screen full of confusion (thank God for lawyers). Don't be alarmed. Scroll down until you see "10K" on the left-hand side. Then click on the button labeled "Documents." Make sure that you don't mistakenly click on "10Q." This will bring up another potentially confusing screen. Again, don't be alarmed.

Next click on the "hot link" underlined in red to the left of the document Type: 10-K. Now scroll down until you find **ITEM 1A. RISK FACTORS**. Take the time to read the risk factors for your chosen business.

Beyond the risks described here, can you think of others? Write down your experience with this exercise in your notebook.

SPOTTING THE MANIPULATION OF ADJECTIVES Over the course of several nights watch the business news (CNBC or Bloomberg TV). Write down any examples of extreme language you hear, especially adjectives. Place in your notebook those news stories described by the station with extraordinary language; put a date next to the story.

Evaluate how often adjectives are used in a story. Is the extreme nature of the adjectives warranted by the extremeness of the facts of the story? Record your observations.

Do you have an emotional response to the business news? If you were to take out the adjectives from the reporting of the story, how would your emotional response change?

As a follow up, how many days did it take for news described with extraordinary language to disappear from the news?

REVIEW

Principle III: *Harmonizing* was central to this chapter. This third principle is about having accord with information, which leads to understanding. To achieve this, the Seven Essential Investor Attitudes were described to help you harmonize your mindset to be more fully in alignment with your right brain.

You learned the importance of focusing on risks before opportunities. Because risks have a tendency to repeat themselves you can anticipate them. Whereas new opportunities unfold in the future and the future is difficult to analyze accurately.

Comfort with uncertainty stresses an acceptance of variance, a form of non-linear, right-brained thinking. Adherence to this Attitude reduces anxiety and opens up the right brain.

Because the cost of pursuing perfection is very high, making good decisions is often greater than or equal to perfect decisions. Again, because the future is difficult to understand it requires relativistic thinking, instead of obsession with perfection. This puts your mind more in accord with the right brain.

Perfection struck again when I demonstrated the importance of forgiving yourself for not being perfect. Accepting that you will make mistakes beforehand reduces the stress of any investment decision. Additionally, forgiveness of a personal mistake allows you to move past the emotions surrounding a mistake and into learning from your mistake.

Both of the Attitudes, You Are Holding Investment Interviews, and Why Does It Have to Be This One, focus your attention on thoroughly understanding an investment. Additionally, both empower you in your investment decision-making. Because it is your money, it is your choice that matters, not someone else's choice.

Finally, I shared with you a number of False Prophets, including misuse of analogies, adjectives, and archetypes. All three are typically used as substitutes and shortcuts for analysis of a real situation. Instead, all three rely upon prejudices and associations to quickly communicate, and often obscure, information.

7

Seven Essential
Investor Behaviors

"Do you want to know who you are? Don't ask. Act!
Action will delineate and define you."

—THOMAS JEFFERSON

SO FAR YOU HAVE LEARNED numerous skills to place you more in accord
with your right brain and to help you understand information. Now that you
understand the information landscape, you must do something with that
understanding: you must take action. The fourth principle, Action, is aptly
named and firmly hands responsibility for investment choice over to you.

In the last chapter I described Seven Attitudes that serve as a permanent structure for increasing the potency of your right brain. However, while
the structure provided by these Attitudes is always present, it is passive.
Now you must take action, this requires activation of the Seven Essential
Investor Behaviors. The Behaviors actively place you in accord with your
right brain and help you to make better investment decisions.

Introducing Principle IV: Action

This principle is defined as:

Effects follow causes.[25]

Those of you with a spiritual bent might recognize this as the Law of
Karma. Those of you with a scientific bent know this principle as Isaac
Newton's Third Law, often stated as: "For every action there is an equal and

---

25 Received via meditations on January 3, 2006 in Dayton, Ohio, USA and March 1, 2006 in Dayton,
Ohio, USA.

opposite reaction." The fourth Principle of Action is the heart of the chapter because of its focus on behaviors, or actions of the mind. Behaving consciously leads to better outcomes and this is the very definition of investing.

The essential core of the Principle of Action is *choice*. This is because choices lead inexorably to action.

Behavior 1: Choose Responsibility

"Money is only a tool. It will take you wherever you wish,
but it will not replace you as the driver."

—AYN RAND

The heart of investing is making conscious choices, and all choices inescapably entail responsibility. Thus, effective Investors choose to be responsible:

re•spon•si•ble (ri-spon'sə-bəl); adjective.[26]

1. Liable to be required to give account, as of one's actions or of the discharge of a duty or trust.

2. Involving personal accountability or ability to act without guidance or superior authority: a responsible position within the firm.

3. Being a source or cause.

4. Able to make moral or rational decisions on one's own and therefore answerable for one's behavior.

5. Able to be trusted or depended upon; reliable.

6. Based on or characterized by good judgment or sound thinking: responsible journalism.

7. Required to render account; answerable: The cabinet is responsible to the parliament.

Investment success is dependent on embodying all of the above definitions, but it requires even more. When most people think of responsibility they think in terms of partial responsibility. But full-responsibility is different. It means having consciousness of personal power and owning the responsibility for choices made when wielding that power. Successful investors do not blame others for failure or believe in bad luck.

---

[26] *American Heritage Dictionary of the English Language, Fourth Edition* (New York: Houghton-Mifflin Company, 2006).

✦ Taking Responsibility for Mistakes ✦

It's November 2001 and my first year as a Portfolio Manager is winding down. I have made many errors that have cost my shareholders money. My annual bonus is predominately determined by my performance relative to my competition; this is known as my non-discretionary bonus. I finish the year in only the 60th-percentile. In response to my situation, I create a document called "Portfolio Management Lessons Learned" that I share with my fellow Davis investment professionals.

My boss, Andrew Davis, compliments me for taking full responsibility for my poor first year's performance as a portfolio manager. He rewards me the full portion of my discretionary bonus. Better still my document, "Portfolio Management Lessons Learned" becomes the basis for much of my future success.

✦✦✦✦✦

This doesn't mean investors have responsibility for everything in the world, but it does mean responsibility for the *power investors have and how they wield it*. People are not responsible for things beyond their power to affect them. Responsibility and power go hand in hand. If a person wants more power then she must be willing to be more responsible. Investing is about growing money. And money is powerful. Therefore, to grow your money you must increase your responsibility. Taking responsibility is in accord with Principle IV, Action, because choosing to behave with responsibility is an action.

Here are some of the choices that investors have full power over:

➤ How much effort to put into uncovering new investment opportunities.

➤ How much analysis to conduct before buying an investment.

➤ Who to trust when considering an investment.

➤ Which information is important in evaluating an investment.

➤ Which investment to purchase.

➤ When to buy or sell an investment.

➤ How much money to invest in an investment.

Because investors hold this power of choice they also simultaneously have the responsibility for those choices; there are no comforting excuses.

The first step in becoming fully responsible is for investors to know exactly what resources and power they have to deploy. Many of the Intuitive Investor's self-assessments and exercises are designed to help you to take inventory of your personal power.

The second step in becoming fully responsible is for Investors to stop rationalizing the negative outcomes of choices and instead choosing to take responsibility for them. An essential part of this is forgiving oneself for not being perfect and learning from your mistakes.

Here is a homily...

"The difference between an investment analyst and an investor is that the analyst aims the gun and the investor pulls the trigger."
—JASON "YOURS TRULY" VOSS

The sole difference between the analyst and the investor is responsibility. Analysis of a prospective investment is interesting; but analysis alone does not make an investor any money. The world is full of armchair investment pundits and "I Told You Sos." This position is an irresponsible one. To buy, or not to buy, that is the question. To have bought or not to have bought is a more responsible position. If investors don't take responsibility for their choices then someone else or something else determines the outcome for them. The burden of choice is responsibility; but conversely, the benefit of responsibility is power (An example of: Principle II: *Paradox)*.

INVESTMENT APPLICATIONS

1. A very simple and empowering formulation: more responsibility = more power, and more responsibility = more money.

2. Taking full-responsibility means avoiding distracting excuses. Excuses disempower you because in your mind you have a "get out of jail free" card that serves as license to be reckless. Full responsibility leads you to greater consciousness of your investment decisions.

3. Awareness of, your full power/the bounds of your responsibility, suggests a path for learning. It also means when bad things happen beyond your power you can forgive yourself and move on.

Behavior 2: Honesty

Equally important to choosing responsibility is choosing honesty. Together, responsibility and honesty create a granite solid foundation for all of the other Essential Investor Behaviors. Because honesty requires a choice, it is in accord with Principle IV, Action.

✦ A Lack of Honesty ✦

In 2001 I am in Boston for a critical meeting with AES Corporation. AES is a U.S.-based global owner of power plants and power distribution. Unfortunately for AES they are experiencing a financial crisis brought on by drought in Brazil. The company bought hydroelectric power production (river dams) from the country of Brazil. In exchange, the country promised to buy its power from AES in exchange for low prices and a guaranteed minimum amount of power production.

Unfortunately, the rain fall in Brazil has been exceptionally low this year. Less rain = less water in the rivers. Less water in the rivers = less water to send through the dam. And that means that AES cannot keep its end of the power production contract. AES' purchase of these assets was financed with debt. That debt has covenants associated with it and one of them says that AES is in default on its obligations if it cannot provide power to Brazil as promised.

All of the big wigs are on hand for the meeting. CEO, CFO, VP of Investor Relations, money managers, and analysts. AES needs to convince its debt holders that it is solvent or the bond owners can put AES in receivership (bankruptcy) and begin selling its assets off. The travails are being followed daily in *The Wall Street Journal* and major business press. Tensions are understandably very high.

After the question, "Are you guys going to survive?" The BIG question is "Are you going ahead with your plans to invest more in your Brazilian money pit?" and eventually someone asks it. AES's CEO, Paul Hanrahan, answers the question with an emphatic "no." But I know he is lying. I actually want AES to invest more money in Brazil and approximately a year later they do.

✦✦◆✦✦

Most people have an understanding of honesty's importance but have never thought of it as an investment tool. But being honest is to be in accord with reality (Principle III, Harmonizing). This uncorrupted clarity allows investors to accurately assess information and to make effective investment decisions.

To clearly see the truth of the universe external to oneself, investors must know the honest internal truth about themselves; otherwise there are distortions. Unfortunately, distortions lead to inaccurate assessments of the information landscape. Those inaccurate assessments lead to mistakes and in turn, those mistakes lead to losing money. Additionally, if investors are not honest with themselves then they are likely to make the same investment mistakes over and over again. Worst of all, investors not knowing their own truth obscures their ability to discern the truth around them.

The truth has a very unique feeling associated with it that is like a flawless diamond cutting through the sticky strands of the obscure. The truth feels like a brilliant and golden light piercing the darkness. When people are honest with themselves they are suffused with the feeling of truth. With practice, when people are honest with themselves they become familiar with the pristine feeling of the truth and recognize its presence instantly. Importantly, when people ultimately shift their awareness outward to examine the universe they can recognize the truth by *feeling* it. When AES' CEO Paul Hanrahan said the company would not invest more money in Brazil I knew he was lying. I knew because *the feeling of truth* was not present in his words. When the mind is free of distortions it results in a nearly flawless truth detector.

INVESTMENT APPLICATION Now when you analyze a business and identify the factors important to you for making a decision, you can use your ability to discern the truth to intuit the truly important factors. It's difficult to overstress the importance of an accurate truth detector in making successful investment choices.

Behavior 3: Balance Intelligence and Wisdom

The next critical Investor Behavior is to actively balance intelligence and wisdom. This is because successful investing boils down to the necessity of balancing the left-brain intelligence and right-brain wisdom when evaluating investments. This magical combination results in the maximum understanding of information and good investment decisions. Because investing is like detective work, equilibrium between left brain and right brain is the skill most admired in detectives and investors. Intelligence is useful for gathering information, and wisdom is used to make decisions. The two brain components, intelligence and wisdom, though opposite are actually part of a greater whole and are complementary (Principle II, Paradox). To actively integrate intelligence and wisdom results in the maximum understanding of information. Actively doing anything is in accord with the fourth principle.

Briefly intelligence and wisdom are:

➤ intelligence – intellectual maturity; its components are:
  ○ knowledge
  ○ memory
  ○ creativity

✦ Intelligence Out of Balance with Wisdom ✦

In 2005 I plan to retire, but I am required to find my successor first. An international headhunting search is conducted that gives Andrew Davis and me many choices. He and I look through a considerable stack of analyst and portfolio manager cover letters and résumés. Most of them work for very prestigious and well-known money management firms. Eventually we interview around ten candidates on the phone. From those we invite a few to Santa Fe for in-person interviews. As a part of the hiring process we ask each candidate to submit a written example of his financial analysis of a company. We do this because we know a hidden secret of the mutual fund business, which is that most firms do not do their own proprietary research. During the course of evaluating the research my colleague Chandler Spears catches two of the candidates plagiarizing research originally published by Standard and Poors!

The plagiarizing job candidates do not know how to do their own financial analysis that is the point of our test. So their choice to plagiarize is intelligent. However, it is unwise.

✦✦✦✦✦

✦ A Word about "Immaturity" ✦

The word "immature" is a loaded word for most. In what follows, the intention is not to create some sort of "in crowd" that separates the mature from the immature. In the current context, immature does not mean juvenile, instead it means not having ripened to one's full sweet potential.

✦✦◆✦✦

➤ wisdom = emotional maturity; its components are:

  ○ feelings

  ○ non-attachment

  ○ intuition

Here is a model of the brain that incorporates the components of intelligence and wisdom:

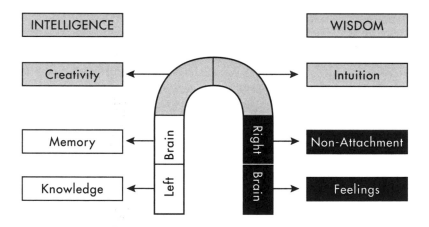

INTELLIGENCE

Intelligence is intellectual maturity. By maturity, I mean a fully seasoned intelligence, characterizing one capable of adapting to most situations and solving new problems. There are three major components of intelligence; namely:

1. knowledge
2. memory
3. creativity

Knowledge and Memory

Knowledge is everything you have ever learned. Anything aiding your storage of information increases your intelligence. This includes items such as a day-planner, a personal digital assistant (PDA), files in a filing cabinet, computer databases, access to the Internet, and lifestyle choices such as proper nutrition.

Memory is your ability to access your knowledge in a timely and accurate fashion. Anything aiding your recall of knowledge increases your intelligence. For example: mnemonic devices; ordering systems, such as alphabetical or numerical; a database's search function; an Internet search engine; proper nutrition; and memory exercises, all help memory.

Creativity

The last aspect of intelligence, creativity, is the most interesting and the most difficult to work with if you limit yourself to only using your left, analytical brain. Creativity happens when the right brain links together with the left brain and recombines pieces of knowledge to provide new solutions to problems. These interconnections are made in a non-linear, organic fashion in accord with the four principles (more on this in chapter eleven).

Creativity is a *natural* function of the mind. Creativity is important to investors because the universe throws many new-to-you problems that require solutions slightly beyond your knowledge's ability to solve them. That is, new problems require new solutions. Because of its unique ability to chart new intellectual territory, as opposed to applying the same old solutions to the same old problems, creativity is the highest expression of the left-brained intellect and marks the point where the left brain merges with the right brain.

The temptation may be to *segregate* creativity into an exclusively right-brained capability, but the brain is an integrated thinking machine. When the knowledge and memory aspects of the left brain reach up and bridge with the intuitive aspect of the right brain, the right brain provides the final, crucial creative juice.

These moments of inspiration are sometimes known as "Eureka" moments. Everyone knows these moments of profundity. The solution to a problem appears out of nowhere. Best, the solution usually is elegant in its effective simplicity. How to do this is the subject of chapter eleven, Cultivating Your Creativity.

WISDOM

You need to have a good understanding of the difference between intelligence and wisdom to properly nurture both. But the difficulty in discriminating between the two is that wisdom is mostly a nebulous topic. You know wisdom when you see it but most people probably cannot be relied upon for a solid definition.

Most think that wisdom is a subset of intelligence. The hole in this logic is that it means only intelligent people are wise. But everyone has known someone simple who is full of wisdom. Similarly, I have known many intelligent executives who have done very unwise things that resulted in the ruining of their careers, the loss of tremendous wealth, and in their imprisonment (e.g., Jeff Skilling of Enron, Dennis Kozlowski of Tyco and Bernie Ebbers of Worldcom). Intelligence and wisdom are not the same thing—not even close. Earlier I said that wisdom is emotional maturity. What this really means is having conscious awareness of your emotions to minimize their distorting effects.

I define wisdom as:

the degree to which you are in accord with reality.

Wisdom can also be described by actions undertaken in accord with wisdom, such as:

➤ The ability to recognize the truth, using Principle II, Paradox, the ability to see/make distinctions

➤ The unswerving willingness to seek the truth, using Principle III, Harmonizing, and its emphasis on understanding, as well as Principle IV, Action, and its emphasis on choice

➤ The willingness to look within oneself, make personal assessments, and change, using Principle I, Infinity and willingness to expand personal boundaries

➤ The ability to see and understand all sides in a given situation, using Principle II, Paradox, and efforts at making distinctions

➤ Recognizing the interrelation and interpenetration of all things, using Principle I, Infinity with recognition of infinite interconnectedness

➤ The ability to float above the flotsam and jetsam of life, that is, to surf the universal flow, in Principle III, Harmonizing, and efforts at having accord with reality

➤ Allowing oneself to harmonize with all of life's possibilities and not just those that are comfortable, using Principle I, Infinity, and its emphasis on vastness

➤ Making conscious, responsible, honest choices, using Principle IV, Action, and its emphasis on choice

Finally, wisdom is your ability to love yourself unconditionally.

Wisdom is important for investment success. For example ... Imagine someone who has constantly received praise for taking big risks. When he downhill skis his friends praise his speed and bravery as he slides down the mountain. And also imagine that his first love praised his risk-taking on the football field. These and other experiences mean he is predisposed/prejudiced to seeking gratification from risk-taking. So his investment style is pre-disposed to risk-taking, too. In fact, he is so pre-disposed that he seeks out investments that have greater risks. This is actually emotionally immature, and therefore unwise, because his investment decisions are unconscious. He is behaving in a way that is comfortable to him, but perhaps detrimental to himself. Additionally, his ingrained behavioral program prevents him from appreciating a low-risk, yet high-return investment, because it does not *feel* risky enough to him. Incidentally, it is equally emotionally immature to steer clear of investments that feel risky too because there is an emotional preference to take fewer risks. The ultimate idea is to understand the information landscape objectively and free of emotional bias (Principles I-III). In turn, this leads to excellent investment decisions (Principle IV).

Here are the component parts of wisdom:

1. feelings
2. non-attachment
3. intuition

Feelings

Feelings, as I defined them earlier, are the basis for the operation of the right brain. Feeling sensations come in many forms, including physical, mental, and spiritual. Exploration of these feelings has been one of the central focuses of the book.

Non-Attachment

Non-attachment means that you have no preferences about either information on the information landscape or about outcomes in your life. When pure feelings are experienced free of ego involvement and emotional reactions, that is, feelings without judgment or preference, accord with reality occurs. Experiencing feelings with non-attachment is one of the keys to cultivating wisdom (accord with reality).

Non-attachment is not detachment because detachment is an active state of disinterest. An example of detachment is when you are young and your mom tells you to paradoxically ignore the kids who are bothering you; this is almost impossible. The more you think about ignoring those kids the more you think about them. The problem with this piece of maternal advice is that the act of ignoring is just that, an act; as in *active*. Non-attachment is a neutral state of being. It is a state of allowing. Non-attachment is a state of readiness where if you have to act, you can.

The essence of non-attachment is difficult to define because most people usually put ideas and concepts on continuums, bounded on both ends by opposite views of the same concept. But non-attachment lies exactly in the middle of a continuum named "reaction." One end of the continuum is labeled as "active reaction," whereas the other end is labeled as "passive reaction." Non-attachment is the middle point, or the fulcrum point between attachment and detachment.

Non-attachment is important because investors cannot afford to color the invaluable information received from their feeling-selves/intuitions with prejudice. Successful investors must experience the world for what it is. So an investor chooses to be neutral/non-attached.

Again, non-attachment is not detachment since this indifference can result in an investor *not* responding to situations that require them to act. This results in missed opportunities, or worse, in a substantial loss of resources if the sale of an investment was called for.

The ideal is not attachment, either. Having attachment means any change in the value of your investment can alter your sense of self-worth. You are not your investment (Principle II, Paradox). Attachment and detachment are both biased and you cannot afford bias in understanding the flow of news from the world. The poor timing of my investment in International Rectifier in the initial days of my career is an unfortunate, personal example of attachment.

INVESTMENT APPLICATIONS

1. Because you have non-attachment you don't feel compelled to either buy or sell an investment just because everyone else is. Non-attachment helps you to avoid the stampede of the herd, olé!

2. You see details that no one else is because you are not overwhelmed with the distorted, emotional hype of an event as covered by the media.

3. You forget past successes and failures so your evaluation of situations is fresh, fully present in the moment and conscious.

4. Best of all, non-attachment means that you see reality clearly. Thus, all of your investment decisions are made with accurate information.

If both of the first two components of wisdom, feelings and non-attachment, are operating then intuition is the natural consequence. The full discussion of intuition comes in chapter twelve, "The Intuitive Investor."

Behavior 4: Judge, But Don't Prejudge

Often behaviors are absorbed via osmosis from society without much conscious choice in adopting the behavior. One of the classic behavioral admonishments is: Do not judge. In fact, the admonishment runs so deep that the word "judgment" is loaded. Yet every time decisions are made, they are judgments. In investing, decisions are made in the hope that the ending stack of resources is bigger than the beginning stack of resources. To maximize the result of choice, rationality demands that all of the possibilities first be judged. Hopefully a good decision is made based on those judgments. How is the need for judgment reconciled with the classic and constant admonishment of "do not judge?"

A close reading of the behavioral admonishment "do not judge" suggests that the real teaching is: "do not pre-judge." The primary difference between

✦ Unbiased Analysis ✦

In the early 2000s I purchase Waste Connections for the Davis Appreciation and Income Fund. Upon telling my Portfolio Management partner, Andrew Davis, of the purchase he is concerned. "Garbage companies are bad investments," he admonishes me. Andrew reminds me of the investment failures our firm has experienced in both Waste Management and Allied Waste. Not only has this happened, but most investors have soured on investments in waste companies. I explain to Andrew that Waste Connections has a radically different strategy from that of the big waste companies. In particular, they pursue waste contracts in small municipalities where it only makes sense for there to be one waste company. This means that Waste Connections does not face competition in over half of its markets. Eventually Andrew holds Waste Connections up as an example of unbiased thinking on my part.

✦✦✦✦✦

judgment and pre-judgment is consciousness. Prejudiced decisions are unconscious and likely based on past, perhaps irrelevant to the current moment, experiences one has had. Alternatively, prejudice may also be conditioned behavior learned from parents or society. Either way consciousness is not present in prejudice. Prejudiced decisions are not in accord with reality and are, by definition, distorted. Distorted decisions are the foundation for poor understanding and ultimately of poor investment returns. The "do not judge" admonishment is really trying to teach the importance of being in the present moment, *with* the current circumstances and set of facts, in order to see the current situation for what it really is. The admonishment is really about the deep need to have consciousness of choices.

We all have free will and the power to choose. This means we need to judge, or to assess. The paradox of free-will cannot be escaped: not choosing, for fear of judging, is to choose not to choose. Paradox arises because you cannot remove yourself from the life you are living—you are a part of reality. This is the essence of Principle I, Infinity—it is impossible to not be a part of the universe. Therefore, it is impossible to not judge. All of life's choices are judgments and they deserve consciousness. Because judgments are choices, they are in accord with Principle IV, Action.

INVESTMENT APPLICATIONS

1. Free from the mistaken notion of "do not judge," you are now empowered to make investment decisions using your full reasoning powers. If you have a "funny feeling" about the executive who heads up a business you are considering an investment in, this is relevant and actionable information, and more importantly, you now have permission to use your judgment in this situation. Your judgment of him is important.

2. Knowing the difference between prejudice and judgment helps you to evaluate whether your choices are made based purely on old patterns of behavior, prejudices, or on seeing reality for what it really is. The investment analogies and archetypes of the last chapter are a form of prejudice and blindness to current investment realities.

Behavior 5: Courage

Here's my favorite quote about courage. It comes from the movie *Three Kings*. The scene is just prior to the characters involved going into battle to rescue a captured comrade:

> Conrad Vig (CV): "Wait, hold on a minute, I wanna go over this plan one more time."
>
> Archie Gates (AG): "You're scared, right?"
>
> CV: "Maybe."
>
> AG: "The way this works is, you do the thing you're scared sh*tless of, and you get the courage after you do it. Not before you do it."
>
> CV: "That's a dumb-ass way to work. It should be the other way around."
>
> AG: "I know, [but] that's the way it works."

The essence of courage is decisions made in the presence of anxiety and fear. Courage is earned **after** you do the thing that scares you, not before. Fears create boundaries around yourself and are usually unnecessary. The decisive and conscious choice to ignore anxiety and fear and push through

✦ Fortitude in the Face of My Peers ✦

In 1999 I am in Palm Springs, California for a Salomon Smith Barney institutional Investors' conference. The conference is massively abuzz because America Online just announced its purchase of Time Warner. The principals involved, Steve Case of AOL and Gerald Levin of Time Warner, are on hand the next day to sell **the** dot.com deal to the pros. But I am on hand because I am interested in, though not infatuated by, News Corp. I want public access to Rupert Murdoch and Peter Chernin of the company because I am considering an investment. It seems to me that much of the investing public is overly focused on News Corp's EBITDA (a poor proxy for cash flow) and to a lesser extent their earnings. My careful reading of the firm's financial statements suggests that a goodly chunk of their earnings comes from tax-loss carry-forwards that are about to burn off. I want a public response to the following question, "Your future earnings projections are above this year's earnings, yet you are going to be losing much of your tax-loss carry-forwards. How will you make up the difference?" Is my non-status quo assessment correct? There's only one way to find out. If ever there were an opportunity to be humbled, it would be now as I nervously ask Mr. Murdoch my question in front of 2,000+ of my peers.

   I am very nervous as I ask Rupert Murdoch my question about the source of future earnings. If my research is not accurate then many of my potential future employers who are on hand will see my foolishness. But I have assessed literally hundreds of businesses and have a good track record of judging them accurately. My faith in myself is unswerving. I ask several trenchant questions that lead to valuable information. Mr. Murdoch acknowledges that News is about to lose its tax-loss carry-forwards. In order to answer my question he needs to publicly disclose the company's future growth opportunities in more detail than he has before. The public nature of his disclosure increases the likelihood of a truthful, complete answer. More importantly, his answer gives me confidence in News' future prospects and I end up buying an interest in the company that serves our shareholders well.

your boundaries is essential for investment success. Choosing courage allows you to explore new personal frontiers. Again, because courage is a choice, it is in accord with the Action Principle.

Perhaps you already have a personal financial advisor, or you rely upon your investment firm's analysis, but now you want to make your own investment choices from now on. However, you are experiencing anxiety and bump up against a boundary: "I've never done this before." Choosing to make investment choices in the presence of anxiety or fear leads to more courage to make even more difficult decisions in the future.

Courage is cultivated by consistently engaging anxiety and fear head on. Additionally, in chapter three the exercises, "Anxiety Review" and "Emotional Inventory," are both helpful in identifying your personal limitations and then the choice is yours as to whether to push through them or not. Courage is not a state of being but an actual behavior. You choose to have courage; you practice courage; and finally you earn courage.

Another way to cultivate courage is to regularly make minor life decisions where uncertainty is present. Such as picking the right apples at the market, or choosing the right route home from work. This sounds innocuous but courage cultivation is a practice. The more you make minor decisions in the face of anxiety, the easier it is to muster courage for important decisions. In short, the process is:

➤ Feeling anxiety or fear

➤ Recognizing anxiety or fear—that is, being conscious of either

➤ Identifying your boundary

➤ Exploring why the boundary is present

➤ Choosing to cross the boundary; this results in the growth of your capabilities

➤ Losing the anxiety or fear and thus, gaining courage

Behavior 6: Conviction

Another of my favorite movie quotes, this time from *A Beautiful Mind*:

"Well conviction, it turns out, is a luxury of those on the sidelines."
—WILLIAM PARCHER to JOHN NASH

Having the courage necessary to make investment decisions leads investors to make choices. However, choice and conviction of choice is not the same thing. Conviction is confidence in your ability to be in accord with reality.

Conviction is a choice and therefore in accord with Principle IV, Action. No one can make you convinced; likewise, no one can un-convince you of anything. It is your choice to believe or not to believe in something, or someone, or yourself. There is no in-between here. But conviction is not blind faith. Blind faith means that you eventually get out of step with Reality as it changes.

Conviction comes from knowing that you assess the universe accurately. True conviction is free of emotion. Conviction is not colored by some misplaced belief in a superior intellect or education or decision-making ability. Conviction is maintained and increased by objectively examining your previous choices in light of the new information that comes from the passage of time. If you made the right choice in the past then your conviction in your ability to perceive reality increases. On the other hand, if you made the wrong choice in the past, you endeavor to learn from the mistakes of past choices. This also leads to greater conviction in your future ability to be in accord with reality. Conviction ultimately comes from knowing yourself.

A way of assessing whether or not you have "it," as in whether or not you are a good investor:

*Do the investments you have judged perform
as you expect them to perform?*

If you pass up buying an investment because of some concern, is your judgment supported by the unfolding story of the investment? If you purchase an investment, does it appreciate in value for the reasons you thought it would? If the answer to either of these questions is consistently a "yes" then you can have conviction that you are understanding information like an investor.

A secret for ensuring that each investment decision you make is suffused with conviction is to treat **"maybes" as "nos."** That is, if you are having doubts about an investment decision and think to yourself that "maybe it will work out," then you treat this the same as "no, I will not purchase this investment." Treating maybes as nos is another way of saying you only invest in yeses, or when you have conviction.

Behavior 7: Assuming There Is a Why

Eventually all investors encounter a set of facts that seem baffling and beyond the grasp of rational analysis. The tendency in our analytically-biased culture is to dismiss such absurdities because they seemingly violate our culture's preference for scientific, rational and certain answers. Yet, as expressed in Principle I, Infinity, everything is part of a greater whole and inextricably linked. This means that there are always causes that underlie the facts of an investment situation.

While the choices (causes) that led to a set of outcomes (effects) may escape your investment analysis, remember that the decision-maker had reasons for her choice. Consequently, investors must always assume *there is a why* for every outcome examined. This empowers investors to pursue reasons and rationales doggedly. This behavior places you in accord with Principle I, Infinity, because it forces you to seek out the interconnections between choice and outcome. Because choice and outcome are alternative ways of expressing cause and effect, this behavior is also in accord with the subject of our chapter, Principle IV, Action. Acceptance of the irrational and assuming *there is always a why* elevates an investor's ability to reveal the truth of a situation.

"Assuming There Is a Why" pulls all of the preceding Seven Essential Investor Behaviors together. Imagine you want to understand an investment before purchase:

1. Your first behavior is responsibility. Before making the investment you take responsibility for your decision to: begin your investigative process; analyze the prospective investment; eventually invest, or not invest.

2. Assuming you analyze the investment candidate then it's critical that you are honest with yourself about your analytical limitations, investment goals and reasons for selecting an investment.

3. In your analysis and purchase decision you use both your intelligence and your wisdom to make an effective choice. This includes using your knowledge; accumulating more knowledge; being creative in your analysis; tuning into your feelings (as opposed to emotions) to discover the truth of the investment situation; remaining

non-attached as you investigate your facts and feelings; and using your intuition to assess the future prospects of the investment.

4. You avoid any prejudices you may have and with the accumulated facts, and your creative and intuitive insights, you judge the investment.

5. Then you muster your courage to either invest or not to invest.

6. After your decision you have conviction that your choice is a good one.

7. All of these behaviors are components of the "why" of why you end up investing.

The Intuitive Investor and You: Self-Assessment

What is your relationship to the word responsibility? Does the word feel burdensome or liberating? Are there reasons for these feelings? Can you imagine a different relationship to responsibility?

Do you feel that you use your full personal power? If yes, in what ways do you utilize it? If no, can you identify some reasons why you do not?

Is your preference to be told the truth? Why is this the case?

Do you do anything on a regular basis to increase your knowledge?

Do you ever feel out of harmony with life? Are you able to identify any consistent sources for your feelings of discord?

Can you remember an important situation in your life where your reaction was neither attached, nor detached, to the outcome, but somewhere in-between these two states? Was the feeling of this state unique or common for you? How does this state feel? Are you able to identify any factors that facilitated your ability to embody this state?

Consider the word "judgment." What emotions surround this word for you? Where did these emotions come from?

Consider your investments. Do you have any perceived prejudices, either positive or negative, about any of them?

Remember a moment in your life in which you made a courageous decision. What emotions were you experiencing prior to your decision? What did you do in the lead up to your decision that helped you to make your choice? How did you feel after the decision was made?

What is your typical response to something that seems strange? Do you reject it, or are you intrigued to find out more?

Exercises

TAKING RESPONSIBILITY

In your notebook, write down the details of a bad investment. Include the reasons for your purchase as well as any reasons you feel are relevant for why the investment did not go as anticipated. Record your response to the outcome.

Now revisit the process you went through before purchasing the investment. Assume now that you are forced to take full responsibility for the outcome, no matter how absurd this may seem. With this new context, now re-examine your choices. Write down anything that you could have done to ensure a different outcome.

ACTIVATING YOUR TRUTH DETECTOR

Place in your notebook the details of a situation in when the truth was not present, but eventually revealed itself. This could be a situation where someone you thought liked you, actually disliked you. Or it could be that your boss was behaving strangely and you didn't know why. Record the details of the situation now. Be sure to include your feelings before you knew the truth, and after.

Next, recall the moment when the truth of the situation was revealed to you. Recall that moment when the person was explaining himself and his actions and just before any emotional response you may have had to the reveal. In your memory are you able to separate out a feeling like "so that's why you said that?" or "so that's why you did that?" How did that feel to you? Describe this feeling in your notes. This is how you experience "the feeling of the truth."

Now harmonize exclusively with that *feeling*—do not attach words to it. Just hold the feeling in consciousness. Now inexorably lock *the feeling of truth* into your memory. At the same time as you are feeling what truth feels like, say the word *"truth"* out loud. Repeat this until it seems silly. You are creating a strong association between the *feeling* of truth with the *word* for that feeling: truth.

PRACTICING NON-ATTACHMENT

Imagine either your most favorite or least favorite sport. That is, the sport that gets your emotions flowing. In your notebook, write down the emotions you experience as you watch the sport.

Next make an effort to watch this sport as soon as you can. Perhaps you go to the Internet and watch footage of a past sporting event. For this to be real it needs to be a sporting event where you are emotionally involved. Now, as you are watching the event, instead of getting involved in the outcome watch it in a state of non-attachment. Appreciate and honor the event for all it's worth: the athleticism, the artistry, the grace, the sensuality, the spectacle, and so forth. See if you can avoid getting emotionally involved with the outcome. After all, you are not an actual participant in the event and despite your emotional response to the event you are not likely directly affected by the event or its outcome.

How did you do? Record your success with this exercise in your notebook. If this was difficult for you, spend some moments exploring the sources of your emotional attachment. Write down any insights in your notebook.

If you are able to embody a state of non-attachment encode this feeling in your memory by saying "non-attachment" out loud as you simultaneously experience the feeling.

REVIEW

In this chapter I shared with you Principle IV, Action. This fourth principle of the Intuitive Investor is all about choices and actions. The ability to be more in accord with the right brain requires active participation. To enbable this to occur, the Seven Essential Investor Behaviors were introduced. Choosing to embody these behaviors allows you to understand information better and consequently to make better investment choices. The Seven Essential Investor Behaviors, taken in order, provide a powerful structure for the effective understanding of information.

Before making an investment you take responsibility for your decision to begin your investigative process, analyze the prospective investment, and eventually invest, or not invest. This is Behavior 1. In analyzing an investment candidate it's critical that you are honest with yourself about your analytical limitations, investment goals, and reasons for selecting an investment. This is Behavior 2. These first two behaviors are the bedrock of embodying Principle IV, Action.

Behavior 3 is balancing your intelligence and your wisdom to make an effective investment choice. This means using your current knowledge and accumulating more knowledge to understand the investment. Behavior 3 also means using your creativity and intuition in conjunction with your intelligence to discover as much of the truth of an investment situation as you can. This leads to better investment decisions.

Behavior 4 implores you to avoid any prejudices you may have and to judge the investment as effectively as you can. Confronted with the decision to buy the investment you muster your courage; this is Behavior 5. Once purchased, you must have conviction that you understood the information well—that is, you must have faith that you were in accord with reality. Each of these behaviors is a component of your reasons "why" you buy the investment. Behavior 7 is also present throughout the analysis process as it pushes you to always understand information even when it seems illogical.

8

The Intuitive Investor Toolkit

NOW THAT EACH of the four principles has been introduced, it is time to combine them synergistically into powerful investment tools for your Intuitive Investor Toolkit. Each of the tools provides a context for understanding information at different points over the life of an investment: before buying, while holding, and after selling.

Your Cousin Vinny provides the context for understanding information prior to buying an investment. The Investment Thesis is a contract between yourself and an investment and is ideal for evaluating investments while you hold them. Thus, it connects you intimately with the investment information landscape. The Lessons Learned List is created after the sale of an investment and is designed so that you avoid repeating your mistakes. In my career I used each of these powerful tools to improve my investment success.

Because each tool is intimately associated with an exercise, keep your notebook nearby so that you can participate.

Context for Understanding Information Before Buying—Your Cousin Vinny

Here's one of the greatest investment secrets. This simple exercise automatically puts you into the proper Investors' mindset before buying an investment. I am certain that you will be surprised at how much investment acumen you already possess as revealed by Your Cousin Vinny.

YOUR COUSIN VINNY

Imagine your cousin Vincent approaches you to invest in a coffee shop that is for sale in your hometown. Importantly, Vinny wants *you* to put up all of the money to purchase the business. So you will be providing all of the cash equity. In return Vinny offers all of his knowledge and labor to run the coffee shop—this is the sweat equity.

What are the questions you **need** to ask Vinny before you are comfortable giving him your hard won dollars for the java shop? You grew up in a capitalist culture and have many years of experience as a consumer. This means you also have a wealth of knowledge to draw on when evaluating the quality of Vincent's coffee shop idea.

Because this is one of the most critical exercises of the entire book, you should really do the exercise. Twenty questions is the minimum number of questions allowed. Write your questions for Vinny down in your notebook right now.

Now compare your questions with my list of potentially relevant questions:

➤ Is Vinny trustworthy?

➤ Is Vinny hardworking?

➤ Does Vinny overwork?

➤ How does Vinny manage stress?

➤ How intelligent is Vinny?

➤ How wise is Vinny?

➤ Does Vinny have experience running a coffee shop?

➤ Should he organize as a corporation, limited liability company, limited partnership, partnership, or sole proprietorship?

➤ What are the benefits and costs of these legal forms of business ownership relative to owning a coffee shop?

➤ What will be the growth of coffee consumption going forward?

➤ What alternative products (substitutes) are there for a cup of coffee?

➤ What will his menu look like?

➤ Will Vinny also sell food?

➤ How strong is his competition?

➤ How much competition does he have?

➤ How will he compete with all of the other coffee shops?

➤ Where is his competition located relative to the shop's location?

➤ Where is the java shop located?

➤ Is this location a good location?

➤ What is the quality of the shop itself? Is it in need of repair?

➤ What is the ambience of the coffee shop?

➤ What does he want the ambience to be like?

➤ How is his coffee, and other products, different from that of his competition?

➤ What will be his primary product? Is it going to be coffee?

➤ Where will he get his supplies and products from?

➤ What will it cost for him to get his supplies and products?

➤ What is the lead time before he can get products that he has ordered?

➤ What prices will he charge for his products?

➤ How did he derive the price for the products?

➤ How will he handle customer dissatisfaction?

➤ How will he handle an explosion of demand for his products?

➤ How will he handle a sudden decline in demand for his products?

➤ How will he handle any seasonality in his business?

➤ What kind of equipment does he need to purchase?

➤ What is the state of the equipment that is already in place?

➤ Does any of the equipment need repairing?

➤ How much depreciation is left on the equipment to take as a tax deduction?

➤ What will be the cost of the monthly utilities?

➤ How much is he going to pay his employees?

➤ Is this wage or salary competitive with other employers?

➤ What other benefits will he provide to his employees?

➤ Who will manage the operations of the business?

➤ Is this manager a good manager of customers, staff, and finances?

➤ Where will he find this person?

➤ How will he compensate this person?

➤ What if this essential employee leaves the shop?

➤ How will he market his coffee shop?

➤ Who will be responsible for the accounting?

➤ How much does it cost to do the accounting for the shop?

➤ To what health department or employer or other regulations does he have to adhere?

➤ What are the environmental risks of the java shop?

➤ What kind of local, state, and federal taxes will he have to pay?

➤ What will he do with profits?

➤ Does he want to grow the business?

➤ How will he pay for the growth?

➤ What proportion of debt will he use to purchase the business?

➤ What proportion of debt will he use to grow the business?

➤ Whom will he do his banking with?

➤ How will you get paid back for your investment?

➤ How much money does Vincent need to make the shop viable?

While this list of questions to ask of your cousin Vinny is very long, it is representative of the important issues confronting most businesses. Feel free to use it going forward in evaluating other investment opportunities.

How'd you do? Was there a lot of overlap between your list and mine? Are you surprised at how many of the pertinent issues you understood and listed? How many of the issues *you* identified did not show up on *my* list? Do not discount these issues as they came from you personally and therefore they are very important in your personal evaluation of an investment.

The "Your Cousin Vinny" exercise is the exact mindset you need as you analyze a business for investment. Over the years I have done this exercise many times with family members, friends, stock brokers and audiences of investors, and no one has ever failed to identify the important issues of a prospective investment. Let me reiterate that point: audiences have never failed to identify the most pressing issues of a prospective investment. More importantly my audiences have also never, ever, come up with questions such as:

"What is the moving average price of coffee shops sold over the last 270 days?"
or
"Have the prices for coffee houses gone up dramatically over the last 3 weeks?"
or
"What are analysts/talking heads saying about coffee houses?"

You recognize these sorts of questions, don't you? These are the types of questions typically asked regarding potential stock market purchases. Interestingly, these sorts of questions don't come up when I ask: "What are the questions you need to ask Vinny before you are comfortable giving him your hard won dollars for the java shop?" Why?

The "stock-market-type-of-question" isn't asked because "Your Cousin Vinny" is the perfect context for evaluating a business for investment. The context is that of an iffy family member wanting to buy a local business. This immediately emphasizes that:

> ➤ You are investing in a business, not a piece of paper (a stock).

> ➤ There is a real chance of loss if you aren't cautious.

> ➤ You have a real choice whether you take on specific risks before investing.

> ➤ You have the innate knowledge necessary to analyze investments.

In other words, there is a profound sense of ownership when the question of investing is asked in this context.

Most importantly, once you take the magic word "stock" out of the question, and say "java shop" then everyone identifies the relevant issues. Investors invest in businesses, not in stocks, bonds, options, real estate, commodities, mutual funds, etc. A stock is just one way to own an interest in a business among many. So what is it about the word "stock" that causes people to go all loopy and to forget themselves, and to cast their intelligence and wisdom out the window?

I feel it has to do with the collective unconscious wherein resides the notion that stocks are equated with huge fortunes won, similar to the winnings from lotteries or in gambling. This is crazy. The only difference between buying a business interest in a private market transaction, like Vincent's java shop, and a public market transaction like the stock market, is liquidity. Liquidity is the ability to buy or sell your interest very quickly and at a fair price. This is the real and *only* magic of the stock market (or bond market or options market or commodities market or …).

> *What the stock market is doing is irrelevant*
> *in your evaluation of an investment.*

After you have become comfortable with the business issues identified in your analysis, then you ask yourself whether or not this is a good business. But, and this is a big but, good businesses do not necessarily make good investments.

> *The only difference between a good business*
> *and a good investment is price.*

Before you make an investment in a business you must evaluate the price of the business. If the price of the business is reasonable, you may purchase an investment in the business. Unfortunately, a complete evaluation of an appropriate price to pay for a business is outside of the scope of this book. However, in the Appendix there is a list of good valuation texts.

Let's look at the four principles that the tool, "Your Cousin Vinny," makes use of:

The first principle of Infinity encourages you to see the many *interrelationships* between Vincent's coffee shop and everything else in the world. The Infinity Principle helps you place all of the facts of a situation on a topographical map. In the "Your Cousin Vinny" exercise, some of those facts are:

> ➤ Does Vinny have experience running a coffee shop?
> ➤ What alternative products (substitutes) are there for a cup of coffee?
> ➤ Where is his competition located relative to the shop's location?
> ➤ Where is the java shop located?
> ➤ What is the quality of the shop itself? Is it in need of repair?
> ➤ What will be the cost of the monthly utilities?

These are all facts that Vincent cannot change about the situation. They are givens and he must accept them if he is going to open a coffee shop with your investment monies.

Yet, even though Vincent's coffee shop is a part of everything as shown in the first Principle of Infinity, it is its own unique entity. So you need to figure out what *is* and *is not* pertinent to your understanding. Now you narrow infinite possibilities to distinctions, shown in the second Principle of Paradox. The "Your Cousin Vinny" tool asks you many questions to establish distinctness, such as:

> ➤ Is Vincent hardworking?
> ➤ How strong is his competition?
> ➤ Is this wage or salary competitive with other employers?

These questions are answerable relative to something else. They help you to narrow the scope of possibilities. The insistence of the Principle of Paradox that interrelated concepts can be opposite gives you good mental integrity for considering all of the relativistic sorts of issues that can affect a business. For example, it could be that Vincent is a hard worker, yet he overworks to such a degree that he is a candidate for burnout. So "hard-working" could be a good thing, or a bad thing. In other words, the second Principle of Paradox lets you know that every strength is also a potential weakness and that every weakness is also a potential strength. Opposite truths are not always absolutely equal in magnitude or importance. It could be Vincent's hard-working nature has a higher probability of being beneficial than the negative probability that he might suffer from burnout. *Continuums* help you to understand these sorts of issues.

Principle III, Harmonizing, tells you that for the coffee shop to be successful Vincent must put in place many "coffee shop-like" structures if he hopes to have a viable business. For example:

➤ How does Vinny manage stress?

➤ Should he organize as a corporation, limited liability company, limited partnership, partnership, or sole proprietorship?

➤ How will he compete with all of the other coffee shops?

➤ What is the ambience of the coffee shop?

Vinny can choose to pattern his stress management on a technique he learned in a book or from a beloved therapist. Vinny can choose an ambiance for the coffee shop that is evocative of his favorite coffee shop in Tuscany. This is the Principle of Harmonizing. This principle also says the easiest way to start a coffee shop is to use other coffee shops as the model.

Lastly, Vincent must choose to act. The coffee shop doesn't open on its own. This is shown in Principle IV, Action. This principle is likely the easiest to understand, but there are several wrinkles. The fourth Principle of Action refers you back to the first Principle of Infinity because it says that effects follow causes. This is another way of saying that everything is interrelated. So if Vinny chooses to open the coffee shop (a cause) then all sorts of things will start happening (effects). Customers could come flooding in. The competition could lower prices. Trusted employees may quit. He could start making a lot of money. You must evaluate Vincent's business *from the beginning* with an eye toward the likely effects of the new business beginning to operate. Principle IV: Action is all about choice. Vinny has all sorts of decisions to make about the coffee shop, such as:

➤ How will he compete with all of the other coffee shops?

➤ What does he want the ambience to be like?

➤ What will be his primary product? Is it going to be coffee?

➤ Where will he get his products from?

These are not the **facts** of the situation, these are choices, and hence, they are subject to the fourth Principle of Action. And "Your Cousin Vinny" makes use of all four principles.

Context for Understanding Information While Holding—The Investment Thesis

Wouldn't it be nice to know the questions to ask of a business's management before investing? Wouldn't it be nice to have such an excellent understanding of a business that when you read the news you actually have an understanding of how that news might affect the business? Wouldn't it be nice to know the criteria that are legitimate reasons to sell your interest in a business? Wouldn't it be nice to make investment decisions more free from emotion? These are among the most difficult things for Investors to apprehend. But one tool helps with all of them: the Investment Thesis.

Earlier in the book I said the investment process is analogous to detective work. Well the investment thesis is your theory of "How the crime was committed." It summarizes:

➤ The facts you believe are important to know about a prospective investment

➤ The facts you choose to trust when you purchase an investment

➤ Your opinion about the quality of a company's management, including their personalities

➤ Your feelings regarding the strengths and weaknesses of the company

➤ Your beliefs about the company's future prospects

➤ A list of the critical points that lead you to invest in the business

You create your Investment Thesis just after you are done with your analyses, but before you call the company and speak with an investor relations professional.

THE INVESTMENT THESIS

The Investment Thesis is the contractual document you write that outlines the relationship between you and your investment. Just like all contracts The Investment Thesis provides the grounds for evaluating the relationship in an objective, legal-like fashion. Because you are the only witness to this agreement you must respect the Investment Thesis with sanctity. This means that if an investment violates the Investment Thesis that you have created then you will agree to sell it, rather than rationalizing a continued reason to own it. The Investment Thesis provides the perfect context for evaluating your ongoing relationship with an investment while you hold it.

Before you can write an investment thesis you need to have evaluated a prospective investment first. However, if you are not currently considering an investment, use an investment that you either made in the past or an investment you currently own.

Most importantly, before writing an investment thesis make sure that you are feeling grounded and not charged with emotions. In particular, you want to be free of elation, fear, or disgust about a prospective investment. The power of the Investment Thesis is that it is written at a time when:

➤ You are in an objective, non-attached mindset. This serves as the basis for evaluating potentially emotionally charged issues surrounding your investment. Examples include bad news about the business, a rapid decline in the value of shares of stock in the business's industry, and a violation of your Investment Thesis. Also, because of the objectivity at the beginning it serves as a check on "mission drift." This is where bad news is rationalized away by an investor. Referring back to the Investment Thesis ensures that no such rationalization can take place.

➤ The knowledge you have accumulated about the business is fresh in your mind. This ensures that you do not forget any information about the business you felt was pertinent at the time of purchase. As time goes on the Investment Thesis will represent the minimum amount of knowledge you have about the business as you will be continually adding information to your document.

Now write down in your notebook the name of the investment and the current date at the top of the document (see the Appendix for a sample investment thesis). Next record your investment time horizon. That is, how long do you expect to own this business? Alternatively, how long do you expect this business to contribute desirable returns to your portfolio?

Write down the strengths of the business—more is better than less at this point. For each strength you record, also include an estimate for how long you feel each strength might be in place. For example, if you feel that the business has a dominate product, write down how many years you feel this product will be dominate. Next, play "devil's advocate" and imagine ways in which the strengths could be overcome by competition or pure chance.

Now write down the weaknesses of the business—more is better than less. For each weakness include an estimate for how long you believe each of the weaknesses might be in place. Play "devil's advocate" and imagine ways that the weaknesses could be overcome by management efforts or pure chance.

The next part of the investment thesis is to record the things about the business that make you feel ignorant. Alternatively, what aspects of the business would you like to understand better? Also write down the things about the business that you feel anxious about.

Now write down a brief list of "The reasons I feel like buying this investment." The list must be brief because restricting the list to brevity ensures that you will only list the most important issues.

In your notebook, make a short list of "The things that *would* cause me to sell the investment immediately." Follow that list up with a short list of "the things that *might* cause me to sell the investment immediately."

Next write down the price you feel is reasonable to pay for an interest in the business.

Now evaluate your investment thesis. How do you feel about this business? Are you comfortable? If not, what things make you feel uncomfortable? Do you need more information? If so, where will you go to get that information? How do you feel about the current market price of an interest in the business, especially relative to the price you feel is worth paying?

If you buy an interest in the business, record on your investment thesis the following:

> ➤ The price you paid for the investment next to your estimate of a price that is reasonable to pay.

➤ The date of your purchase next to your estimated investment time horizon.

Your investment thesis is a *living document* so you must update the thesis to reflect new and pertinent information that affects any aspect of the thesis that is already written down. Importantly: this does not give you the power to radically change the thesis as artificial support for your emotional connection to an investment!!

INVESTMENT APPLICATIONS

What Else Do I Need To Know?

If after creating your investment thesis you are still uncertain of a decision, it's a sure indication of two things: you don't have enough information to make a decision, or else your emotions are getting in the way of you being decisive. These are the very issues addressed in chapter three, "The Infinite Possibilities of the Information Landscape."

The investment thesis helps to highlight these issues for you so that you can move through them. Upon further personal reflection it could be the case that you have no legitimate reason for experiencing the emotions of feeling ignorant, in which case you make a decision: buy or not. But it could be that your emotional reactions about ignorance are entirely justified. In that case, you seek out more information until you feel you have just enough information to make a good decision (maximize the ignorance).

Because the investment thesis summarizes the information you know and do not know about a prospective investment, it serves to highlight appropriate questions for a company's management team. These are the types of questions such as: who is the firm's strongest competitor; what are the sales forecasts for each of the next five years; what key new products will be unveiled over the next several years; what mistakes has the business made and how did it learn from them. Frequently these questions cannot be answered easily by publicly available information. So a thorough investment thesis naturally suggests which questions should be directed to a firm's "investor relations" department, which nearly all publicly traded businesses employ. Look for the appropriate phone number or e-mail address on the company's website or on the bottom of the company's press releases.

Overcoming "I Can't Decide"

The investment thesis is created and you are about to invest. You are confident you have the right amount of information to make a good choice.

However, you just can't decide. This is a sure sign you are experiencing either anxiety or fear. In this case you use the exercises outlined in chapter three to identify the true cause of your indecision. If you are experiencing anxiety then you muster your courage and choose to buy or not.

If upon reflection you are legitimately experiencing the intuitive emotion of fear then this is a strong sign that you should either not invest or that you should sell the investment if you already own it. Because you put these things in writing when you create your investment thesis, it helps you to make easier and better decisions.

News Flow Evaluation

The Investment Thesis is the *basis* for your investment and thus it is what you compare news flow to in order to evaluate the effect of news on your investment. Say for example you are invested in an "exploration and production" company, that is, an oil company. Then say you read in *The Wall Street Journal* that the U.S. Government is going to provide massive tax breaks for businesses that invest in hybrid vehicles for their vehicle fleets. How do you evaluate this piece of news? You compare it to your investment thesis.

In your thesis you not only include the business strengths, but also the importance of time in your evaluation. If you feel the news violates any of the strengths, or reasons for buying that you listed on your thesis then you have very good *cause* for evaluating the investment's continued viability.

Just because a part of your thesis is violated does *not* automatically result in you selling the investment. However, if the news falls under the category of "things that would cause me to sell the investment immediately" then you *do sell immediately*. If the news doesn't violate the thesis, or if you feel that management can respond to the news event in a timely and intelligent fashion then your thesis is not violated. Therefore, you continue to hold the business. Or if you have not already bought an interest in the business then you buy.

Less Emotional Decisions

Because the investment thesis is created at the beginning of your ownership in a business and I insisted that it should be created at a time when you felt free of emotions surrounding the business, it serves as the objective basis for evaluating situations as they unfold in the future. If you choose to honor the sanctity of your investment thesis and allow it to trump any feelings you currently have about the investment then it acts as an unswerving check on your emotions.

Learning From Your Mistakes

The thesis allows you a rapid way of evaluating your mistakes so that you learn from them, and (hopefully) never repeat them. During my career most of my mistakes were made because I either did not create a comprehensive thesis from the outset, or because I ignored the information in my thesis.

If your mistake is not having a comprehensive enough thesis then the lesson is obvious: next time you are more diligent! If you feel your thesis is comprehensive, but you missed something, then the next time you invest in a similar business then you include these new factors in your decision-making.

The mistake of ignoring your thesis is the most painful and the most difficult to overcome. This is because you are your own police officer and only you can choose to obey and enforce the law of your own thesis. This powerful tool is made impotent as soon as you elect to ignore it or revise it to suit your current emotional needs.

Context for Understanding Information After Selling: The Lessons Learned List

---

While it may be comfortable to sit in a decision-free zone to ensure you never make a mistake, this is also likely to have the result of your never growing as an investor. If you invest, you will make mistakes. So rather than avoiding mistakes by never making decisions, as an investor your goal is to never *repeat* your mistakes. The tool for accomplishing this is the creation of "The Lessons Learned List." The list is the embodiment of the age-old adage of: "Fool me once, shame on you. Fool me twice, shame on me." The lessons learned list also provides the perfect context for evaluating an investment after you sell it (see the Appendix for a sample).

The lessons learned list should be created at two important times in the life-cycle of an investment:

1. At the end of each year even if you haven't sold an investment, and ...

2. Upon the sale of an investment

During the course of my career I made a list at the end of each and every year. But I would also update the list during the course of a year with any new lessons learned or important observations. So the lessons learned list is a living document that gathers together your accumulated investment wisdom. In fact, much of the content of *The Intuitive Investor* came from my collection of lessons learned.

For the list to be fully potent requires you to honestly and unabashedly confront your mistakes so that you do not repeat them. This sounds simple enough, but the process can be brutal. In fact, it's critically important to be 100% honest with yourself. After all, you are the only witness.

EXERCISE: CREATING "THE LESSONS LEARNED LIST"

Upon either selling an investment or a calendar year having passed, make a list of the investment mistakes you made. Then carefully review the mistake so that you identify why and how you made it. Now use your creativity to imagine a remedy to the mistake. Write the lesson down on your Lessons Learned List.

Now list all of the lessons you learned, not just those arising from mistakes. Perhaps the lesson is just a simple observation or a mistake you avoided making because of a powerful insight.

The Lessons Learned List is very straightforward in concept, but having the fortitude to make your list each year and upon the sale of an investment is tough. If you make creating "Lessons Learned Lists" a habit, then each year your list gets shorter as you learn from your mistakes and avoid others.

REVIEW

In this chapter I shared with you three powerful tools, each of which should occupy an important place in your Intuitive Investor Toolkit. Each tool addresses a different part of the investment life-cycle, before buying, while holding, and after selling.

Your Cousin Vinny provides the context for understanding information prior to buying an investment. Its secret is that it emphasizes that you are the owner of your capital investing in a business whose issues you likely understand well. The context of this tool ensures that you focus on the correct issues. Consequently, you avoid issues such as the daily gyrations of the stock market, or feelings of inadequacy regarding your ability to evaluate an investment.

The Investment Thesis is a contract between yourself and an investment. Thus, it connects you intimately with the investment information landscape. This contract provides the appropriate context for you to evaluate your investments while you hold them. This tool mainly helps to provide you with an objective framework for evaluating all of the news and emotional issues surrounding an investment.

The context of The Lessons Learned List is after the sale of an investment. The tool ensures that you learn from your mistakes by creating a living document that accumulates your investment wisdom. The primary goal is to avoid repeating a mistake in the future. Importantly, you may add any learned wisdom to your list.

Section Review

In Part Two of *The Intuitive Investor*, "Activating Your Intuition for Wealth Manifestation," I first shared with you the Seven Essential Investor Attitudes. The Attitudes are like subconscious mental programs that are always active. Accord with the Attitudes puts your mind more in alignment with the right brain. The Seven Attitudes were: Focus on Risks Before Opportunities; Comfort With Uncertainty; A Good Decision Is Most Often ≥ The Perfect Decision; Forgive Yourself for Not Being Perfect; You Are Holding Investment Interviews; Why Does It Have To Be This One?; and Beware of False Prophets.

Next I revealed the Seven Essential Investor Behaviors. These are active mental programs that help to remove the majority of the distortions that prevent your right brain from functioning at its full capacity. The Seven Behaviors are: Choose Responsibility; Honesty; Balance Intelligence and Wisdom; Judge, Don't Prejudge; Courage; Conviction; and Assuming There Is a Why

Principle III, Harmonizing, was introduced in part two. Accord with the third Principle is the crucial step that allows an investor to understand information as you harmonize with something to understand it. Next, Principle IV: *Action* was introduced. It emphasizes the power that lies in both responsibility and choice.

PART THREE

Putting the Four Principles to Maximum Use

HOPEFULLY YOU HAVE COME a long way in becoming an Intuitive Investor. As powerful as the techniques, skills, and tools have been so far, they do not compare with the most powerful techniques of creativity, intuition, and wealth manifestation. Use of these skills puts the four principles to maximum use. But for this to happen the four principles must be explored more in depth and expanded to provide the necessary capacity for supporting the ultimate right-brain investing tools. Doing this means that the Intuitive Investor will enter radical territory within the context of the modern scientific status quo. But my promise to you remains that each skill I share with you is something that I have personally used for investment success.

With more robust four principles in place I will explore the power of meditation, the ultimate intuitive vehicle. Because many people are intimidated by the idea of meditation I will show that the meditative mind state is an entirely natural state of mind that most people enter each day. I will describe powerful techniques for uncovering what you already do to enable you to enter a meditative state. Knowledge of when and how you meditate will allow you to enter the state at any moment of your choosing.

Next, I will share with you some of the secrets for increasing your creativity. Techniques for accessing the right brain's creative function virtually at will are demonstrated. Following on the heels of creativity is intuition, another of the right brain's hallmarks. I will show you clearly how to access you intuition to better understand information. In turn, this ensures that you make better, more lucrative investment decisions.

All of the skills taught in the book combine together to form A Radical Guide for Manifesting Wealth. The five steps needed "to get what you want" are shared. Additionally, some of the secrets of refining your ability to manifest what you want are shared. *The Intuitive Investor* concludes with "Reports from The Field." This is a collection of anecdotes from my career that demonstrate the use of the full powers of the right brain and its creativity, intuition, and manifestation skills.

9

Increasing the Potency
of the Four Principles

*"...It is important to realize at the outset that
the principles of material realism are metaphysical
postulates. They are assumptions about the nature of
being, not conclusions arrived at by experiment."*[27]

*   *   *

*"One becoming two, the two becoming three,
the three becoming the fourth that represents the One."*

—MARIA PROPHETISSA, Ancient Egyptian alchemist

So far the four principles have been dealt with in a limited way. To realize their full potential requires an expansion of the understanding of their operation. Then the four principles need to be integrated together into a "sum-is-greater-than-the-parts" whole. A caution to the deeply scientific or deeply religious: this material may be challenging. My solemn promise is that I am sharing only those things that I have experienced and utilized with success.

One way to amp up the volume on the four principles is to make a move from the secular to the sacred. Don't be alarmed, this is *not* brainwashing. The purpose is to discuss experiences that all human beings have but for which there is not widespread scientific acknowledgment. I also want to avoid scientific and religious dogma that might confuse the *clear signal of experience.* But, by definition, the universe is larger than science and religion.

---

[27] Amit Goswami, Ph.D., with Richard E. Reed, and Maggie Goswami, *The Self-Aware Universe: How Consciousness Creates the Material World* (New York: Tarcher Penguin, 1995), 17.

"The picture of quantum tunneling from nothing [i.e., the birth of the universe] raises another intriguing question. The tunneling process is governed by the same fundamental laws that describe the subsequent evolution of the universe. It follows that the laws should be 'there' even prior to the universe itself. Does this mean that the laws are not mere descriptions of reality and can have an independent existence of their own? In the absence of space, time, and matter, what tablets could they be written upon? The laws are expressed in the form of mathematical equations. If the medium of mathematics is the mind, does this mean that mind should predate the universe?

"This takes us far into the unknown, all the way to the abyss of great mystery. It is hard to imagine how we can ever get past this point [i.e., what existed before the birth of the universe]. But as before, that may just reflect the limits of our imagination."[28]

Principle I: *Infinity*

Earlier I secularly described the Principle of Infinity as:

The universe is infinite.

With this definition investors identify their positioning relative to everything else. This first principle also helps investors to know that everything is interconnected. But to tap the power of the right brain fully, and to experience what many describe as psychic phenomena, I need to broaden the Principle of Infinity.

Here is the non-secular definition of Principle I: *Infinity*:

The only God worth believing in is an Infinite One.

As a former atheist I am fully cognizant of the strong repulsion many people have toward the word "God." The word is chosen because of its utter lack of ambiguity. "God" is the most widely known word for: the universe, the Void, Nothingness, the Totality, the One, Infinity, YHWH, Allah, Great Spirit, the Dream Time, 1, 0, the Zero Point Field, etc. For those comfortable with God this likely is not a difficult word to accept. For those

---

28 Alex Vilenkin, Ph.D., *Many Worlds in One: The Search for Other Universes* (New York: Hill & Wang, 2006), 204–5.

of you who are atheists or agnostics or non-believers or just indifferent, this concept is likely to pose a challenge. Let's explore this a bit more so we can move past any prejudices and fully activate our brains, right and left.

The second category of readers described above, the non-believers, likely place their trust in science and science alone. Most typically this unswerving belief in science is a belief in the power of the physical sciences. The physical sciences are those such as physics, astronomy, chemistry and biology—the hard sciences where many answers are very certain and adhere cleanly to linear mathematics. This unswerving belief in hard, mathematical answers has a name: *material realism.* This philosophy is also some times called *determinism* because it assumes that all things are mathematically determinable if you know two things:

1. Mathematical formulas precisely describing phenomena, and ...

2. The initial state of the universe.

But determinists are the classical scientists of yesteryear; they are those shaped by seeing the world as a series of mathematical certainties, and those shaped by the theories of René Descartes and Sir Isaac Newton. But in the 19th Century a new physics emerged that had greater *explanatory* power than Cartesian-Newtonian physics: quantum physics. Many people remain unaware of the ways that quantum physics describes experience. This is because determinism has been so preeminent in educational institutions for the last 300 years. The problem is that the old classical science of the determinists does not explain nature as well as does quantum physics, especially with regard to states of consciousness that underlie the creative and intuitive functioning of the mind. To ensure that you and I are on the same page, a brief overview of the state of Cartesian-Newtonian physics is in order.

The material realist/deterministic scientific philosophy rests on five key assumptions, to be examined in light of quantum physics:[29]

1. Strong objectivity

2. Causal determinism

3. Locality

4. Material monism

5. Epiphenomenalism

---

[29]Amit Goswami, Ph.D., Richard E. Reed, and Maggie Goswami, *The Self-Aware Universe: How Consciousness Creates the Material World* (New York: Tarcher Penguin, 1995), 15–8.

Strong objectivity is René Descartes' philosophy known as dualism where he divides experience into two parts: the objective and the subjective. In Descartes' view the objective realm falls under the purview of science. The preoccupation of science is the examination of matter; as in: atoms, the book in your hands, whatever you are sitting on; the stars; and anything that is considered "out there" and separate from your mental experience of the world. The subjective realm Descartes considered as under the purview of religion. He felt that the preoccupation of religion is the mind. In short, Descartes and most of the scientists following him believe objects are separate and independent of the mind. This thinking is sometimes referred to as Cartesian after Descartes. In fact, Descartes envisioned the world as a huge machine with extraordinarily complex inter-workings.

Causal determinism is the view of the world that says if you know the initial conditions of a system, and the fundamental laws of nature that all matter obey, you can then predict what will happen in any future moment. So if you sneeze at some point while reading the book? That is predicted by knowing the state of the universe just after the Big Bang and the formulae that govern the workings of the universe. You then wind the machinery of the universe forward up to the time you sneeze. Not only that, but you can wind the machine backwards, too. You can observe the conditions present now and work backwards mathematically to know what happened just after the beginning, too.

Locality means for one object to influence another it must have contact with the other object. For example, if you hop in your car to go to the grocery store you actually must traverse the space between. You can't just disappear from your home and reappear at the store (teleportation). What's more, the maximum speed for your trip to the store is the speed of light—nothing in the universe moves faster than this according to Einstein's theory of relativity. An implication of *locality* is that objects are constantly acting upon one another in a chain of cause and effect. But for cause and effect to be connected objects have to be local to one another.

The next assumption of most adherents to the hard sciences is *material monism*. This means that everything in the universe, including your consciousness, is made of matter. In other words, every thing is material, there is no such thing as the immaterial.

The final foundation of material realism is *epiphenomenalism* and it attempts to account for one of the true anomalies that material realism does not explain well: consciousness. Epiphenomenalism says that consciousness is explained as arising from the complex chemical and physical reactions of matter. According to material realists, we should someday be able to create a fully functioning brain with consciousness artificially in a lab.

Unfortunately for material realists these assumptions are undermined by quantum physics. Let's take them in turn again and learn a little bit about quantum physics, too.[30]

The first assumption of the material realists is *strong objectivity*. Scientists have overwhelmingly demonstrated that merely looking at electrons immediately changes their nature from behaving like a wave to behaving like a particle. That means that electron behavior cannot be predicted objectively unless you include your subjective choice, to look or not look at the electron, in your calculations. Strange, right? Not really. If you understand Principle I, Infinity, then you know that the electron is not separate from you—everything combines as a part of the seamless whole. Clearly, since subjective choice determines electron behavior then material realism's *strong objectivity* does not hold.

Next up is *causal determinism*. Again it has been exhaustively demonstrated that when you examine an object, say a car, that you can never determine both its velocity and its position simultaneously with absolute accuracy. So there is always an error in your knowledge of the initial conditions of a system. That means that causal determinism cannot be stated in absolute terms, only in relative terms. This is evidence for Principle II, Paradox. It's a probabilistic universe, not a causal one. The only absolute is the Universe. Since objects and their characteristics cannot be definitively described mathematically and simultaneously, the material realists' *causal determinism* is also violated.

What about *locality*? It has been shown definitively in the laboratory that when the state of one of two correlated electrons is altered, *no matter how far apart*, its correlated electron is affected identically even if it is on the other side of the solar system. This change in the state of both electrons happens instantaneously and in violation of the speed of light! So clearly the action is taking place outside of what we think of as material reality. This is known in the scientific parlance as nonlocality and it violates material realism's *locality* assumption. The correlated pairs of electrons are evidence for Principle III, Harmonizing.

What about *material monism* and *epiphenomenalism*? These two points combine to try to explain the anomaly of consciousness. As you saw above, in order to understand an object (an electron) you have to make a

---

subjective choice, to view or not view the object. By viewing it you change its nature. It doesn't make sense that an epiphenomenon, a supposed by-product of chemical interaction, can actually feedback on the very matter that created it in order to affect its state. Consequently both material monism and epiphenomenalism fail to adhere to their own deterministic set of logical scientific assumptions.

You may think these anomalies are unimportant but science cannot *leak* intellectually, even slightly. Cartesian-Newtonian physics has irrevocably been shown to be only a special case of quantum physics that holds mostly for the reality that human beings seem to occupy—the gross-level material world. In other words, the old science is incomplete.

The physical sciences are an exploration and explanation of the world solely describable by numbers and words, the purview of the left, analytical brain. They have explored thoroughly almost all phenomena describable in this fashion. But science fails to describe the full richness of experience. So why believe solely in science? Many answer "because that described by science is verifiable and replicable." Yet not all that is verifiable and replicable is described by science. Science has as its goal to describe all of experience, but everyone experiences things for which science has no explanation. Because of this, these experiences still await scientific explanation, and thus scientific *acknowledgment*. Science is not the basis for our lives, *experience* is.

There is tremendous resistance among scientists to acknowledge a wider realm of experience beyond materialism, that is, belief in things beyond what can be seen, heard, smelled, tasted, felt, and measured. Yet in chapter two, I discussed that a full experience of the Greatest Sunset exceeded numbers and word's, and hence science's, ability to explain it. So why do skeptics have such a difficult time with valid experiences that fall outside the realm of sensory perception and outside of Cartesian-Newtonian science's ability to describe them? As we will explore in depth shortly, these experiences by definition take place outside of the linear mind. Not coincidentally, skeptics spend a disproportionate amount of their conscious time in the realm of the linear mind. Yet, this is exactly the reason for the inability to experience the so-called psychic phenomena discussed in depth here in part three.

It has been my experience that there is a near-perfect correlation between dogmatic skeptics and those who cannot achieve extended periods of silence in their linear minds. Cut off as they are from a silent mind—

a mind free from the meanderings of numbers and words—skeptics rarely experience the states of mind that the right, non-linear mind, makes possible. All of us must believe in our experiences, so skeptics must be forgiven for not believing in phenomena experienced by a great number of the rest of us, if not by them. The problem is that many skeptics have turned their skepticism into *beliefs* so strong that they have created their own scientifically-based religion. Furthermore, because of an unswerving association of scientific reasoning with linearity skeptics spend most of their lives empowering the very thing (the left brain) that cuts them off from a fully mindful human experience of existence.

> *Unequivocally stated, my religion is the*
> *collection of my experiences.*

My experiences are the only incontrovertible part of my life, or anybody's life, really. You know what you have experienced, even if you cannot explain those experiences fully. But you should still believe in them even if science and religion cannot explain them fully either. Other people's experiences you should trust, but you also should verify that you are capable of experiencing them too. That is all I am asking you: *believe in your experiences.* We will continue to explore right-brain possibilities with exercises that are vehicles for experience. We will also explore a methodology for how the experiences work, and this methodology is scientific; meaning that it is verifiable by your experience.

The scientific method first demands you experience something before you begin to consider it as real. Those experiences lead to theories. Then those theories are rigorously tested to ensure their ability to explain your experiences and to make predictions about the future. The right-brain techniques explored are verifiably real and replicable and you are in accord with the scientific method. Science does not give us a complete explanation of how the techniques described work; yet because they *do* you must maintain scientifically open minds.

There exists the possibility of a middle ground between science and spirituality: a belief in experience. Abraham Maslow, an important psychologist wrote:

> "If there is any primary rule of science, it is, in my opinion,
> acceptance of the obligation to acknowledge and describe all
> of reality, all that exists, everything that is the case ... At its

best it [science] is completely open and excludes nothing. It has no 'entrance requirements.'"[31]

Forgive the detour, but it's important that as many of us as possible are open to new possibilities. So what is the implication of: "The only God worth believing in is an infinite God?"

A critical implication in accepting that God is infinite is that the ineffable You is a part of It. Seeing yourself as separate from God means God is infinite except for you. That clearly does not make any sense. A further implication is that because you are a part of God you are interconnected with everything.

The revised definition of Principle I using the mystical (to some) and all-encompassing concept of God creates a greater sense of interconnection: with everything. Feeling this profound interconnection between ALL things allows you to connect to life in a larger, vaster way. With this great sense of interconnection comes a greater source of information, intuition, which benefits your investment returns.

I am not alone in embracing Principle I, Infinity. Many revered and renowned scientists believe in the unbroken interconnectedness of everything. For example, Dean Radin, Ph.D. has written an excellent book entitled *The Conscious Universe: The Scientific Proof of Psychic Phenomena*, in which he provides a sweeping overview of the very strong scientific evidence for psychic phenomena. Radin says regarding interconnectedness, "The studies described here support ideas about deep interconnectedness espoused by physicists, theologians, and mystics. Mind and matter may be part of what physicist Victor Mansfield describes as 'a radically interconnected and interdependent world, one so essentially connected at a deep level that the interconnections are more fundamental, more real than the independent existence of the parts.'"[32]

So who is Dean Radin, Ph.D.? He is the Director of the Consciousness Research Laboratory at the University of Nevada, Las Vegas and he has done parapsychological research for AT and T, Contel, Princeton's department of psychology, the University of Edinburgh, SRI International and the U.S. government. To that effect he says, "During the Reagan administration, the House Science and Technology Subcommittee released a report

---

[31] Amit Goswami, Ph.D., Richard E. Reed, and Maggie Goswami, *The Self-Aware Universe: How Consciousness Creates the Material World* (New York: Tarcher Penguin, 1995), 145.

[32] Dean Radin, Ph.D., *The Conscious Universe: The Scientific Truth of Psychic Phenomena* (New York: HarperSanFrancisco, 1997), 172.

containing a chapter on the "physics of consciousness." The report stated that psi research deserved Congress's attention because "general recognition of the degree of interconnectedness of minds could have far-reaching social and political implications for this nation and the world."[33] Let alone your investment portfolio.

But Radin is not alone in his belief in the interconnectedness of the universe. In his book, "The Holographic Universe," Michael Talbot describes in depth the many scientists who share this viewpoint. In particular, he focuses on David Bohm, Ph.D., a protégé of Einstein's, and his views as described here:

> "An aspect of quantum reality that Bohm found especially interesting was the strange state of interconnectedness that seemed to exist between apparently unrelated subatomic events. What was equally perplexing was that most physicists tended to attach little importance to the phenomenon. In fact, so little was made of it that one of the most famous examples of interconnectedness lay hidden in one of quantum physic's basic assumptions for a number of years before anyone noticed it was there.

> "That assumption was made by one of the founding fathers of quantum physics, the Danish physicist, Niels Bohr. Bohr pointed out that if subatomic particles only came into existence in the presence of an observer, then it is also meaningless to speak of a particle's properties and characteristics as existing before they are observed. This was disturbing to many physicists, for much of science was based on discovering the properties and characteristics of phenomena. But if the act of observation actually helped create such properties, what did that imply about the future of science?"[34]

And here I pick it up a little later ...

> "During this same period of his life Bohm also continued to refine his alternative approach to quantum physics. As he looked more carefully into the meaning of the quantum

---

33 Dean Radin, Ph.D., *The Conscious Universe: The Scientific Truth of Psychic Phenomena* (New York: HarperSanFrancisco, 1997), 193.

34 Michael Talbot, *The Holographic Universe* (New York: Harper Perrenial, 1992), 35.

potential he discovered it had a number of features that implied an even more radical departure from orthodox thinking. One was the importance of wholeness. Classical science had always viewed the state of a system as a whole as merely the result of the interaction of its parts. However, the quantum potential stood this view on its ear and indicated that the behavior of the parts was actually organized by the whole. This not only took Bohr's assertion that subatomic particles are not independent 'things,' but are part of an indivisible system one step further, but even suggested that wholeness was in some ways the more primary reality."[35]

Continuing on…

"Indeed, because the quantum potential permeates all of space, all particles are non-locally interconnected. More and more the picture of reality Bohm was developing was not one in which subatomic particles were separate from one another and moving through the void of space, but one in which all things were part of an unbroken web and embedded in space that was as real and rich with process as the matter that moved through it."[36]

And further…

"…despite its apparent materiality and enormous size, the universe does not exist in and of itself, but is the stepchild of something far vaster and more ineffable. More than that, it is not even a major production of this vaster something, but is only a passing shadow, a mere hiccup in the greater scheme of things."[37]

And lastly, regarding Bohm …

"In a universe in which all things are infinitely interconnected, all consciousnesses are also interconnected. Despite

---

35 Michael Talbot, *The Holographic Universe* (New York: Harper Perrenial, 1992), 41.

36 Michael Talbot, *The Holographic Universe* (New York: Harper Perrenial, 1992), 42.

37 Michael Talbot, *The Holographic Universe* (New York: Harper Perrenial, 1992), 52.

appearances, you are beings without borders. Or as Bohm puts it, 'Deep down the consciousness of mankind is one.'"[38]

And even Erwin Schrödinger, a founding father of quantum physics once said:

"Consciousness is a singular for which there is no plural."[39]

It's important to note that the Principle of Infinity was received by me in my personal meditation practice and therefore is sourced exclusively in my experience. However, I am shocked by the large number of scientists who corroborate the same realization. This makes sense, though, since we are all tapping the same source as the grounds for our realizations, the source of reality. Because I do not want to replace dogma with further dogma, please know that you are allowed your skepticism. The exercises following in subsequent chapters provide the necessary framework for proof of the principles described. These in turn help you to unlock the power of the right brain. My request is that until each of you, even the skeptics, can perform the exercises well, then criticism must necessarily be forestalled until then.

So here is the full set of words/lenses associated with Principle I, Infinity:

The only God worth believing in is an Infinite One. *Anything less than this is not infinite. This means that* you *are all a part of It. This means that everything is interconnected and part of the Whole.*[40]

The Principle of Infinity embraces the concepts of possibilities, completeness, and interconnectedness. And oddly enough science and spirituality seem to agree.

Principle II: *Paradox*

Earlier I secularly explained the essence of Principle II, Paradox, as:

The secret to understanding the universe is accepting paradox.

---

38 Michael Talbot, *The Holographic Universe* (New York: Harper Perrenial, 1992), 60.

39 Michael Talbot, *The Holographic Universe* (New York: Harper Perrenial, 1992), 86.

40 Received via two meditations: October 21, 2005 in Dayton, Ohio, USA and July 19, 2008 in Albuquerque, New Mexico, USA.

That explanation is secular. Now I am going to redefine Principle II to align it with the new, non-secular version of Principle I, Infinity.

Non-secularly the essence of Principle II, Paradox, is:

The secret name of God lies in Paradox.[41]

Let me expound on the meaning of Principle II starting with the fragment: "the secret name of God." How do you wrap your mind around the infinite essence of God? The secret, unpronounceable, name of God lies in Paradox. This means that to experience the essence of the Infinite, of the Universe, of God with equal clarity to hearing the name of your most beloved, you put your mind into a state of Paradox. In chapter four's exercise, "Experiencing Paradox," I asked you to ponder the paradox of "This sentence is false." This is the feeling you have when your analytical mind shuts down and is still and silent, allowing you to tune into the essence of the universe. The reason for saying "the secret name" is that the name of God, the essence of God, is ineffable and thus unpronounceable. It cannot be experienced in the limited form of a word. Yet, the feeling and essence of God is accessible by embracing paradox. This is one of the linkages between Principle II, Paradox and Principle I, Infinity.

You might be tempted to say, "Paradoxes are interesting, but I'm not sure I see them as fundamental to an understanding of the universe." Ah, a good point. But believe it or not, scientists and mathematicians alike have spent inordinate time studying paradox and here is one of the most remarkable things found:

> "Logical typing was invented by two mathematicians, Bertrand Russell and Alfred Whitehead, to keep logic pure ... What another mathematician, Kurt Gödel, *proved* [emphasis mine] is that any attempt to produce a paradox-free mathematical system is bound to fail if that system is reasonably complex. He proved this by showing that any system of reasonable richness is doomed to be incomplete. You can always find the statement within it that the system cannot prove. In fact, the system can be either complete but inconsistent or consistent but incomplete but can never be both consistent and complete ... So right out the window went a number of ideas, including the

---

[41] Received via meditation on March 6, 2005 in Santa Fe, New Mexico, USA.

possibility of a complete and consistent mathematical system like Russell's and Whitehead's theory of logical types."[42]

The implications of this are vast. In other words, all logical systems, all mathematical systems, all attempts at formulaic determinist science are always incomplete. The only way to make them robust enough to describe the experience of reality is that they must always contain paradox. Why is paradox omnipresent? That's right, because paradox is the essence of the infinite universe, where all things are possible, including seemingly contradictory phenomena.

Remember using continuums to make sense of the paradoxical nature of the universe? You also use continuums to zero in on the probabilities of a situation since the universe is probabilistic. Here is a more complete list of common continuums to familiarize yourself with:

➤ Detachment and Attachment—to help hone in on non-attachment

➤ Tangible and Intangible—to help you break free of a pure sensorial experience of the universe

➤ Relative and Absolute—as in the value of a business (e.g., P/E-based valuation vs. discounted cash flow-based valuation)

➤ Infinite and Finite—as in stepping down from vast possibilities to probabilities (Principle I down to Principle II)

➤ Substance and Form—to help you understand the necessary structure (form) for understanding something, but also the essence of something (substance); substance and form should be in *equal* proportion

➤ Quality and Quantity—especially of information; sometimes it is appropriate to pursue quantity of information; sometimes it is quality you pursue

➤ Return and Risk—ideally you desire the paradoxical investment low in risk and high in return

➤ Future and Past—investing unfolds in the future but sometimes you use the past to help anticipate the future; knowing when to emphasize future vs. past requires wisdom

42 Amit Goswami, Ph.D., Richard E. Reed, and Maggie Goswami, *The Self-Aware Universe: How Consciousness Creates the Material World* (New York: Tarcher Penguin, 1995), 183.

➤ Subjective and Objective—especially with regard to analyzing your investment process; you need clarity as to what information is factual (objective) and which is based on opinion (subjective); can also be used to parse another's analysis

➤ Feelings and Thoughts—feelings are the language of the right brain, thoughts are the language of the left brain

➤ Nothing and All—understanding that both of these are in operation simultaneously helps you tune into the paradoxical nature of the universe

➤ Destruction and Creation—useful for processing where a business is now in its life cycle; is it in a decline where old solutions are not working (destruction); or in a phase where a new business plan is being implemented (creation)?

➤ Death and Life—another variation of destruction and creation

➤ Feminine and Masculine—particularly in the Eastern yin-yang sense; feminine energies are receptive; masculine energies are activating

➤ Yes and No—a variation of yin-yang

➤ Passive and Active—a variation of yin-yang

➤ Breadth and depth—with regard to information; sometimes you need lots of cursory information (breadth); sometimes you need a lot of information about a single subject (depth)

The goal is accepting that both continuum ends are simultaneously operating and valid. All things are possible in a moment, if improbable.

Taken together, Principle I, Infinity and Principle II, Paradox describe the intangible aspects of experience. You begin at the ultimate with Infinity and then step down that vastness to Paradox. For paradox is generally how the left brain/analytical mind experiences the Infinite. You experience the universe as infinite distinctions, such as: me and you; friend and enemy; woman and man; hot and cold; good and evil, and so on. These distinctions result in a feeling of separateness driving your perception of the universe. So the interconnectedness of the first Principle of Infinity is difficult to apprehend. In fact, when confronted with a feeling of the Infinite, the left brain typically short-circuits and in a similar fashion to trying to evaluate the truth of the statement "This sentence is false."

Principle I of Infinity is the Higher description of the universe. Whereas, Principe II of Paradox is the Lower description of the universe. And by lower, I do not mean less important, I mean more in accord with how most of us experience life. The truly useful distinction between the first two principles is that Principle I is about infinite possibilities and Principle II is about making distinctions within infinite possibilities.

Principle III: Harmonizing

I earlier secularly explained the meaning of Principle III: Harmonizing as:

> "The secret to increasing your personal power is to harmonize with what you want to understand or embody and then you become it."

Stated for the purpose of cultivating your creativity and intuition, the new, non-secular meaning of Principle III: Harmonizing is:

> *The secret to the power you seek is to harmonize with that which you wish to become and you shall become it.*[43]

The new definition of the meaning is not that different from the earlier version. But I feel the newer version is purer with more potency, but the essence remains the same. The third Principle of Harmonizing is about *understanding*.

As we descend down each of the four principles we need less modification and explanation of the principles because we get closer to the material realm that is most familiar to most of us. There is a little bit of information that I can add to Principle III, Harmonizing, but not much.

Some things are difficult to harmonize with. For example, to embody the essence of a physician requires many years of knowledge accumulation so that you may fully harmonize with a physician's knowledge. Anytime you learn in life there is a period of knowledge accumulation where the knowledge feels separate from you. Then all at once you feel that the knowledge becomes one with yourself. At that point you have become what you envisioned becoming.

---

43 Received via a dream on June 29, 2006 in Dayton, Ohio, USA.

Here's what science has to say about the third Principle of Harmonizing:

> "...Jahn and Dunne [two renowned psychologists] propose that [mind over matter] actually involves an exchange of information between consciousness and physical reality, an exchange that should be thought of less as a flow between mental and material, and more as a *resonance* between the two."[44]

Additionally, here is a quote from a medical doctor named Dr. Brugh Joy:

> "I believe that reaching expanded states of consciousness is merely the *attuning* [emphasis mine] of your central nervous system to perceptive states that have always existed in you but have been blocked by your outer mental conditioning."[45]

Again, Principle III, Harmonizing was received in a dream and yet the principle seems universal. None of us discovered it; we all are just recognizing how the universe operates and then describing it.

The third principle of Harmonizing works with the first two principles to make you a better investor. Let's return to the story about AES Corporation from earlier.

> Among the most successful investments I make as a professional money manager is in AES Corporation. AES is one of the world's largest private owners of power plants. The Company has spent years buying up government utilities as they sold them off to raise money. I came to own AES by plumbing the depths of investment possibility looking for critical demographic factors that were immutable.

How? I began with Principle I, Infinity, and its universe of *possibilities* and created a mental topographical map of the state of the world at the time. I then tuned into the world to *understand* it accurately using Principle III, Harmonizing. What I saw were a number of demographic-trend-mountains *distinct* from other features on the map (using Principle II, Paradox). In 2000 here is how I went about my process:

> The first demographic-trend-mountain I harmonize with is the huge increase in technology to solve all problems. Never

---

[44] Michael Talbot, *The Holographic Universe* (New York: Harper Perrenial, 1992), 125.

[45] Michael Talbot, *The Holographic Universe* (New York: Harper Perrenial, 1992), 174.

mind computing, many refrigerators are beginning to have mini-computers on board and some can be linked via wifi to the Internet. Each morning I use an electric sonic-vibrating Superstar toothbrush. I have a cell phone, an electronic organizer and an electronic music player, all three of which accompany me everywhere. My entertainment room has a flat panel TV that uses as much electricity as an electric car hurtling down the highway at 60 miles per hour! And on and on. In short, the amount of electronic gadgetry is growing very rapidly.

This is an increase in the breadth of the electronic technology and one end of a Principle II, Paradox, continuum. What about the other end, depth?

As Third World nations' economies grow their people buy as many electronic gadgets as does the First World. This means that as the Chinese become wealthier they have the purchasing power to buy microwave ovens, refrigerators, ovens, stoves, blenders, toasters, sonic tooth brushes, personal computers, televisions, stereos, etc.

This is an increase in the depth of technology use and the other end of the continuum. Let's continue on with the AES example:

Things are growing out and up meaning there is a new investment Everest forming on the investment landscape. There is huge potential for money making because the creation and construction of anything in the universe, like a demographic mountain, requires resources. To make money you follow the resources. So how can I capture the entire trend with a single business rather than having to own every end manufacturer of every electronic gadget?

Because of my knowledge of the first Principle of Infinity I knew that to identify a single company I would need to explore the *interconnections* of the trend.

The underlying interconnection is that all of these gadgets need electricity to work. Who owns electricity? Utilities own electricity. But the trend is about depth and breadth. In the

First World, people already have electronic gadgetry, but the breadth is increasing. That is, we are all using more electricity to power more electronic gadgets. Yet, I want to capture the entire trend of an increase in breadth **and** depth. So I need to look for a global power company because the Second and Third World countries are where the depth portion of the trend is predominately located.

At this point I began to discriminate in accord with Principle II, Paradox, to find a single company that fit all of the criteria. That led me to AES and several other companies. Continuing further ...

I analyze the strengths and weaknesses of each of the investment candidates. I believe AES is the most attractive candidate for investment.

Here I used the second Principle of Paradox to make distinctions between the resource choices made by the various companies (resource managers). Then I evaluate the positive and negative consequences of those choices. This is Principle II, but also Principle III, Harmonizing, because I tried to *understand* the consequences of management choices. Here is more explication about AES:

The positives for AES are that they own power plants all around the world; in the First World and in Second and Third World countries where the depth of electronics is increasing rapidly. They also generate lots of cash—over a $1 billion each year. AES also has diversified power generation assets (i.e., power plants), including coal, oil, hydroelectric and geothermal plants. So they are not dependent on one source of power and thus subject to volatile price fluctuations in the raw material costs of generating power. AES owns power distribution assets (i.e., power lines) as well. This diversified revenue stream is a form of an insurance policy against a drop in power demand.

Principle II, Paradox insists I establish the proper context for understanding some of AES' strengths and weaknesses. The fact that they own plants and power lines is obviously good, but why? Because it is: "a form of an insurance policy." Notice, I found an analogy that worked well and thus, it revealed important information. This is Principle III, Harmonizing, at work. The benefits of owning AES were not the only aspects to focus on:

The negatives for AES are that they have a funky, super-decentralized management structure. You know the kind, that odd Silicon Valley, romper room kind, wherein employees are seemingly more important than management. I feel this could be either a good thing or a bad thing. There is a time and a place for decentralized management, and centralized management. But I will be watching. Another negative is that AES is mostly financed with debt. Unfortunately with debt you must always make your interest payments lest you be forced into bankruptcy by your creditors.

But again, there are positives for every negative (the Principle of Paradox) because debt financing is cheaper than equity financing.

Thus far, I had yet to break out a calculator or a spreadsheet to analyze AES all of this analysis was mostly right-brained. Yet I had an excellent understanding of the business coming from an appreciation of, utilization of, and mastery of the first three of the four principles. Yes, I had made use of facts, but they were all in service to the creativity and intuition of the right brain. The left brain was useful where a structure to the analysis was needed, or when a quantitative assessment needed to be made. But it would be how AES performed in the future that would make my shareholders money. That assessment of the future was all right-brained and involved the identification of the growing resource mountain of electronic gadgetry; and the sizing up of AES. Let's keep going:

> The next step I undertake is to examine AES' past performance by crunching numbers. I need to know if the numbers support in a non-prejudicial fashion both my intuitive feeling about the business as well as the annual report's claims made by management.

This previous step is outside of the scope of this book. But notice that the number crunching is in service to the right-brain's assessment. Here are more AES details:

> I like AES' past performance as indicated by their numbers. I create a valuation model to determine an appropriate price to pay for a share of stock in AES. The Company is trading at a discount to its fair value. I am interested enough in AES to conduct an interview with management.

My valuation model of AES mostly utilizes my creativity as I try to properly model AES's future performance and capture the essence of how that performance will turn into value for the Davis Appreciation and Income Fund's shareholders. My interview with management was almost entirely a right-brained, intuitive assessment of the people that ran AES. I evaluated whether I liked them, was comfortable with them, and whether I felt they were competent (notice all of the proceeding verbs are linked to feelings, a right-brained activity).

> I like AES management, but I do not looooove it. Nonetheless, I know enough about AES to be confronted with the ultimate investor decision: buy or not buy?

Principle IV: Action

Principle IV is *Action*. The full definition of the principle is:

Effects follow causes. [46]

This is both the secular and non-secular definition. I did not contrive it to be this way. But as the principles are stepped down from *Infinity* to *Action* there is a secularization of the principles. They move from formless to form. They become dense. So there is no way to state Principle IV in a non-secular way. The Action Principle is also known as the Law of Karma, which is non-secular. The meaning of "effects follow causes" is self-evident.

The Action Principle also encompasses the paradoxical concepts of free-will and destiny. It works like this:

➤ You have the free-will to make choices within your personal power.

➤ These choices are the "causes" in your life.

➤ Those choices generate "effects" that are largely out of your control.

➤ This is the destiny of your life.

In turn, you are then free to choose how to respond to these new "effects" by choosing again. These new choices then become new "effects." This

---

[46] Received via meditations on January 3, 2006 in Dayton, Ohio, USA and March 1, 2006 in Dayton, Ohio, USA.

karmic cycle goes on and on. Unfortunately, without consciousness in your choices then you wield your personal power without full potency and are subject to effects/consequences that return to you from that unconscious source. This strongly suggests that with consciousness you gain greater power in your choices and also greater effects/investment outcomes. Thus, having consciousness of your investment choices is really a way to maximize both your personal power and your Karma.

Principles I, Infinity and Principle II, Paradox are the intangible principles. Whereas, Principle III, Harmonizing, and Principle IV, Action are the tangible principles. Further, and interestingly, Principle IV naturally flows back into Principle I because the Action Principle is about the **interconnection** between action and reaction, causes, and effects. And of course the Infinity Principle is about the interconnectedness of all things. Because the first Principle of Infinity is just that, infinite. It encompasses all of the other principles. Yet, Principle IV circles back to reconnect with Principle I. This is not a coincidence. For these principles to be principles they must be general and encompass all possibilities. To be useful they are specific, hence their individual distinctions.

Principle III, Harmonizing is the Higher version of the principle of action. Whereas, Principle IV, Action is the Lower version of the principle: action. The distinction is that Harmonizing is passive or surrendered action, but Action is active action. When you are *Harmonizing* your only action is to surrender yourself to the action of someone or something else. With *Action* the choices are exclusively yours—it is active action.

Reviewing my examination of AES notice that Principle IV suffused every step along the way. This is because each part of the AES analysis required action on my part. It required that I choose to act and that I choose which actions to take. Thus, Principle IV, Action is almost infinitely in operation, and in this way it also points back to Principle I, Infinity. Let's pick up the story of AES again:

> I end up purchasing AES and immediately lose massive amounts of money for my shareholders—over half of the initial investment! There is drought in Amazon-dominated Brazil and 40% of AES's entire business is generating hydroelectric power there. No rain fall means there is no power. No power means there is nothing to sell. Nothing to sell means no revenues. No revenues means no profits. No profits means no

shareholder return. No shareholder return means I have made a mistake. No power being sold also means AES is violating a contract it signed with the country of Brazil to deliver a fixed amount of power at a certain price each and every year. Ouch!

Principle IV, Action is in operation throughout the AES analysis; effects follow causes irrevocably. Yet, until I took action and chose to invest my shareholders' money in AES there was no interconnection between AES and my shareholders' lives. This is the power inherent in Principle IV, and the responsibility. The Action Principle is all about responsibility and owning those choices. So what did I do?

> I reevaluate AES and its prospects. This means I reassess my universal map to see if I have misunderstood the interconnections between AES and that mountain of opportunity: growing electricity use.

Reevaluating the interconnection was Principle I, Infinity in operation. But it was also Principle II, Paradox, because I reassessed the return versus risk of AES. Principle III, Harmonizing was operating too because I had to evaluate how my decision had gone horribly wrong and to learn from my mistake.

> I want to buy more AES. My trader at Lehman Brothers, Mr. J.V.O., asks me as I am buying more: "Dude, are you sure you want to do this? You are the only buyer today!" He means that I am the AES market today—it's me pumping all of the cash in as every-one anxiously sells AES.

My decision that day, when I bought the majority of my position in AES, resulted in a many times multiple appreciation in the value of my shareholders' AES holdings. What did I see on the investment topographical map that gave me such confidence to take *Action* when every seller could only see risk and ruin from amongst all of the possibilities?

> I say to JVO: "AES generates $1 billion in cash every year." "Everyone needs electricity. It isn't an option any longer to not use it." "Rainfall in the Amazon is almost always a given." "AES' crisis is causing them to change their crazy super-decentralized management structure."

Yet, none of the preceding facts answered the question as to whether or not to sell AES or to continue buying. *That* decision was an emotional decision to trust the facts that my right brain had determined were the pertinent facts from amongst all of the possible facts of the situation. That discrimination and discernment was the result of the application of the four principles. Without them I would have been what every seller of AES was that day: a fearful mob, and not an investor.

In summary, there are four principles: Infinity, Paradox, Harmonizing, and Action. The operative words for each principle help your understanding of their individual functionings, as well as the power of their integration. The operative words are: possibilities, distinctions, understanding, and action. You begin with an investment landscape full of infinite possibilities. You then begin to *distinguish* the interconnections and what is important. Then you seek to *understand* what you have identified as important. Then you take *action* based on your understanding. And lastly, within the framework of each principle you have learned specific tools to help you take advantage of each of the principles. Understanding the principles and the tools activates and takes advantage of your right brain. The result is understanding information. Ideally this leads to new and greater investment success.

Seamless Integration

As mentioned Principle I, Infinity and Principle II, Paradox, are Higher and Lower versions of the same principle: the Universe. So you can reduce the two principles into one: the Universe.

Principle III, Harmonizing and Principle IV, Action are Higher and Lower versions of the same principle: Action. *Harmonizing* is passive action, whereas *Action* is active action. So you can also reduce the final two principles into one: Action.

Consequently, there are really only two principles: God and Action. Or, if you prefer: Destiny and Free Will. Both are paradoxically in operation at the same time. But can these two principles, *God* and *Action* be combined into an Ultimate Principle? Yes. It's helpful to know that some cultures around the world refer to God as "The First Cause," and still others refer to God as the "Causeless Cause." Thus, ultimately there is only One Principle: God.

REVIEW

There is an essential element hidden in the structure of the four principles directing their application. This is like the DNA inside each of your cells directing your cells' creation and renewal. The hidden element is: that excellent use of the four principles is dependent upon excellent use of creativity and intuition. Fortunately for you, the four principles also underlie the cultivation and utilization of your creativity and intuition. The concepts all feed back into one another. You might say this is paradoxical. You might say this is mystical. And that is where we are headed ... into the mystic of meditation.

10

Meditation: The Ultimate Intuition Vehicle

"... the common thread in all these [psychic phenomenon]
experiments ... [was] some sort of relaxation technique
(through meditation, biofeedback, or another method);
[that] reduced sensory input or physical activity;
dreams or other internal states and feelings;
and a reliance on right brain functioning ...

"It seemed that when the left brain was quieted
and the right brain predominated, ordinary people
could gain access to this information."[47]

Meditation suffers from misunderstanding, misinformation and aversion. This unfortunate situation has limited its use as one of the most powerful tools for understanding information. While it may seem as if I am leading you astray from investing, I am not. Because meditation is a state where the right brain and left brain dissolve into One, it maximizes the full power of both.

The meditative state is a *natural* state of mind and is the doorway to a fully activated and conscious mind. It is meditative states that allow you access to creativity, intuition and wealth manifestation. Exploration of this topic opens up an entirely new world, one rich with skills for making you richer.

In a general sense, meditation is the four principles run in reverse, starting with Action and moving to Infinity. In a specific sense, meditation is

47 Lynne McTaggart, *The Field: the Quest for the Secret Force of the Universe (updated edition)* (New York: Harper Collins Publishers, 2008), 134.

like cutting a pathway through the jungle to an ancient temple to find treasure. In other words, creating a meditative practice that removes the ego's obstructions of the meditative state, where you find inspiration, imagination, and wealth manifestation.

The chapter concludes with self-assessments and exercises to help you become better meditators. In turn, that will help you to more easily access the powers of creativity, intuition and wealth manifestation.

The Meditative Process

The four principles run in reverse is meditation.

1. Principle IV: *Action* You *choose* to want to enter a meditative state.

2. Principle III: *Harmonizing* Then you begin to harmonize with the meditative state.

3. Principle II: *Paradox* If the ego is still functioning you are not One with the meditative state, but are separate.

4. Principle I: *Infinity* When you are able to harmonize fully with the meditative state you become One with Everything, and enter the meditative state.

Notice that the meditative state occurs in Principle I, Infinity. In fact, the two are the same thing.

Meditation Is a Natural State of Mind

When most people hear the word meditation I am guessing that most envision a shaven-headed cave dweller sitting silently for hours, staring at a blank white wall or a candle flame. This image makes most people feel bad because this image seems ridiculous and unachievable. Everyone would like more time in their lives to spend life in deep contemplation of the profundity of the color white. Okay, maybe not everyone would, but many would. The shaven-headed cave dweller image also makes normal people feel foolish, too. Many try "meditation" and are not able to still their minds while staring at a candle or a white wall. Thus, most people feel that they have failed and they believe (wrongly) that they just aren't meditators. Meditation is one of life's most valuable practices but sadly the misunderstanding surrounding meditation is so large that most people never utilize its potential.

Where did this image of meditation come from? I feel it came from the Western World's initial connections with the Eastern World's meditators starting in the late-19th Century, but especially in the late 1950s and throughout the 1960s. Meditators were monks and gurus who devoted their lives to the practice. At a particular time in history, Western seekers met people whom they felt had answers. Because these folks wanted to be like these monks and gurus they employed Principle III, Harmonizing, aping the practices of the monks and gurus. The problem is that this naïve view focused almost entirely on the details of meditation and not the substance of meditation.

To alleviate the confusion surrounding meditation, I want to explore some definitions.

From the American Heritage Dictionary[48]...

> **med•i•ta•tion** [měd′i tā′shən]; noun.
>   1. a. The act or process of meditating.
>   b. A devotional exercise of or leading to contemplation.
>   2. A contemplative discourse, usually on a religious or philosophical subject.

Of these definitions, I feel only 1b is okay, "A devotional exercise of or leading to contemplation." However, that definition is just as incomplete in its understanding as most of the Western World is about meditation. Let's look at another ... from Wikipedia ...[49]

> "Meditation is a mental discipline by which one attempts to get beyond the reflexive, "thinking" mind into a deeper state of relaxation or awareness. Meditation often involves turning attention to a single point of reference. It is recognized as a component of many religions, and has been practiced since antiquity. It is also practiced outside religious traditions. Different meditative disciplines encompass a wide range of spiritual and/or psychophysical practices which may emphasize different goals—from achievement of a higher state of

---

48 *American Heritage Dictionary of the English Dictionary, Fourth Edition* (New York: Houghton-Mifflin Company, 2006).

49 Wikipedia, http://en.wikipedia.org/wiki/Meditation

consciousness, to greater focus, creativity or self-awareness, or simply a more relaxed and peaceful frame of mind."

This description is a vast improvement over the standard, dictionary one. The person writing the Wikipedia article is obviously a meditator. In particular I like the inclusion of, "... one attempts to get beyond the reflexive, 'thinking' mind ..." part. I also like that the description says there are "Different meditative disciplines ..." Here the definition includes some of the basics, in my mind, of ...

What Meditation Is

Here's what I believe meditation is:

Meditation is a natural state of mind that occurs when the egoic mind[50] is diminished or turned off.

Why do I humbly feel this is the ultimate, earth-shaking definition? For starters, meditation *is* a natural state of mind. Everyone meditates naturally, but most just don't know it. This is one of the most important points of the entire book so let me repeat that:

Meditation is a natural state of mind.

This is important because most people think of meditation in the same way the dictionary and Wikipedia think of it, as: "A devotional exercise ..." or "... a mental discipline ..." These things are true about meditation as a *practice*. But meditation is like running. It's a natural thing for you to know how to run, but some are better at it naturally. Still others practice a discipline of running and become "Runners." The shaven-headed cave dwellers are the meditation athletes; those folks who make meditation a discipline and a practice. But this doesn't mean you do not meditate. Should the fact that you are not Olympic runners diminish your enjoyment of running? Of course not. Feeling that way is foolish.

Now, regarding the other half of the definition above, "... when the egoic mind is diminished or turned off." Recall that the egoic mind is the set of behavioral defenses people erect to protect their vulnerable, feeling selves. By doing the book's exercises you have subtly been dismantling your egoic minds all along.

---

50 *Egoic mind* means the state of mind where a sense of "I," or a sense of separateness from the interconnectedness of the universe, exists.

In the Anxiety Review you explored the way strong emotions, in this case anxieties and fears, can indicate personal boundaries that need examination; and maybe dismantling. The Emotional Inventory was a retelling of your personal biography, designed to help you identify your emotional connection to the events of your life. Later, I taught you a technique for tuning into what the truth feels like, a crucial skill. All of this work was done because the meditative state is always operating, but it is obscured by the static of the egoic mind. The exercises begin to quiet your emotions and help you to access the meditative state. Said another way, when the egoic mind is turned off, you meditate. It's that simple.

I am going to break with the convention of having exercises at the end of the chapter. I want to demonstrate convincingly that everyone is a meditator, but just doesn't know it.

PROOF THAT EVERYONE MEDITATES

Consider the following question: What things do you do that rejuvenate you? Write each of your rejuvenating things down in your notebook. Now take a moment to record what it is about each activity that rejuvenates you. How do you feel when you do these activities? Put these responses in your notebook too.

If you are having trouble thinking of anything, here is a short list of the many things people over the years have shared with me that they do to rejuvenate:

➤ Sports: golf, fishing, running, swimming, football, basketball, martial arts, skiing, hiking

➤ Gardening and yard work

➤ Doing the "Honey, Do" list

➤ The arts: music, dancing, drawing, painting, sculpture

➤ Cooking

➤ Cleaning: sweeping the floor, doing the dishes, mopping the floor

➤ Bathing or showering

➤ Driving

➤ Jigsaw puzzles

➤ Praying

Predominately these activities are rejuvenating because they put you in a meditative state. These are activities where the normal hustle of your mind is quieted. These activities trigger a different way of being that is outside of normal routine. Yet, think of how you feel when doing things that rejuvenate you. Are these feelings unnatural? Or is it more the case that these feelings feel extraordinarily natural? These things rejuvenate because they put you in your natural meditative state.

To further demonstrate how often you are in a meditative state, write answers to the following questions in your notebook. What do you do to relax? Next, consider what it is about these activities that relaxes you? Lastly, and most importantly, how do you feel when you do these activities?

These activities are relaxing because they help you to turn off the noisy buzz of the egoic mind. Even watching TV can induce a weak meditative state.

Now consider the following questions for contemplation:

➤ Have you ever driven somewhere and upon arriving at your destination you don't remember the drive but now you know why your mom said something to you many years ago? Or something similar?

➤ Have you ever done the dishes and suddenly understood how to solve a nagging problem? Or something similar?

➤ Have you ever swept the floor and suddenly you feel rejuvenated and energized? Or something similar?

If you answered yes to any of the questions then you now know that you naturally meditate. Importantly:

Being in a meditative state is meditating.

This is why I say with confidence there is so much confusion about meditation in the Western World. People get so overwhelmed by the trappings of meditation (the monasteries, the monks, the robes, the incense, the white wall, the candle flame) that they overlook the fact that they already meditate! Obsession with meditative form over substance is a disaster as most people believe they can't meditate. Yet, everyone has been meditating for their entire life. Sadly the belief that you don't meditate shuts you off from an enormously valuable practice. You feel great, refreshed, and rejuvenated when you meditate. Most importantly, many of life's most important lessons, realizations, explorations, creations, and intuitions happen when meditating.

In the above questions for contemplation you discovered the sorts of things that can happen when you meditate. The situations in the questions for contemplation are examples of finally accessing information about the world that had always been present but that were hidden by the ego. These realizations happen because in these moments the full power of the right brain is unshackled from the ego. That is, you gain conscious awareness, you finally see, and understand information! Because life is a continual series of decisions, or of continual investments, meditation is at the root of ultimate investment success. Meditation ensures you use more of the power of your mind to make conscious decisions.

So how does someone make meditation a practice? How does someone move from being a meditator to becoming a Meditator?

Meditation is generally taught horribly. Meditation instructors ask you to change before working with what you have already got. So let's start with what you already have and then stretch the bounds of who you are to encompass something new. That means you begin with your own unique meditative substance and only then do you add meditative form.

Let's return to the arch model that graphically demonstrated the components of intelligence and wisdom. The diagram is the same as before, but notice now that "meditative state" is the space where intelligence and wisdom meet. The meditative state is also where the left brain and right brain resolve themselves and become One. Said another way, in a meditative state paradoxical separation dissolves into infinity. The meditative state is Principle I, Infinity.

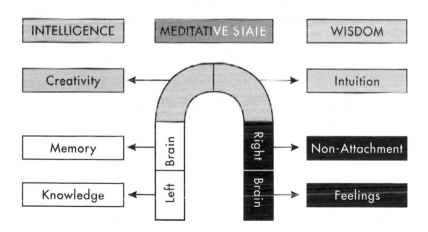

A Powerful Analogy

Here's an analogy to help you become a Meditator:

*Meditation is like cutting a pathway through the jungle
to an ancient temple to find treasure.*

These are the correspondences:

➤ the Pathway = the meditative practice (the form)

➤ the Jungle = the ego

➤ the Temple = the meditative state/meditation/the feeling realm
(the substance)

➤ the Treasure = the fruits of meditation

In the beginning, before you have a meditative practice, you stand before a dense, dark, scary Jungle. Somewhere in the middle of the jungle resides a beautiful, splendorous, vast Temple. Assuming you find a way into the temple you discover enormous Treasure. Now let's discuss this in meditation terms.

Earlier I said meditation is about connection (the pathway); a connection to the purest version of yourself (the temple), uncorrupted by the defensive and largely unnecessary constructs of the ego (the jungle). By connecting to your subconscious or feeling self (the temple) you are able to dismantle the ego's constructions (the jungle) that no longer serve you. When you take down these constructions (the vines and trees of the jungle) you more fully connect to your feeling self (the temple) with the result being that you gain greater access to your creativity, intuition, and wealth manifestation (the treasure).

So the first question is: How do you cut through the jungle? The second question is: What does the temple "look" like? And the last question is: What kinds of treasure exist; or why do you care to cut through the jungle in the first place?

The Ego (The Jungle)

The ego is like HAL 9000 the computer in Stanley Kubrick's film, *2001: A Space Odyssey.* HAL, an artificial intelligence computer, is designed to help the astronauts by managing the routine functioning of the ship and to protect the astronauts in case of danger. Unfortunately, HAL malfunctions and gets out of control. The computer actually ends up killing most of the astronauts it is designed to protect. The ego is similar to HAL as it also frequently malfunctions and slowly disables you by shutting off access to the rejuvenation and magic of the meditative state. Most importantly for our purposes, the unconscious ego obstructs access to creativity, intuition and wealth manifestation.

You may be tempted to hack away at the ego jungle to destroy it entirely. In fact, many spiritual traditions have as a focus the destruction of the ego. But when functioning normally, the ego naturally protects the deeply sensitive feeling-self (the temple). That feeling-self is your connection to the vast, interconnected universe and the apparatus that is the source of your intuition. Without the jungle the elegant architecture of the temple is more exposed to the elements and overrun with indifferent tourists. Eventually the temple becomes corrupted.

The point of meditation practice is not the destruction of the ego, it's to get to the temple and uncover the treasure lying inside whenever you want to. The problem of the ego is that unless you have consciousness and control of the activation of its defenses, then your feeling-self (the temple) remains hidden and inaccessible behind the ego's dense jungle protections. So the ego is a welcome source of protection when used consciously; and an unwelcome, overgrown, obstructive jungle when not used consciously.

Here is an example of the mind in a state of meditation: watching an engrossing movie and being emotionally moved by that movie. Let me explain. Is the movie real? No, it is a fantasy. Unless a person participated in the creation of the movie or the movie is about that person's life or someone else's life that they know, the movie has no *direct* bearing on that person. So how is it that a person ends up laughing, crying, or getting excited by a movie?

The reason is movies are a safe haven where many people are comfortable turning off their normally very active egoic patterns, as well as their rational left brains. In other words, people surrender to the fantasy that is the movie. If a person doesn't surrender, the left brain processes the experience like this: "The results of this system are interesting. Light is created by a filament lamp and that is reflected by a mirror through a strip of plastic that has emulsion on it. That emulsion is a facsimile of real light waves that struck the emulsion. Hmmm. Fascinating." That's the pure left brain take on a movie.

But most people grant themselves permission to enjoy movies for what they are: one of the few safe playgrounds for the entire brain, especially the right brain, to play. In this state people dial down the ego and the left brain and have direct access to their feeling selves. In this meditative state the movie becomes your life, too. Often, the result is tremendous enjoyment.

Have you ever wanted to cry during a movie but fought it off? That is the ego at work. It's likely your feeling-self felt a deep connection to what was transpiring on the screen and was vulnerable. Just as you were about to cry the ego flew into action cutting off the direct feeling experience of the movie. Perhaps instead you were chastised as a child for crying and your ego fires up the old defensive "do-not-cry program" that was created to ease the passage of childhood. These moments where the ego suppresses emotion feel very strange, even in the body. The ego has many ways of protecting your feeling-self which is what can make gaining consciousness of them difficult work.

Whatever method your ego uses it is trying to serve its purpose: to prevent the very sensitive feeling-self from being hurt. This is not a problem as long as your not crying is a *conscious* decision. And by "decision" I mean that you could cry if you wanted to. If your ego absolutely won't let you cry while watching a movie, there is then no decision to make because there is no power to decide. And furthermore, this reaction clearly indicates a limiting personal boundary. Many situations in life are like the movie; people operate with the same old programs. Yet there is actually nothing in the present moment to fear, so no ego protection is necessary.

For most folks, the ego is like an overgrown jungle where new experiences lead to new jungle seeds being planted or fertilizer being added to the already existing jungle. The overgrowth of the jungle is so extreme and entangled that organisms/experiences well below the canopy/surface are starved of light. The jungle eventually overruns and obscures everything except for the top surface area of experience.

It's not that the jungle isn't alive and wonderful, nor that it doesn't contribute to the health of the ecosystem, it's that it is dangerously overgrown and needs to be cut back. In nature, unexpected catastrophes like drought and fire cull the forest. In life, the jungle that is the ego frequently gets culled by unexpected catastrophes, too. These include losing a job, breaking up with a boy/girlfriend, divorce, being diagnosed with a disease, or a death of someone significant. When these catastrophes strike they are very damaging to the jungle/ego and especially so if it is massively overgrown. Overgrown egos provide lots of kindling for catastrophic life fires.

Our goal with regard to the ego is to consciously control it, allowing it to serve its function, but not to become unnecessarily overgrown.

The Meditative Practice (The Pathway)

Some of the earlier exercises revealed a few of the wonderful feelings, experiences, and knowledge you can have when meditating. These meditative Treasures are contingent on reaching the Temple (meditative state) via a Pathway (meditative practice) through dense ego Jungles.

In search of treasure, people are often tempted to cut a straight, unswerving path directly through their egos to the temple. But this kind of pathway incurs perfection's tremendous costs. Such as meticulously leveling the ground, uprooting stumps, and paving the pathway regardless of the actual topography, density, and obstacles of the jungle.

Creating this kind of meditation practice is analogous to being obsessed with proper meditative form before feeling as if you can properly experience meditation. The problem is the topography of each person's jungle is always uneven and denser in some places than in others. It's just not efficient to bull your way through the constructs of your ego.

When you create your meditation practice to cut through your ego to attain meditative states you need to be flexible. Some portions of your ego are so intense, multi-layered and dense that if you insist on bullying your way through them you actually do more harm than good. This kind of attitude toward your ego is unhealthy and is similar to being at war with yourself. Not only that, but it is just inefficient and actually leads to you spending a lot of unnecessary time fighting yourself. A healthy relationship with your ego accepts ego's role in your life. This choice is analogous to changing the course of your pathway slightly to accommodate major features of your personal topography.

Your goal is to create as direct a pathway through the jungle as is efficient, not as direct a pathway as is possible.

How do you find a pathway to get through the jungle to the temple that contains the treasure? It's important to know that every meditation practice seeks to accomplish the same thing: diminishing, switching off, or gaining control of the ego.

What follows are meditative practices that will help you to access your meditative state more naturally.

WORK WITH WHAT YOU HAVE

The earlier "rejuvenation" exercise demonstrated the unique meditative practices you already use to achieve a meditative state. You have been to the temple before. So when you need to meditate to solve a problem, say to gauge the "mood" of the financial markets, then you simply do what you already do to get to the meditative state—that is, do the thing that rejuvenates you. This method works with what you already have and is stupendously simple. The easier this is then the more you will use meditation as a tool and the more you will think of yourself as a Meditator. There is no reason to make this more complicated than it needs to be.

A version of "making it more complicated than it needs to be" is the huge amount of time many meditators spend trying to get the right meditative posture. This is foolishness. The proper meditative posture is: whatever works! Would you prefer to meditate and have one of the most amazing experiences of your life, but have poor meditative posture? Or to have perfect meditative posture and … and … and … nothing significant happens?

The problem is that many meditators (small 'm') and meditation teachers (small 'm') feel as if a Meditative Experience is not possible without perfect posture. I can flat out say this is nonsense.

Turning off the ego is the only condition for achieving a meditative state, posture is not. Is posture important? It can be. Does it supersede substance? No. Meditative form, posture, is important only as a refinement once you achieve meditative substance. So-called "proper" meditative postures are simply the postures others have used to help themselves achieve a meditative state. Unfortunately, meditative forms are frequently taught to beginning meditators inflexibly and unconsciously. If a swimmer and golfer both achieve meditative states while playing their sports, how important can posture be?

I said posture can be important, so what postures are legit? Any posture that works. My favorite way to meditate is lying down before I go to sleep. However, I have a good friend who is a great Meditator who falls asleep if he tries to do this. His preferred method is to sit on a couch with his back supported against the couch. Still others prefer to sit on their meditative gear (all modern activities have official gear), the zafu and zabuton. Some sit on their gear in a lotus position, while others like me, kneel. Still others like to meditate without any sort of gear and they do so in a full lotus position with a perfectly straight spine and a tucked chin with their eyelids slightly open and a soft focus about three feet in front of them. By the way, *this* is the traditionally dogmatic correct meditative posture. For me, that just doesn't work. Some people, because of preferences, prejudices, and ego convince themselves that anything but *The Posture* is cheating. No worries. The universe is Infinite so every posture potentially will work.

GAIN CONSCIOUSNESS OF THE EGO SYSTEMATICALLY

The first meditation technique was to "do what you already do" to achieve a meditative state. But there are other ways to expand your meditative possibilities. Since meditative success is dependent on dialing down the intensity of the ego, or having the ability to turn it off (or on) at your will, a natural place to begin expanding your meditative practice is the culling of your ego.

Here is an exercise that is the spiritual equivalent of growing many arms and hacking away at your ego jungle with very sharp machetes. It is very effective, but can be hard work. Take a deep breath and spray on some bug repellant …

Recall a time when you felt **strong** emotion, but that is no longer so strong for you. This could be the profound love you felt for someone else. It could be the anxiety you felt before giving a speech. It could be the blow up you had while driving home from work before a holiday weekend. It could be the moving compliment you received from a close friend. Whatever your choice, put that emotion back into your mind's eye.

Record the circumstances of the emotional moment in your notebook. What were the facts of the situation? What things contributed to your deeply felt emotions? Perhaps this was the timing of the event or perhaps it was the culmination of many emotional events.

Even if you felt that the emotions you felt were positive, take a moment now to examine any preferences or prejudices you might have brought to the emotional moment. This may be tough, but identify them anyway. Write these preferences or prejudices down in your notebook. These are architectures of the ego.

An example of this type of egoic preference infiltrating a positive moment would be a romantic evening with your partner where you placed conditions that needed to be fulfilled for the night to be "perfect." Those conditions/preferences might have included wanting to eat at the right restaurant, or wanting to actually eat out at a restaurant, or wanting to order the right wine, or wanting the chef to replicate your favorite meal the way she did three years ago when you first met your partner, or wanting a new necktie to increase your dapperness, and so forth.

An example of ego preferences occurring in a negative moment might be an argument you have with your partner where you place restrictions on what can be discussed. It could be that your partner is specifically communicating to you what is upsetting to the partner about you but that you would prefer they say it differently before you will acknowledge his or her opinion, or you prefer to have the discussion at another time, or you prefer that your partner not engage in name calling, or you prefer that he or she not bring up past situations again, and so forth.

Now imagine the situation again, but this time imagine it having happened without your preferences and prejudices. How does this change your experience of your powerfully emotional moment? Record your observations. What should be left after removing the ego are your feelings, not your emotions.

Does removing your ego out of the situation help you to see aspects of the situation that eluded you previously? Any new observations are to be put in your notebook.

Once you identify the emotional/ego influence on your feelings, you will have gained consciousness over your ego and how it operates in these types of situations. To gain conscious *control* requires that you be able to feel the "springing into action" of your ego so that you can choose in the moment to prevent it from obscuring your feeling-self.

The point of this exercise is not to feel soulless and neutral about everything, like some mechanical automaton; the point is to dismantle our *unconscious* ego responses. Once the unconscious responses are identified we can then have the power to **choose** to do whatever we want with them.

DISTRACT THE EGO

One way to avoid the entangling nature of the ego jungle is to distract it while meditating. A wonderful thing about the analytical, left brain is that it is hard wired to handle only two *conscious* thoughts simultaneously.

You may be thinking, "But I do things that require more than two thoughts at a time. Like driving." Yes, there are many more than just two things to consider when driving. But most of those things are a part of the subconscious. Long ago these skills were made a part of the brain's autonomic systems like muscle memory.

You can use this limitation of the left brain, its inability to process more than two conscious things, to your meditative advantage. What you do is put two innocuous things into your conscious mind. Then you just sit back and relax and let the meditative state unfold, usually shortly thereafter. This is why activities like sweeping the floor, doing the dishes and driving facilitate meditative states. The analytical brain occupies itself with innocuous activity. Meanwhile, the right, intuitive brain sneaks its way to the forefront of consciousness and its powers begin to flow.

You may have heard of, or used, mantras. Mantras are the repetition of a word or series of words over and over again. Mantras also work to distract the ego and to free up the meditative function of the mind. Eventually, the repetition of the mantra becomes unconscious and then the meditative state is achieved.

All of these variations of the tool can be effective. Choose which variation works. As an investment application, when you want greater insight into your investments do something that occupies your analytical brain, like anything identified in the Rejuvenation Exercise, to unlock the creativity and intuition of your right brain.

HAVE A VECTOR

When meditating, people frequently have a specific meditative goal. That may be to relax; understand an important relationship; figure out whether or not to invest in a business; hack down the ineffective parts of the ego jungle; improve a golf swing; etc. But almost inevitably, the egoic mind will kick into gear. This is the equivalent of finding yourself in the temple, lifting the lid on the treasure chest, when WHAM, you think to yourself something like: "Gosh those cupcakes at work were good!" It's virtually guaranteed to have these kinds of meditation moments. Another likely outcome is in the midst of meditating you suddenly realize that for the last ten minutes you have been reordering your "to do" list. How do you overcome the distractions of the ego?

1. Don't sweat it. These things are natural, even for experienced Meditators, so don't be upset with yourself. If you are, it is like being at war with yourself and it has the unintended consequence of contributing additional preference and judgment (that is, more ego) to

your experience. That, in turn, just creates more meditative work for you to do later.

2. Instead, give your left brain an affirmation to focus on because it works better with a vector. Here's the evidence … Try to do the following impossible task: Don't think of an elephant! This is impossible since the mind, because of memory, is designed to work with substance, not eliminate it. In other words, you cannot erase your memories. So you give your mind something affirmative to focus on, a vector or a task.

Because the left brain prefers the substantial, rather than the in-substantial, affirmations work to distract it. This aspect of the left brain is one of the reasons why aspiring meditators and Meditators stare at white walls and flickering candle flames—it gives the left brain something disciplined to do. While certain kinds of vectors consistently work well, the ultimate vector is: whatever works.

One vector that I find works well is having a purpose for meditating, even if that reason is: I am just practicing. But there are an infinite number of reasons to want to gain access to your right brain's powers by meditating.

So, in summary, it's like this, when you meditate and end up way off the pathway and are lost in your jungle, you do not chastise yourself. Instead you put back into your mind's eye the point of focus (in **bold** below) of your meditation. For example:

> Lahdy-dee-dah. I'm meditating. I'm meditating. **I need to figure out why I got so mad at my boss last week.** [Several minutes later.] The Yankees are going to rock this year. Now that they have a left-handed relief pitcher they will be unbeatable. Lahdy-dee-dah. [Several minutes later.] Oh, I got way off track there. **I need to figure out why I got so mad at my boss last week.** [Moments later.] Oh, my goodness, now I know why! I am still frustrated with my mom because she always babied me and I felt she was disrespecting me and I feel like my boss does that, too.

Vectors give your meditative mind a focus that allows you to get back on track.

Another form of a vector is guided meditations. Some of the most powerful meditations I have experienced are guided. The guidance can be in the form of a compact disc or being led by a meditation instructor.

In summary, there are as many forms of meditation (Pathways) as there are practitioners. Do not be limited by the list above. Everyone has license to explore their own meditation practice to discover unique pathways through their ego jungles.

Like anything, practice turns meditation from a haphazard occurrence into an on demand skill.

The Meditative State (The Temple)

So you've created your own unique meditative Pathway by hacking through the obstacles of your ego Jungle. Suddenly you arrive at an illuminated clearing in the Jungle and arrive at the Temple: the substance of meditation—the meditative state. The Temple is a metaphor for your very sensitive feeling nature. Some call the meditative state a clairvoyant state because in this state you are able to harmonize with anything in the universe as long as you can map it and then distinguish it.

The temple is a realm where you sit at the nexus of a vast realm of information, all communicated to you by *feeling*. This is where you harmonize with the Infinite and all things are possible in direct proportion to your ability to turn off the ego. The less ego is present the more sensitivity in Knowing. The giant caveat is that to function at its full awesome power, your feeling-self needs to feel absolutely safe.

How do you know when you are in a meditative state? Couldn't you have gotten lost along the way and deluded yourself into believing you are meditating? Couldn't your ego have tricked you?

You know you are at the temple when you experience: rejuvenation; general mental stillness; feelings of contentment; feelings of interconnectedness with other things, other people, and perhaps with Everything. You may also feel elation and vastness, like you are flying or unlimited in potential.

You may also experience direct knowing. The intuitive strike may feel like one of those vaunted, "Aha!" moments, or "Eureka!" moments. Also, it may be that when you turn your attention to something, say an executive at an investment you are considering, then a specific, unique and very subtle feeling arises within you and *without* words. In this case the *feeling* is that of the executive. If these kinds of feelings are occurring then you are definitively in a meditative state.

A SIMPLE, POWERFUL, MEDITATION PRACTICE

Think back to the rejuvenating activities you identified earlier, the ones that help you enter a meditative state. Without words, recall how you feel when you are finally in that condition. Remember how your awareness feels. Also, concentrate on the feeling that exists in your body when you are in the meditative state. Once you have this feeling in your mind's eye say out loud the word "meditation." Repeat the word until you feel there is an association between your feeling and the word.

Now describe those feelings with words and write them down. But don't let the words dictate your feelings because feelings are vaster than words. Describing these feelings with words helps because the analytical brain will codify the experience and record them into your memory for future recall.

On the surface this exercise is about identifying the feeling of the meditative state. But there is more. The more frequently you meditate and learn what it feels like to be in a meditative state, the easier it is to get to the temple rapidly. Metaphorically, when you tread the Pathway frequently the Jungle does not grow back to cover the Path *and* eventually you *know* your way to the Temple. In Intuitive Investor speak: you harmonize with the feeling of the meditative state to enter a meditative state.

Technically:

1. You identify the feeling of the meditative state, then ...

2. You memorize this feeling so it's part of the "memory" part of your intelligence, then when you want to enter the meditative state ...

3. You recall the feeling of the meditative state from memory and harmonize with the feeling. That is, you allow yourself to be suffused with the feeling of the meditative state. Then ...

4. You are instantly back at the temple.

With a little practice eventually it *is* this easy to enter a meditative state.

REMEMBERING AWE

Awe also puts you into a meditative state almost instantly. It works because when you are confronted with something overwhelming in its importance or scale (for example the night time sky full of stars, the Grand Canyon, or the birth of a child) the left brain short-circuits in its efforts to describe, codify, and understand the experience. Remember, the left brain can only consciously handle two things at once. Awe renders it useless. In effect, trying to comprehend vastness gives the left brain nausea. So it automatically stops trying to analyze and what remains is your powerful, right-brained feeling-self!

Thus, another technique for recording the feeling of the meditative state is to remember awe. If you allow yourself to harmonize with that feeling such that in the moment you are again suffused with the feeling, then you will automatically be in a meditative state.

Even after you have hacked through your ego jungle you sometimes discover your temple has remnants of the jungle on its steps, so you cannot experience its full rich majesty. This is like the meditative state achieved naturally and automatically by everyone; and also like that described in previous exercises. However, when you *methodically* hack through the jungle, create a *well-worn* pathway, then when you arrive at the temple something very different awaits you. There will stand the full, rich, awe-inspiring majesty of the temple. You know this moment because you feel overwhelming awe and you feel absolutely everything. At this moment you are in the mystic. As you become a better and better Meditator, you will have many deep and meaningful experiences rivaling anything experienced external to yourself. This is why non-secular definitions of the Four Principles were needed in order to orient you with their vast possibilities.

The Fruits of Meditation (The Treasures)

While the full majesty of the temple is awe-inspiring, fun, and interesting, it is *not* the sole point of Meditation. The ultimate point is the *Treasure* inside the temple. The treasure is the information and lessons that powerfully affect your life. What kinds of treasure? *Anything is possible.* But I will share with you in the upcoming chapters three of the most powerful treasures as applied to investing: creativity, intuition, and wealth manifestation.

A Sample Meditation Practice

I have outlined the four main steps involved in a meditation practice, but let me make it concrete and describe a sample meditation practice.

MAKE TIME FOR IT

The best way to get better at anything is to invest time and resources into the activity; Meditation is no different. However, meditation is different because the only things necessary are a little bit of time and a desire to meditate. It is the ultimate portable activity. I strongly recommend for those just beginning a meditation practice to only meditate when feeling like it. This ensures that your association with meditation is fun and not a chore.

Ideally, in the beginning you set aside a minimum of 15 minutes for a meditation. As you get better you can enter a meditative state almost at will and less time is needed. The maximum amount of time to meditate is up to you. My maximum time is generally 1.5 hours, two times per week. However, I have meditated for up to 10 hours. Ultimately, the moment dictates the length.

GOAL?

The next step in your meditation session is to decide if you want a goal. I choose a goal about 50% of the time. Maybe you have a stressful day or week or conversation and want to examine the causes of the stress. In this case, you have a goal. On the other hand, you may feel wonderful and feel like letting the universe provide a spontaneous and serendipitous experience. That is, you let the Flow take over. While often fantastic, this meditation is frequently more difficult because without a vector the ego is more likely to interrupt the Flow. It's important to experiment and be flexible. Make whatever choice feels right. In the context of investing you will almost always have a meditative goal as you try to understand a specific part or parts of the information landscape.

GET COMFORTABLE

This seems self-explanatory, but comfort must absolutely *pervade* your meditation practice. Your body simply must be comfortable otherwise your body will distract you until it is comfortable. So, you may sit in perfect lotus, you may sit in an easy chair, you may lie down, you may do whatever you feel aids your comfort. In turn, this aids your meditation practice. Physical comfort also means you are not hungry or experiencing indigestion either. You also need your environment to be comfortable. So the temperature and noise level need to be amenable. Meditation is easier if you enter meditation already a little bit relaxed. If you have a distracting amount of Herculean things to do, it may make sense to meditate when you are less distracted. But meditation is also a powerful relaxation practice so don't let this become a prohibition. Comfort also means that if you feel embarrassed to be meditating then you don't meditate—say if your family or friends are not supportive of your practice. In short, because your egos are enough of an obstacle to meditative success, you don't add anything in that is extraneous.

HARMONIZE: PRINCIPLE III

Now that you have the time and you are comfortable you can get down to business. You can begin anywhere, but for beginners I highly recommend harmonizing with the same feelings you experience when you do the things that rejuvenate you. Those feelings should be your initial point of focus because they already **are** your Temple. Those feelings naturally identify your pathway through your jungle. Harmonizing with your feeling of the meditative state is the most direct and natural way of getting past your egoic mind.

If you are harmonizing with the meditative state then things happen quite spontaneously and without you seemingly causing them to. You may get a creative inspiration. You may get an intuitive insight. Importantly, there is no end to the depths of experience—there is no end.

PARADOX: PRINCIPLE II

Over time, as you repeatedly walk and create your pathway you experience the resolution of paradoxes; that is, it all starts to make sense. You understand and unravel how self-contradictory things can be simultaneously true. Arrival at this point is accompanied by feelings of humility, awe, clarity, and the truth, the likes of which are infrequently experienced by non-practicing meditators. With persistence, this road marker exists *along* everyone's meditative pathway.

INFINITY: PRINCIPLE I

Past the road marker of paradox you experience a profound sense of unity with everything in the universe. Here all things are possible and you know absolutely that they are. This realization is very likely to be accompanied by feelings of absolute bliss. Here are the stories of two Apollo astronauts; notice how each of them went through the four principles in reverse (that is, from Action to Harmonizing to Paradox to Infinity); and also note the consistent use of variations of the word "feeling:"

"I felt that I was literally standing on a plateau somewhere out there in space; a plateau that science and technology had allowed me to get to. But now that I was seeing it and, ever more important, what I was feeling at that moment in time, science and technology had no answers for. Literally no answers. Because there I was and there you are. There you are: the Earth. Dynamic. Overwhelming. And I felt that the world was just … there's too much purpose. Too much logic. It was just too beautiful to happen by accident. There has to be somebody bigger than me. And … and I mean this in a spiritual sense, not in a religious sense. There has to be a Creator of the universe who stands above the religions—that you yourself create the god in your lives."

—GENE KERNAN, Apollo 10 and 17 Astronaut[51]

And …

"The biggest joy was on the way home. In my cockpit window every two minutes: the earth, the moon, the sun and a whole 360 degree panorama of the heavens. And that was a powerful overwhelming experience. And suddenly I realized that the molecules of my body, and the molecules of the spacecraft, and the molecules in the body of my partners were prototyped and manufactured in some ancient generation of stars. And that was an overwhelming sense of Oneness, of connectedness. It wasn't them and you, it was: That's me! It's all of it. It's … It's One Thing. And it was accompanied by an ecstasy; a sense of, "Oh my God. Wow! Yes! An insight. An epiphany."

—EDGAR MITCHELL, Apollo 14 Astronaut[52]

Further Exploration

Here are some helpful hints if you want to explore this vast topic more thoroughly.

---

[51] From the DVD "In the Shadow of the Moon;" directed by David Sington; Velocity/Thinkfilm; 2008; at the 1:32:00 mark.

[52] From the DVD "In the Shadow of the Moon;" directed by David Sington; Velocity/Thinkfilm; 2008; at the 1:25:15 mark.

THERE ARE NO LIMITS

I have meditated for many years and have yet to find the end of the possibilities. I am still absorbing, processing, and trying to make useful many of the experiences I have had. My career success and this book bear witness to the possibilities.

One of the things I have discovered while hacking through the jungle of my ego is that there is more than one temple. In fact, I have discovered ever taller, greater, more spectacular temples. And each time I discover a greater, more awe-inspiring temple, there is a richer, more splendid, more useful treasure contained inside.

My meditation practice always grows in fits and starts. Sometimes it feels like 5 steps forward, 4 steps backward an—evolutionary advance. While other times it feels like 10 steps forward, 0 steps backward; a revolutionary advance. However, it is always rich. So I encourage you to keep at it and never assume you have reached the end—it just isn't possible because you are exploring the depths of an infinite universe.

MAKE THE TIME

This point is so important it makes a second appearance. Hopefully by now you can see how valuable meditation is as a tool. Like all investments, to earn returns on meditation you need to invest your resources, especially time. The reason is that most people, me included, have dense jungles that need the attention of a machete. By the time you read this book you already have a life time's worth of jungle. So there is probably a lot of culling necessary. However, you have explored many extremely valuable secrets for improving your meditative success and with an investment of time you will access the full richness of your right brains.

STUDY

If meditation is something of interest to you, then study it. This natural brain state receives short shrift in our culture and people have ignored its power. One of the ways to catch up is to start reading about the subject of meditation. There are endless tomes that have been written over literally, millennia. However, in the Appendix there is a list of recommended readings and I strongly encourage reading at least one of these books.

Additionally, many cities now have meditation venues. Seek out a group. Many yoga studios have some form of meditation. There are formal meditation groups that practice, though they often do not advertise and they can be insular. A limited number of martial arts studios also practice meditation, though the number is shockingly small given the history of the arts. Beware that meditation charlatans abound even if they don't know they are charlatans. Let your feelings guide you in your choice. If you are uncomfortable with the situation and your instincts tell you to RUN then do just that. There is no Meditation Police Force roaming around.

The Intuitive Investor and You: Self-Assessment

What things do you do that rejuvenate you? What sorts of insights have come to you when you have been doing these activities?

Does meditation now feel like a natural state of mind to you? How does it feel when you are in a meditative state?

In what ways has a meditative state helped you to make important decisions in your life?

How has meditation assisted you in making investment decisions? What can you do to incorporate meditation more into your decision making process?

Exercises

MOVIES AS A WAY OF CHARTING THE EGO

The next time you watch a movie notice how you respond to what you see and hear. Is there only a limited range of permissible responses to a movie for you? Is it okay to laugh, to cry, to be outraged, or to get excited by a movie? If you notice any limitations, put those down in your notebook.

If you, in fact, have a narrow range of movie response possibilities, spend some time examining why this is true. Write any observations down in your notebook. Use the reasons you have discovered as a point of focus in your meditation practice. The goal is to gain control of your defenses so that they are only up when you want them up.

HELP IN DISMANTLING UNNECESSARY CONSTRUCTS OF THE EGO

This is intended to be an ongoing practice, not a one time exercise. So, in effect, it is like spiritual weightlifting or jogging. Making this exercise a part of your weekly life will help to make you a better meditator. Just like physical exercise it also makes you happier and healthier.

Recall a moment over the last week when you felt strong emotions. Detail the *facts* of the experience in your notebook. What judgments or preferences did you add to the experience? What stimuli triggered your emotion? Is this emotional response typical when this kind of stimuli is present? If you answered "yes," it's likely that you have identified a program created by your ego.

When did your response to stimuli like this begin? It may be helpful to start with the deeply traumatic events of your life as the possible source of when the ego created this automatic behavioral response. Write down any observations you may have.

Once you have discovered the source of your emotional response, which may take many meditative sessions, ask yourself: "Is this program still serving me?" If the answer is no, then ask yourself: "Am I really still in danger after all of this time has passed?" If you feel that the egoic program *is* still serving you then ask yourself: "Can I improve on the old emotional technology of this defensive program, or is this the very best I can do to protect my feeling self?"

If the program is *not* serving you then here is a technique for changing how you respond. Imagine the exact same situation happening again but, this time imagine responding differently; in the way of your choosing. If needed, repeat this technique until you sense that the next time this kind of event happens you are able to respond without the ego being involved. Alternatively, if the ego's defensive program is necessary, then repeat the exercise until you respond to the stimuli with the new and improved protective program.

This exercise is a continual exercise in humility for me because dismantling my ego is tough work. However, this is one of the single greatest investments of my life and its benefits far outweigh the costs.

REVIEW

The secret of accessing the meditative state is using the four principles in reverse. You first elect to take *Action* when you make time for meditation, set meditation goals, and get comfortable. You next begin *Harmonizing* with the meditative state, your Temple; this is your Pathway through the Jungle of the ego. It's then that you begin to uncover the Treasure lying at the heart of the temple: creative inspiration or intuitive insight. The more deeply you explore the temple the more likely you are to discover that the underpinning of the universe is Paradox. And even further still you experience profound bliss and unity with everything. In this state you have unique creative inspirations and intuitive insights.

11

Cultivating Your Creativity

"You must be clear that when it comes to atoms, language can be used only as in poetry. The poet, too, is not nearly as concerned with describing facts as with creating images and establishing mental connections."

—NEILS BOHR, quantum physicist

The Intuitive Investor has been dedicated to sharing the right-brain investment treasures that I have uncovered from both my years as an investor, and from my years of creative problem solving as an investor. But I want for you to have the ability to create solutions to any investment problem you may encounter. This requires a general tool. Fortunately, creativity is a general tool, radically broad in its applications. In fact, the active solution to any new-to-you problem comes from the creative process. So knowing the secrets of the creative process is a must.

Creativity is one of the hallmarks of the brain and is, in my opinion, the highest expression of intelligence. Unfortunately, a lack of understanding of how to systematically access creativity abounds. In turn, this limits its full development and utilization. In this chapter, I will share with you secrets for systematically accessing your creativity.

Creativity occurs when the knowledge and memory of the left brain merge with the non-linear, intuitive essence of the right brain. The creative process can be generally described as the four principles worked in reverse with a starting place in the left brain's knowledge. When looking for creative inspiration to solve a particular investment problem, you simply make that problem the point of focus in a meditation.

To improve creativity three things must be done: knowledge increased, memory improved, and your ability to achieve a meditative state improved. Techniques are demonstrated to improve each area. The chapter concludes with self-assessments and exercises.

Creativity Defined

Creativity is a natural function of the brain and it happens when you are in a meditative state with a specific problem as a part of your focus. Creativity is a literal act of creation! Meaning that the treasure you bring back from your meditative process brings into existence that which did not exist before. Your creative solution, because it is something new, actually expands the boundaries of the universe. This is possible because of Principle I, Infinity—that is, you are a part of the universe, thus as you expand, the boundaries of the universe also expand.

The Creative Process: Four Principles–Style

Creativity is generically the Four Principles run in reverse, but grounded in your left brain.

1. Knowledge You begin with your knowledge because it is the root of creativity.

2. Principle IV: *Action* Then you *choose* as your meditative focus the problem you want to solve.

3. Principle III: *Harmonizing* Then you begin to harmonize with the meditative state with your point of focus being the problem for which you want a creative solution.

4. Principle II: *Paradox* At this point, you are not one with the meditative state; you are separate.

5. Principle I: *Infinity* When you are able to harmonize fully with the meditative state you become One with everything, activating your imagination very purely. Eventually you receive creative inspiration.

The creative process is that simple.

The Creative Process

The creative process is a specialized meditative state with a problem as your point of focus. Here, very specifically, are the steps of the creative process:

1. Do your research

2. Have a point of focus

3. Create time and space for yourself

4. Relax!

5. Enter a meditative state

6. Put the problem into your mind's eye

7. Relax more!

8. Don't try to force an outcome

9. Record the information

10. Have understanding

11. Choose to do something with your understanding

DO YOUR RESEARCH

To maximize the creative process you need to have done research to get a sufficient amount of knowledge. This knowledge about your problem is the raw material for the creative process. The more information you have pertaining to your problem the more likely it is that you'll come up with a creative solution. If you feel that you don't have enough knowledge about the problem then you must go get more before engaging in the creative process.

HAVE A POINT OF FOCUS

You begin the creative process with a problem you would like to solve. For example: a new investment idea; a way of asking a question of an executive to get important investment information you want; connecting disparate ideas into a new large investment theme; creating a mathematical description/ formula of a real world phenomenon; or understanding the business story behind the business data. This problem becomes the point of focus of your meditation. In my experience, the more specific you are in stating your investment problem, the more creative your right brain's solution.

So the creative process begins grounded in the knowledge realm of your left brain. Then you ascend the Four Principles with Infinity as your destination.

CREATE TIME AND SPACE FOR YOURSELF

Next, set aside the time to meditate on creative solutions to your problem. Not a lot of time is necessary, just enough to access the meditative mindset. You also need appropriate space. In other words, you need an environment conducive to being relaxed. This is different for each person. There is a time and space to do the activities that rejuvenate you—that is, that put you into a meditative state.

RELAX!

Meditation works best if you are relaxed. In the presence of freneticism the ego tends to fire up to protect your feeling-self. So it behooves you to relax, since this aids your ability to bypass the ego and enter the meditative state. This also means that you do not try and *force* a creative outcome. It also means that if your creative process seems stymied, you don't get frustrated. Creativity is a natural outcome when the right brain has a point of focus and is in a relaxed state.

ENTER THE MEDITATIVE STATE

Now when you enter the meditative state, you have entered Principle I, Infinity. The meditative state is where opposites are resolved into Oneness. In the creative process you bring your personal creative point of focus and dissolve it with God.

Once you feel yourself generally in the midst of egoic stillness, you gently put the problem you are trying to solve into your mind's eye. One of two things will happen.

One, your egoic mind kicks into gear. You know this is happening when you are *thinking* about something unrelated to the problem you are trying to solve. In this case relax and return to the meditative state.

Two, something magical starts to happen. You either have a solution pop into your mind—EUREKA!—or a thought process related to your problem begins. If your right mind begins working on a creative solution, then let the process unfold.

RELAX MORE!

After floating your problem into the meditative-ocean you relax more. If you have difficulty staying in the meditative state, continually focus gently on the pristine feelings of the meditative state until you are back at your temple. Once back, you re-introduce your problem to your mind's eye until the solution comes.

BE GENTLE

You are gentle with yourself at all times and do not try to force an outcome. The right mind *does* respond to method. So if you have adhered to the method I have outlined so far, you just need to be patient. If you are capable of creating a solution to your problem then it will happen eventually. Depending on the size of the problem (global warming, world hunger) it may take many trips to the meditative state to generate a creative solution.

Be encouraged. Creativity *is* a natural function of the mind. You do not need to be "creative" to solve problems creatively. In my opinion, when we say that someone is "creative" what is really being said is that someone has the natural ability to access the meditative state to solve problems. But everyone naturally has creative capacity.

EUREKA!

You know you have the creative solution to your problem when it's accompanied by an exalted *feeling* of truth and simplicity. EUREKA! This is raw creative inspiration and happens in accord with Principle I, Infinity.

RECORD

To transform the creative inspiration from a feeling into a thought so that you can get your left brain involved, too, you need to describe the creative solution with something the left brain understands, most likely words. So you need to record the results of your creative inspiration.

When you *separate* creative inspiration from its original feeling with words to make it *distinct* then you activate your imagination, or your creativity. Imagination is inspiration with mental grounding; this is Principle II, Paradox. So creativity is one side of the meditative state, the side grounded in the left brain.

UNDERSTANDING

Now that you have the investment information provided by the creative process spend time trying to understand the information. That is, spend some time harmonizing with it to ensure that you "get it" and that the information is made potent. This is Principle III, Harmonizing.

CHOOSE

Now that you have a creative solution to your investment problem you have to do something with it. That is you need to choose what to do; and of course, this is Principle IV, Action.

SUMMARY OF THE CREATIVE PROCESS

In summary, the creative process is a trip up the four principles and then back down from the four principles. From the starting place of your left brain's knowledge you ascend the four principles into the meditative state, Principle I, Infinity. There you receive creative inspiration as a solution to your problem from which you step back down into reality until you make a choice, Principle IV, Action.

Improving Creativity

To become more creative you need to strengthen each component of your arch. So if you strengthen your knowledge and memory then your creative process is also strengthened. In turn, if you strengthen your access to feelings and practice non-attachment then your intuition is improved, which strengthens your creativity. And lastly, if you want to improve your creativity you improve your ability to achieve a meditative state. The meditative state is the alchemical mixing bowl where each of the necessary creative components mixes together so that substantive and radical permutations occur. The left-brain distillate of this process is creative treasure.

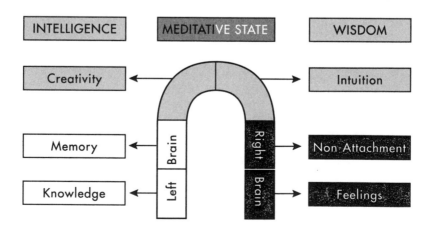

Let's start the improvement of creativity with the intelligence side of things by reviewing the components of intelligence:

➤ *Knowledge* is everything you have learned and stored in your brain.

➤ *Memory* is your ability to access your knowledge in a timely and accurate fashion.

➤ *Creativity* is pattern recognition, where your knowledge and memory mix with your right brain to provide solutions to problems.

IMPROVING INVESTMENT AND BUSINESS KNOWLEDGE

Knowledge is the raw material of the creative process. Think back to a creative solution you have come up with in your life. Were you able to understand the solution? If the answer is yes, then it means that the solution was within the bounds of your knowledge. So to increase your creative abilities then you need to increase and improve your knowledge.

To improve your knowledge in order to make better, more creative investment decisions you increase your:

➤ Quantity—breadth of information

➤ Quality—depth of information

➤ Personality—uniqueness of information

Quantity: Breadth of Information

To further empower your creativity you increase the amount of your knowledge. The more raw material you make available to your creativity the greater your chance of making the essential connections amongst the information that are necessary to reveal a new way of doing something, through creativity. In essence, each piece of information is an individual tile in a mosaic that you build. Engaging the creative process leads to pictures emerging out of the mosaic. The more mosaic pieces, the more emergent pictures. The greater your knowledge, the greater the potential for you understanding information.

When I was a mutual fund portfolio manager and my responsibilities were large, I spent most of my day increasing my knowledge. I read nineteen newspapers daily, the three major business news wires, several business and investment magazines, and had software that scoured the Internet for real time, actionable information. You do not need to read this much information. As my family's investment manager, a blog writer, and author, I only read three news sources, taking me less than 30 minutes each day. Some days I choose to read more and on some days, less.

Another way of improving your breadth of knowledge is to be conscious of the world around you by "seeing your world differently." There is important and investible information everywhere. The great thing about this choice is that it doesn't require any additional time on your part, just more Investor consciousness.

Libraries are a great low-cost way of improving the breadth of your knowledge, and thus your creativity. Examples include the local library, the local university's business school library, or your own library of business, economics, and investment books (see the Appendix for help with this). The Internet is the greatest repository of knowledge ever created. In fact, in my professional career the Internet was how I accessed all of those newspapers, newswires, magazines, and search engines. Another knowledge resource is databases. If you are crazy-interested in investing you may purchase access to investment databases, although this is an expensive choice. Another source of information is magazines. Then there is television, too. And on and on.

Quality: Depth of Information

There is value in having a shotgun (quantity) approach to increasing your knowledge because you never know when something you have read will be the missing link in your creative process. However, there is also tremendous value in a rifle (quality) approach, too. Above, I did not talk about what types of information to consume. But an efficient way to improve the investment knowledge fueling your creative process is to focus your attention. So at least half of the information you consume should have an investing context. After all, it's unlikely that a romance novel contributes to your knowledge about the prospects of fossil fuel energy in the next fifty years.

Any understanding of economics, businesses, finance, financial analysis, or the nuts and bolts of investing are all beneficial. You don't need to be expert in each topic, but you do need to know enough to understand the language of business and investing. This is true of anything; if you want to understand auto repair then you need to understand the functioning of the alternator.

The best place to start improving the quality of your knowledge is to read beneficial investment books (see the Appendix). As mentioned before, libraries, both local and university, are excellent sources of quality information. Then there are business newspapers, magazines and the Internet, too. Investment databases abound and are also a great source of raw material for the creative process.

Personality: Uniqueness of Information

You have been keeping a notebook through *The Intuitive Investor*. No doubt, during the course of your reading of the book you have had some creative and intuitive realizations about you and your investment process. I strongly encourage you to always have a way of recording your life's important observations, such as in a notebook. Doing so makes your knowledge permanent and it contributes to your continued effectiveness as a person and as an investor. Best of all, these introspective insights are unique to your personality and consequently, they serve you and your investment process directly.

In short, to improve your creativity you increase your knowledge.

IMPROVING BUSINESS AND INVESTMENT MEMORY

The importance of recall is that knowledge is impotent if you cannot access it when it is needed. Fortunately, there are many ways to improve memory.

Internal Technologies

1. Create multiple pathways and use mnemonic devices
2. Exercise your memory

Create Multiple Pathways and Use Mnemonic Devices

In ancient Greece, if someone wanted to record knowledge for posterity it was very expensive. Carving the information in stone was laborious and costly. Parchment was also expensive, and paper was unknown to the Greeks. So the solution for many ancient Greeks was to go for a walk. They would first outline the information they wanted to recall. Then as they walked they would intentionally associate noteworthy features of the journey with the pieces of the information they wanted to memorize. So when they wanted to recall a portion of their knowledge they would simply imagine going on the walk and the information would come out as they came to the noteworthy points in their minds.

You don't need to be as elaborate as long as you understand why the Greeks' technique worked. The secret was that they used the power of

Principle III, Harmonizing. By associating knowledge with noteworthy points on a memorable journey the Greeks created multiple pathways to their knowledge: the outline of the knowledge itself (an abstract memory) and the hike (sensory memories). This technique works because much of memory is keyed off of the senses and feelings, too. So a practical memory-improvement technique is to engage multiple senses when you are learning something so that you have multiple pathways to your knowledge. Thus, it's more easily recalled.

For example, you are reading this book and you could choose to take notes. If the notes are in your own words then you engage multiple aspects of your senses and feelings as well. You have your vision, the tactile sensation of your pen moving, and any feelings you have about the information. Likewise, when listening to a lecture and taking notes you hear the information, and see the information as you write it down. This is why note taking aids in memory recall, and ultimately creativity, too.

Another multiple-pathway technique is to intentionally recall the information multiple times. This creates separate pathways to the knowledge, improving recall. And still another technique is to read something aloud so that you have an aural memory as well as a visual memory. The genius of most of these techniques is that they do not require additional time on your part. You just need to be cognizant when you are learning something to experience the information in multiple ways so that your memory is improved.

Mnemonic devices are similar to creating multiple pathways. In fact, the ancient Greek, "go for a walk" method is a form of a mnemonic device. You are all probably familiar with Every Good Boy Deserves Fudge as a mnemonic device for remembering music's treble clef. Less common is Roy G. Biv as a mnemonic device for remembering the colors of the spectrum: red, orange, yellow, green, blue, indigo and violet. You can create your own mnemonics. For example, to memorize the names of the Four Principles you could create the following mnemonic: IPHA. That's short for Infinity, Paradox, Harmonizing and Action. You could then create the mnemonic device: Investment Paradise Here Awaits!

Exercise Your Memory

One way to improve memory is to exercise it. Because information in the current era is so easy to record, usually in an electronic device, most people's memory muscles are weak. You can improve your memory by remembering phone numbers, holidays, birthdays and anniversaries the old fashioned way: memorize them.

External Technologies

Dozens of solutions now exist to improve your ability to come up with the exact knowledge you need NOW to help you solve a problem or answer a question. For example:

1. Organizational structures (for example, alphabetizing, Dewey Decimal System, and so forth)

2. Database's search function

3. Internet search engine

4. Electronic devices

Organizational Structures

Deceptive in its simplicity, alphabetizing is an organizational structure that helps you to record and recall information quickly. Files in a filing cabinet or on a computer can be organized alphabetically or by broad subject or by function or whatever. The easier information is to access the sooner it becomes part of the raw material for the creative process.

Database's Search Function

Most computer database's have a search function allowing you to rapidly find information you search for. The ability to recall information so easily is a tremendous aid to your creativity.

Internet Search Engine

The Internet links millions of computers, and their vast information, in an ad hoc network. With a search engine this public information becomes your personal source of information. The combination of the Internet with a search engine is, after meditation, probably the single greatest creativity-enhancing invention of all time. You already know about search engines, but do you know how to do a Boolean search? If not, look at any search engine's search primers to improve search results. The more precise your recall of knowledge, the more focused your creative process.

Electronic Devices

Today's technology allows you to nearly have the full functionality of a personal computer in your pocket. These portable devices (BlackBerry, iPhone, SmartPhone, and so forth) keep your: date book, phone book, memos, word processing documents, spreadsheets, voice notes, photographs, and have Internet access. So you are free to learn new knowledge, recall past knowledge, and engage in the creative process virtually anywhere. These devices make you hugely productive.

IMPROVING BUSINESS AND INVESTMENT: RIGHT BRAIN SIDE

There are four more areas that can be improved to better the creative process: access to feelings, practicing non-attachment, intuition, and the meditative state. Chapter ten was all about improving the meditative state, while the next chapter, "The Intuitive Investor," has a thorough discussion about how to better access your feelings and practicing non-attachment. The natural consequence of embodying these two aspects of the right brain is intuition. Each of the concepts learned so far in the book now begin to inter-penetrate and violate a strictly linear layout to the book.

The Intuitive Investor and You: Self-Assessment

Think back to what you feel was a creative solution you came up with in your life. What was going on around you at the moment of the solution? What was going on within you at the time of the solution? Record your answers in your notebook.

Take a moment to recall a "Eureka!" moment that you had in your life. In your notebook write down answers to the following questions: What was your mind state when this moment occurred? What sorts of realizations did you experience? How important were these realizations? Is there any reason why the conditions present in these moments cannot be replicated?

In what ways are you a creative investor? Do you feel that the world of investing is full of vast possibilities, or do you feel constrained by it?

Who do you know that has creative investment ideas? What is their process for generating these ideas?

Exercises

First, make sure that you have at least 30 minutes of private, relaxation time. Next, in your notebook, write down an investment problem that you would like to solve. This could be wanting new creative investment ideas to explore, a new method for examining a business, or a way to understand vast information flow about a business. Now take several moments to write down the knowledge you have about this problem.

Now set your notebook down and begin to relax. You are going to follow the steps outlined in the Creative Process Overview. So you begin by putting the problem you want a creative solution to in your mind's eye.

Next, begin harmonizing with the feeling of the meditative state. Eventually your egoic mind will still itself. Be patient. If you get off track and begin thinking about something superfluous, just return your problem back to your point of focus. Then still your mind again. The goal is not stillness. The goal is for your right brain to begin mixing with your knowledge to generate a creative solution. If these sorts of thoughts remain in your mind's eye then the creative process is functioning.

Write down any solutions to your problem in your notebook.

REVIEW

The secret to being able to access creativity at will is to understand the conditions that make creativity possible. Creativity is simply the Four Principles run in reverse, but grounded in the left brain.

Improving your creativity requires a strengthening of each of the components of your brain, left and right. On the left-brain side you need to first, have creative raw material, knowledge, which fuels your right-brain's creative process. There are three general ways to improve your knowledge: increase the breadth, improve the depth and write down your own observations. Second, you need to improve your ability to recall what you already know. You can do this with internal and external technologies. Last, and most important, you enter into a meditative state with an investment problem as your point of focus. Once the creative solution appears you descend back down the four principles. First you record your creative insight. Then you seek to understand it. And last, you take action regarding your understanding of the new creative insight.

12

The Intuitive Investor

"It appeared that the unconscious mind somehow had the capability of communicating with the sub-tangible physical world—the quantum world of all possibility." [53]

In mapping the brain's frontiers, intuition is the least charted. Many people consider it to be a version of an informed guess. But intuition, like meditative states and creativity, is a *natural* brain function. Intuition is the highest flowering of the right, organic mind and it happens when the formless quality of the right brain bridges with the left, linear brain's ability to distill, structure, and describe. In short, intuition is the Four Principles run backward, but grounded in the right-brain's feelings. I call it "tuning into the cosmic radio station." Each of the steps necessary for accessing your intuition at will is fully described. The chapter concludes with self-assessments and exercises designed to make you a more Intuitive Investor.

Intuition Defined

Besides the highest expression of the right brain, what is "intuition"? Intuition is defined as [54]...

> **in·tu·i·tion** [in-too-ish-uhn,-tyoo-]; noun.
>
> 1. direct perception of truth, fact, etc., independent of any reasoning process; immediate apprehension.
>
> 2. a fact, truth, etc., perceived in this way.
>
> 3. a keen and quick insight.

---

[53] Lynne McTaggart, *The Field: the Quest for the Secret Force of the Universe (updated edition)* (New York: Harper Collins Publishers, 2008), 121.

[54] *Random House Dictionary* (New York: Random House Inc., 2009).

4. the quality or ability of having such direct perception or quick insight.

5. *Philosophy.*
   a. an immediate cognition of an object not inferred or determined by a previous cognition of the same object.

   b. any object or truth so discerned.

   c. pure, untaught, noninferential knowledge.

6. *Linguistics.* the ability of the native speaker to make linguistic judgments, as of the grammaticality, ambiguity, equivalence, or nonequivalence of sentences, deriving from the speaker's native-language competence.

My own personal definition of intuition is:

> *the **natural** ability to harmonize with the universe and experience direct knowing.*

Because of the interconnectedness aspect of Principle I: *Infinity* you can tune into and sense anything that is transpiring in the universe at any time. This is only limited by your ability to describe what is happening. I strongly encourage you to conduct your own intuition experiments to verify these facts for yourself.

Where Intuition Takes Place

One of the reasons intuition feels like happenstance to people is that they look for it to happen in the thinking realm. Or they expect a full-fledged, word-based transmission. But it's that very utilization of the analytical, left brain that stands in the way of an intuitive experience. When the left brain is used, with all of its concepts and structures and rigidity, it activates the ego and its defenses of the feeling self—thus squelching feelings. And *intuition takes place in the feeling realm.*

Why Intuition Works: Unifying Principles I-IV

Intuition works because everyone is a part of the universe. Because we are all a part of the same reality we can harmonize with any portion of reality and feel it. Remember, by feelings I do not mean emotions, but instead the information received when tuning into the universal flow. This is the unification and blurring of the four principles into one: tuning in. When you feel it—that is, what you want to have an insight about—you have just that: a feeling. The feeling does not come neatly packaged in numbers or words. Instead, it is up to you to translate that pure feeling into numbers or words. There are two very tricky aspects to overcome when tapping into intuition: our culture's huge investment in the development of the left brain and the resultant ego structures that make experiencing a true, pure, clear signal very difficult; *and* the difficulty of translating feelings into words so that intuitive insights can be better understood and be worked with.

WHY INTUITION IS USEFUL

Those unused to tapping the power of the intuition, or who have written it off as a euphemism for luck, need some explanation as to its power.

Intuition is valuable because an evaluation of the present moment cannot solely be reduced to a set of linear problems. Reality is larger than its linear approximations. Intuition is an ideal tool for understanding those aspects of reality that are non-linear and vast. So intuition is a natural complement to the knowledge and memories of the left brain. Additionally, by tapping into your intuition you can identify the information in front of you that is actually pertinent to an important decision.

Intuition can clearly demonstrate what people are really thinking and feeling. This is not just reading body language, as intuition can work even if you cannot see or hear the person in question.

Intuition can also often reveal the natural outcome of a set of entangling structures that are in place. For example, a business makes a number of products all of which are successful. It sells these products all over the world. Yet, its CEO has just retired and a new CEO is brought on board. She believes that the competition for the company's most important product is only going to increase. Therefore the CEO invests tremendous amounts of capital into the development and launch of new products that are slightly outside of the expertise of her company. Will the company succeed; if so, for how long?

This problem, which is so typical of investment problems, is an entanglement of a number of linear, logical problems as well as non-linear dynamics problems. Intuition can, and often does, provide the universal solvent for disentangling this mess so that you see the underlying probabilities of the probabilistic universe. In other words, because the world is an organic, non-linear place then you must use an organic, non-linear tool to help you comprehend reality and to act accordingly. This is why intuition is powerful.

In chapter fourteen, "Reports from the Field," anecdotes from my career will demonstrate some of the real world applications of intuition.

The Intuitive Process

Intuition is generically the Four Principles run in reverse, but grounded in your right brain.

1. Feelings You begin with your feelings because they are the root of intuition.

2. Principle IV: *Action* Then you *choose* as your meditative focus the information with which you want to attune.

3. Principle III: *Harmonizing* Then you begin to harmonize with the meditative state with your point of focus being the feeling with which you want to attune.

4. Principle II: Paradox At this point, you are not one with the meditative state; you are separate.

5. Principle I: *Infinity* When you are able to harmonize fully with the meditative state you become one with Everything, activating your intuition very purely. Eventually your intuition generates an intuitive answer.

So intuition is the Four Principles in reverse, but grounded in the right brain.

Steps in the Intuitive Process

Just like any tool, you need procedures and methods to ensure proper intuition use. While you can use a screwdriver's handle as a hammer it functions better as a screwdriver. You may use intuition to solve all sorts of problems, but let's first learn to use your intuition most naturally.

Here are the steps in the intuitive process:

1. An analogy—tune into the cosmic radio station.

2. Choosing the station—use intention to direct your feeling-self to what you want to understand or harmonize with.

3. Tuning in by turning off—let go of the egoic mind.

4. Hearing the signal—surrender to the feelings present.

5. Listening to the signal—pay attention to the feelings experienced.

6. Translation—describe your feelings with words.

7. Evaluation—how closely do your words match your feelings?

8. Decide—make a decision based on those feelings.

A POWERFUL ANALOGY

Intuition is:

tuning into the cosmic radio station.

This analogy elegantly captures the nature of the intuitive process. Keep it in mind and tie each intuition step back to this analogy moving forward.

CHOOSING THE STATION

Before you can enter the meditative state you need to know which piece of information you want to attune with and to eventually understand. That is, the *feeling* you want to become One with. This could be the "mood" of the financial markets; the character of a CEO; the public's perception of a company's product; the state of the economy; the feeling the public has about the future; and so on. Whatever you choose this becomes your *intention*, and is akin to choosing the cosmic radio station you want to tune into.

Intention is humbly focusing your mind on a situation or problem for which you want an intuitive insight. The word "humbly" is very important because for the process to work best you need to be humble. This is because in a state of humility there is no ego present and thus intuition is more able to flow.

So the intuitive process is grounded in the right brain's *feelings*.

TUNING IN BY TURNING OFF

With a feeling intention you now need to tune into the cosmic radio station. You do this by ascending the four principles and entering a meditative state; this is Principle I, Infinity. Recall that the meditative state is where opposites are resolved into Oneness. Here you bring your personal intention and merge it with impersonal Allness. The success of the intuitive process is in direct proportion to your ability to turn off the egoic mind. That is, to your ability to be non-attached.

HEARING THE SIGNAL

Once you have tuned into the cosmic radio station you need to hear the signal. You do this through *surrender*. Surrender is a state of receptivity as free of ego as you choose it to be. That is, you allow yourself to vibrate as purely as possible with what you want to understand. You want to become One with your intuitive intention. When you do, you will have that "EUREKA" sensation and you will have tuned into the cosmic radio station and received information.

Again, your ability to hear the signal in an intuitive state is directly proportionate to your ability to turn off the ego. Put another way, distortion of your intuitive signal is directly proportionate to the strength of your ego. Strong ego = strong distortion. Strong surrender = strong intuitive signal.

Now that you have become One with your intuitive intention, now you must use your awareness to examine how you feel. That is, you must listen to the signal.

LISTENING TO THE SIGNAL

Now you are tuned into the cosmic radio station. The signal is practically free of static (ego) and you are hearing a clear signal from the cosmic radio station. Now you need to listen to the signal if you want to comprehend its meaning. In other words, you need to *pay attention* to the feeling experi-

---

✦ An Example of a Surrendered State ✦

Have you ever had the experience of walking down the street and you see someone with a funny look on his or her face and a funny feeling to go along with it; and what ends up happening is that for a moment you take on the expression, feeling, and demeanor of the person? You literally morph into them for just a moment. This result happens because when you are surrendered and in a meditative state the mind is formless. So someone else's strong vibration can shape you almost instantaneously. This is the kind of experience you want when you are tuning into the cosmic radio station and trying to "hear the signal." If this kind of experience feels scary, that's the ego kicking in because it either senses a loss of a sense of self, or because it detects that the feeling-self is negatively affected by morphing.

enced in your surrendered state of Oneness with your intuitive intention. Importantly, your memory can store feelings, not just numbers or words, so put the feeling into memory.

TRANSLATION

The second hardest part of the intuitive process, after diminishing the ego, is *translation*. This is where you take the feeling information you received while tuning into the cosmic radio station and put it into words. This is an optional step. It is possible to just store the feeling in your memory without translation. However, translation is where the intuitive right brain merges with the left brain and invokes the left brain's very strong ability to identify, codify, describe, and record. This is translation's advantage.

When you translate the information you separate it from intuitive inspiration. This is Principle II, Paradox. The separation is accomplished by

✦ Absolute Surrender Is Frightening ✦

Perhaps cryptically, I said that surrender is as free of ego as you *choose* it to be. It is possible to experience absolute surrender, or an absolute state free of ego. This means you temporarily disintegrate your ego and its artificial boundaries by removing all form and structure from your mind in order to let yourself be one with what you want to understand.

But the ego does not like absolute surrender and frequently it will trigger terrifying emotions just before a state of absolute surrender that sometimes can seem like death. The reason it feels like death is that you have quite literally never been on the other side of the precipice and to move to that spot requires that you "die" to your old self and faithfully enter a new space.

In my years of teaching meditation, many people have approached this terrifying precipice for many years and have turned away each time, unwilling to let the full egoic self go. By no means am I demeaning the choice to turn away. Speaking from personal experience, the precipice is genuinely the most terrifying precipice I have ever chosen to cross. Why would someone want to cross this precipice? Because on the other side is personal growth and perhaps someday, absolute bliss. A measure of one's ability to surrender is the degree to which one can overcome these terrifying anxieties put in place by the ego.

✦✦✦✦✦

✦ Tuning into the Truth ✦

Sometimes what you want to tune into and listen to is the truth. You know you are harmonizing with the truth because it feels like a crystal clear, adamantine diamond cutting through obscurity. Sometimes the truth feels like an "empty spot" or "nothingness." You suddenly get this sense of a void, or vacuum, and because the universe abhors a vacuum, you feel yourself pulled in the direction of the empty spot. These feelings are the source of the classic king of all Buddhist conundrums: emptiness. Given the limitations of a linear language these words are actually apt descriptions because this is what the truth feels like.

writing down or voicing the words you feel best capture the essence of your cosmic radio station feelings. This likely takes some practice. And it may sometimes be the case that your feelings about a situation are never able to be fully translated into words. This is because the universe is extraordinarily complex and some feelings and problems are beyond your ability to comprehend or describe them. So the largest disadvantage of translation is the difficulty of a precise translation.

EVALUATION

Once you have translated the signal of the cosmic radio station into a linear format you need to evaluate it—a left-brain strength. Importantly, you compare the information received from your intuition to see if it matched your initial *intention*. That is, you make sure that you were harmonizing with what you wanted to understand; this is Principle III, Harmonizing. If not, then you have one of two choices: repeat the intuitive process, or move on in your investment decision-making process without intuitive insight.

You also must evaluate the effectiveness of your intuitive process. Where did it breakdown or suffer? What aspects of the steps need improvement?

DECIDE

Now that you have intuitively derived information, you need to decide what to do with it in Principle IV, Action. Information is not interesting in and of itself. Information is interesting as applied to a decision. Buy, hold, or sell? Get more information? Focus on other information? You need to decide.

SUMMARY OF THE INTUITIVE PROCESS

In summary, the intuitive process is a trip up the four principles and then back down the four principles. From the starting place of your right-brain's feelings you ascend the Four Principles into the meditative state, Principle I, Infinity. There you receive intuitive inspiration as a solution to your problem which you step back down into reality until you make a choice, Principle IV, Action.

Investment Applications:
The Intuitive Investor in Action

ASSESSING MANAGEMENT CHARACTER

You gather all of the necessary information about a business. You do all of your investment analyses and you are almost ready to invest. However, you know every business's success depends on management and its choices. You see numerical evidence of management's strengths and weaknesses but are uncertain of its integrity. So you use intuition to tune into the CEO's character.

Your meditative intention is "XYZ Corporation's CEO's integrity." To aid in your ability to harmonize with the CEO you listen to a company webcast to hear his voice. Alternatively, you look at a picture of the CEO from the annual report that you download from the Internet. These things help you locate him topographically amongst the cosmos. You then harmonize with the CEO and become One with his vibration. You get the feeling that he is self serving, arrogant, and sleazy. Now you need to act/decide. Maybe you gather further evidence or maybe you tune back into the CEO on a different day to confirm your intuitive sense. Maybe you make an investment in the business anyway.

FEELING WHAT THE FUTURE MAY HOLD

You read the news about a business for many months. It wants to take advantage of the growing appetite among consumers for alternative, non-fossil based, energy sources. You know the business has some tangential skills that *might be* extended into this new venture. However, you are uncertain.

Your feeling vectors are: the future of alternative energy; and the ability of the company to take advantage of this future. You tune into the cosmic radio station. Regarding the first vector, the *feeling* you get is of a decreased use of fossil fuels. The second *feeling* you get is of accord and harmony. You conclude the company is able to make the transition successfully. However, you are not stupid. You then endeavor to conduct all of your regular investment analyses. Even though the business is likely to be successful in its new endeavors the price per share of the company may be too expensive. So you watch the company to see if the price gets to a point where you should buy. You also continue to evaluate your intuitive insight about the business to see if it is confirmed by its news.

This type of intuitive exercise can also be used for an industry, the financial markets, a national economy, or the international economy.

IDENTIFYING THE IMPORTANT ISSUES OF AN INVESTMENT

You are invested in a business and feel you know it fairly well. Yet, the stock's appreciation never matches your positive view of the business. Of all the possibilities, you want to know which factor is the one troubling other investors the most.

Your intuitive station is: the thing scaring other investors. You turn off your ego, enter the meditative state, review the factors you are aware of, and listen. You learn that investors are worried about interest rates. You couple this intuitive insight with your knowledge that interest rates may soon shift—this is why other investors feel uncomfortable with this business.

Next, you evaluate whether the fear is justified. That is, your intuitive station is: the likelihood that interest rates will shift in the next six months. You conclude the interest-rate fear is unwarranted and take advantage of the depressed share prices and buy more of the business.

SURMISING THE "MOOD" OF THE MARKET

A recession is underway and the financial markets are collapsing. The media is entirely negative saying that a Depression is imminent. You want to take advantage of the drastically low prices of businesses but want to know if the market has bottomed.

Your intuitive intention is: the mood of the market. An alternative intention is: has the market bottomed? You tune in intuitively and learn that the most fearful market participants have already exhausted themselves with their anxiety and that they have sold their investments. Optimism is returning. Alternatively you may learn that "yes," the market has reached a bottom. You choose to invest in businesses you have analyzed and watched for several years.

A caveat: Intuition gives you insight into the probabilistic topography of the universe. It reveals the structural entanglements *already* in place and the likely natural effects of those structural entanglements unwinding that is suggested by your understanding of cause and effect. That is, intuition suggests a natural and likely outcome given a specific time's conditions. But because free-will exists the probabilistic landscape will change as people exercise their free will. This means that the market may fall further once the causes you have interpreted *today* have changed in the *future*. So you must continually evaluate. See the case study in chapter fourteen.

IDENTIFYING THAT WHICH IS HIDDEN

You like a prospective investment but can't seem to get conviction. Your intuition suggests you shouldn't invest. But you want to be absolutely sure you aren't just being paranoid.

The cosmic radio station is tuned to that which the business doesn't want you to know. Your process suggests the business has a difficult relationship with someone else. Depending on your sensitivity (determined by how little the ego is present) you can determine that the bad relationship is with another business to whom the company owes money. The ultimate in sensitivity might reveal to you that the relationship is with the company's short-term creditors. This strain means the business may soon face a cash crunch. You decide not to invest.

Note: Tuning into the relationship with "short-term creditors" requires that you have knowledge of this part of the Cosmic Topography. In other words, you need to build up your knowledge of the business to even recognize this as a possibility. Otherwise, when you tune into the cosmic radio station you get feelings/signals you cannot translate into words. If you can't translate your feelings into words it may be an indication that you need to increase your knowledge of the business until your feeling harmonizes with some aspect of the business you know about and to which you can relate your feelings.

IDENTIFYING IMPORTANT SHIFTS THAT ARE UNDERWAY

The current economic expansion is over five years old. This is highly unusual. You want to know if there are any important shifts underway not appreciated by the broader market.

Your intuitive focus is: important shifts underway that people are missing. You discover everything is ok. This period of growth is a rare period where the economy is in balance and evolving naturally. At this time you are comfortable with your investments and choose to do nothing.

A FINAL WORD ON INTUITION

Intuition's possibilities are endless. In my mind, intuition is the most powerful investment tool available to anyone. This is because of its absolute flexibility and its ability to deliver *feelings* about the actual state of the universe at a given moment in time. I use intuition on a daily basis and with ever greater success.

The Intuitive Investor and You: Self-Assessment

Do you know anyone that has intuitive investment insights? Have you ever asked them how they do "it," that is, how they make intuition work? What successes has your acquaintance had with intuition? What failures have they experienced?

Have you ever had what you felt were intuitive insights with regard to your investments? If so, how was the information received in your intuitive process different from a lucky guess? What did you do with your intuitive insight? How did your choice affect your returns?

Exercises

FEELING OTHER PEOPLE Choose the person with whom you have the most complicated relationship. Write his or her name down in your notebook.

Now take several moments to get into a meditative state. Once you are relatively still, tune into the feeling of the person. Do *not* assign words to your feelings. Just pay attention to him or her until a pure sense of the person forms. Keep your feeling in your mind's eye.

Now try to assign words to the overall feeling of that person and write them down in your notebook.

HELP WITH TRANSLATING FEELINGS Imagine your very favorite meal. Now, without words, begin to experience your meal with each of your five senses. Begin with how your favorite meal appears. Next, experience the meal's aroma. Now move on to what it sounds like as you chew each delicious bite. Now move on to the textural feeling of your favorite food in your mouth. Lastly, imagine the flavor of the meal in your mouth. Remember, do not use words—just experience the feeling of the meal in your imagination.

Now I want you to write down the myriad feelings of your favorite meal in your notebook. The goal is to talk about the feeling of your favorite meal in the same way that a somlier talks about her favorite wine. This exercise should help you at translating complex feelings/experiences into linear words.

SHARPENING YOUR INTUITION For each person you encounter in the upcoming week pay attention to the different way that each person "feels." That is, what is the vibe of each individual? Begin to see if you can make distinctions between each person. How often are you correct in your assessment of strangers? What differences do you note? Record your observations in your notebook.

SHARPENING YOUR INTUITION, PART 2 Pay attention to the way the objects you encounter on a daily basis feel to you. Does metal feel the same as plastic? How does a hamburger feel, relative to a salad, relative to a candy bar? Again, I am not talking about how these things feel tactilely, but energetically. Record your observations of the distinctions.

SHARPENING YOUR INTUITION, PART 3 For the next week, try to feel the driver in the car in front of you on the road. Try and feel what they are about to do. How successful are you at discerning what they are about to do? What other information from your senses aids you in your judgments? What knowledge do you bring to bear to help you understand? Place your thoughts in your notebook.

SHARPENING YOUR INTUITION, PART 4 Have someone that you trust who is good at acting (projecting energy) put the energetic intention of imminent movement into one of her limbs, but without giving anything away via body language. Try to feel which limb they are intending to move. Confirm to see if you are correct. Record your observations.

SHARPENING YOUR INTUITION, PART 5 Have someone you trust, who is good at acting (projecting energy) harmonize with a strong emotion without giving anything away via body language. This could be anger, mercy, love, fear, and so forth. Try to feel what the person is feeling and confirm that you are right. Track your successes, failures or observations in your notebook.

REVIEW

In chapter twelve, "The Intuitive Investor," I defined intuition as the natural ability to harmonize with the universe and experience direct knowing. In an overarching sense, intuition is simply the Four Principles in reverse, but grounded in a feeling state. Within the structure of the Principles it is possible to refine the process to aid in tapping the intuition at will. The process I described was "tuning into the cosmic radio station."

First was "turning off" where you let go of the egoic mind. Next was "choosing the station" where you choose something that you want to understand; this becomes your intuitive intention. Next you have to "hear the signal" where you allow yourself (surrender) to become One with your intuitive intention. Then you use your awareness to evaluate how you feel, this is called "listening to the signal." These feelings can be left untouched or translated into a linear format. The advantage of translation is that you can then use both halves of your brain, left and right, to begin to understand the information. After you have collected intuitive information you have to "evaluate" it in order to have understanding. Lastly, you must decide to do something with the information you have gathered.

13

A Radical Guide for Wealth Manifestation

"Genius is the ability to put into effect what is on your mind"

—F. SCOTT FITZGERALD

Manifestation is the ability to materialize what you desire. It has been written about extensively in many books, so what can be gained from a further exploration of this concept from the standpoint of an investor? Investing is omnipresent in every decision you make. Investing is making conscious decisions where benefits outweigh costs and this *is* manifestation. This close relationship between manifestation and investing means that one of the book's central topics is manifestation.

In a general sense, manifestation is the four principles run forward. Just like all of the other topics of Part III there are details to add within that overarching structure. The manifestation steps are: inspiration, imagination, thought, word, and deed. When each of these five steps is honored and the sequence adhered to manifestation occurs. Radical Wealth Manifestation is a perfect description of the normal investment process coupled with the powers of inspiration, imagination and thoughts balanced between the right brain and the left brain.

The Manifestation Process

Generally, manifestation is the four principles run forward.

1. Principle I Infinity When in a meditative state you receive an intuitive inspiration. At this point the inspiration remains seminal, but undescribed.

✦ Manifesting an Inspiration ✦

In the fall of 2002 I am out dancing in Santa Fe when suddenly it occurs to me that I should write a book for a general audience about investing that reveals some of the secrets of investing I have discovered. I scoff at the absurdity of this inspiration. I am a portfolio manager of a mutual fund and to disclose some of my secrets will be handing them over to my competition.

In the summer of 2005 in the lead up to my retirement from investment management, my friend Stephen asks me what I am going to do in my retirement besides study martial arts. I say, "Maybe, write a book." In return, he asks, "What kind of a book." My reply is, "I can't decide. Either a book about investing or about spirituality." Essentially, Stephen replies, "Why can't it be the same book?" I spend the next several years imagining what this book would look like. I generate lots of material that I present to friends and to strangers in public lectures. I am gauging the response of the material and how it activates people.

It's April 29, 2007, and I have awakened from a dream with a powerful inspiration. I have the entire introduction to a book in my mind. I race to my computer and begin typing up an e-mail that I send to myself to record the inspiration.

February 1, 2008, I finally sit down at my laptop computer and begin writing my investment opus. My working title is "The Discerning Investor." In it I will disclose the secrets of success from my Wall Street career. It's my feeling that this success was derived from blending the knowledge of my left brain with the intuition of my right brain. Within two months of writing I have over 400 pages of material and I feel that I am only half-way through my book. The material is just flowing out of me, but more interestingly, things are flowing toward me, too!

That is, people whom I have never met before begin appearing at dinner gatherings, from my wife's professional connections, and from random places, to assist me in my manifestation efforts. With the input of these people I know that the most important book I can write is about the right brain, because it has been almost completely ignored in the investment lexicon.

Over the next two years my book is rejected by almost every major publishing house. Some of the feedback is encouraging and quite a lot of it is discouraging. However, I continue to invest my life's energy into the creation of what has become, *The Intuitive Investor*.

Eventually my book and life's passion finds a willing publisher who understands my vision and wants to encapsulate my original inspiration in a book. *The Intuitive Investor: A Radical Guide for Wealth Manifestation* is published in the fall of 2010.

✦✦◆✦✦

2. Principle II Paradox Your inspiration is stepped down into your imagination by translating into either numbers or words. By cleaving the inspiration into two halves, the formless feeling of inspiration and the words that allow inspiration to form in the imagination, you can begin to think about it creatively.

3. Principle III Harmonizing Here you are able to think about the original inspiration in a grounded, real world way. Once satisfied as to its potency, you commit to live the inspiration; that is, to harmonize with it.

4. Principle IV Action Once you choose to live the inspiration you put it into action in your life.

So manifestation is the Four Principles run forward. It's that simple.

Radical Steps for Wealth Maninfestation

Every single one of The Intuitive Investor's skills comes together to help you manifest wealth. Manifestation is the ultimate investment skill: turning straw into gold. The steps for wealth manifestation are:

1. Inspiration This is intuitive inspiration about what you should do.

2. Imagination This is creative imagination of what to do and how to do it.

3. Thought This is structuring your inspiration and imagination into a plan.

4. Word This makes your inspiration more material, it is a commitment to the plan.

5. Deed This is making manifest your initial inspiration.

All five steps are equal in importance and all must be present in order for manifestation to occur.

INSPIRATION

Manifestation begins with inspiration, that is, with Principle I Infinity. We tread this ground in chapter twelve, "The Intuitive Investor," which was about intuitive inspiration. Specifically, you learned a method for how to generate inspiration. Those EUREKA moments are unique; they are where something you have never imagined or created *pops* into your consciousness, accompanied by inspirational feelings.

You must honor inspiration.

The feeling of that eureka moment is a powerful indication from the universe that you should be paying attention, so it must be honored. That inspiration is the magical seed of manifestation and it often points people in the direction of change. Unfortunately, the ego doesn't like to have the earthquake of change shaking its foundation. So another essential key to manifestation is to unshackle from the emotional limitations of the ego. In this way inspiration flows and directs the manifestation process.

> In my creation of *The Intuitive Investor* my initial crystal clear inspiration occurred in the fall of 2002 while dancing. However, my ego shut the inspiration down and refused to let me honor it.

IMAGINATION

Once inspiration has occurred then you need to begin to mix its power with what you already know. This is imagination, this is creativity, this is Principle II, Paradox. Now you let the right brain and left brain dance together. The creative process outlined in chapter eleven, Cultivating Your Creativity, is a natural assist to this process.

Again, you must be ever vigilant for the protestations of the ego. The ego will attempt to sabotage the creative process unless the creative process is engaged with consciousness. The voice you will hear will try and convince you that what you are imagining is impossible, foolish, not necessary, and/or not truly unique. If you begin to hear these voices in your head then a bad thing and many good things have occurred.

The bad thing is that the ego is engaging in self-sabotage. One good thing is that there is awareness of the self-sabotage, so the ego may be turned off. To have self-sabotaging thoughts is also a powerfully good indication that you are in the midst of a creative process. This process likely involves real personal growth for if real personal growth isn't what is at stake, then the ego and its limiting barriers would not need to activate.

Eventually, natural, elegant structures will begin to form out of the nebula of your imagination.

> In the summer of 2005, I can not imagine what my investment book will look like until my friend Stephen admonishes me about my limited view of the possibilities. This allows me to break through the bounds of my ego and begin engaging my creativity. Some initial structures begin to take shape from the mixture of my inspiration and my imagination.

THOUGHT

Once inspiration and imagination begin their dance with one another, forms will begin to emerge from the manifestation nebula. Among these structures will be: a plan for manifesting what you want, as well as obvious next steps for action. The presence of these structuring thoughts is the indication that the left brain is beginning to take over the process—a very good thing. If you cannot think it, then you cannot do it. The thought stage is, in effect, the organizing stage.

Now you begin adding form to substance in equal proportion. Thinking about the process begins to make inspiration more material, more real. It allows you to understand the inspiration and imagination, of Principle III, Harmonizing.

At this point you can begin to bring your full knowledge to bear to manifest what you want. Additionally, you begin to see your knowledge and emotional limitations and this suggests a natural course for action: get more information and get help. But thoughts are not valuable unless you do something with them.

> I spend the time from the summer of 2005 to January 2008 thinking about what my book will be like. I think endlessly about different structures and approaches. I am mixing my inspiration and imagination with my knowledge. Consequently, I begin creating the architectures to support my material.

WORD

Because words are lenses for thought energy you want a clear and focused lens for your inspiration. This is the stage where you make a commitment to make your inspiration, imagination and thoughts real. Word is where you inject your personal interest in with the initial inspiration. This is where you become committed to guide your life by your initial inspiration. So Word is both, Principle III, Harmonizing: you become your inspiration, and Principle IV, Action: you become committed to realizing your inspiration.

You can formally write your idea down or you can talk about your idea with someone. When you voice what is in your thoughts your ideas immediately develop density, they take weight. When you give your thoughts the breath of life they are born and become separate from you. Your thoughts become their own entities.

Imagine you are deeply in love with someone and thinking privately about marriage. What happens to the idea of marriage once you voice it to your partner, or to a friend, or to a family member, or to your parents? Once voiced, the thought of marriage is difficult to make go away. This is because "word" makes thoughts real and separate from you. Another (unfortunate) example of "word" is the e-mail that as soon as you send it you regret it. Your thoughts are instantaneously real when you write them down or give them voice.

Think of "word" in terms of the powerful promise: "I give you my word."

> I share my material with friends and their responses are overwhelmingly enthusiastic. Encouraged, I begin to create presentations for my material and share my ideas with the public. Again, the response is overwhelmingly enthusiastic. These responses are so powerful that I commit myself to writing a book.

DEED

The last manifesting step is actually doing the deed, Principle IV: Action. This step likely takes the most time because the material world's physics are denser than those of the inspiration, imagination, thought, and word realms. In the above marriage example, suppose you end up planning to get married. Most marriage ceremonies are months in the making and require lots of resources/energy. Deeds take time.

Deed is where your internal world fully bridges with the external world. Deed is where the order of your plan meets the chaos of the real world. To ensure that you are able to manifest what you want your plan needs to be living and real to you. That means that you continually inject your personal energy into your manifestation plan to make it real.

> I start writing February 1, 2008, and begin engaging in the steps necessary to make the book more than just a personal, internal exercise. That is, I begin engaging the external world. That engagement immediately begins shaping the course of the book. My initial inspiration now is something wholly separate from myself and has a life of its own. Advocates and nemeses descend from many unexpected places.

Finer Points

There are many finer points to pay attention to in order to manifest what you want.

GRAVITY

Because the universe is probabilistic, if you want to manifest something then you need to increase the probability of it happening. One way to do this is to do things that are known to have a high probability of working. You also do these high probability things *often* in order to increase the probability of manifesting what you want. You also are persistent because persistence increases the probability of your manifestation dreams continuing to live on until they are realized in the future.

In a sense manifesting is about creating density and gravity around what you want. As Einstein demonstrated the greater an object's gravity the more space warps around the object. The result is an increase in the probability that other things fall in toward the dense gravitational object and cannot escape it. Among these falling "objects" are the things you want to manifest.

> My book is rejected by almost-every publisher. Some of the feedback I receive is positive, but much of it is negative. But I have a proven strategy, including having surrounded myself with advisers who each have track records of helping authors create successful books. My life has become getting the book published. This means that as the real world buffets me I do not get knocked off my center-of-gravity. Not only that, but I am persistent. This creates additional gravity and momentum that helps me to overcome the real world's inertia.

ACCORD

Critically, manifestation must be suffused with accord to work. When your inspiration, imagination, thoughts, words, and deeds are in alignment things that you want become real.

Recalling my purchase of AES Corporation, it was the result of my desire to uncover an excellent investment candidate. First there was the inspiration: in the future the world will need to generate lots of electricity. Next, I merged inspiration with what I knew and engaged in an imaginative process: for me to fully capture the benefit of this power trend I need to invest in a business that can capture both growing electricity use, and also the increase in the number of devices using electricity. Then I had to begin thinking about which investment candidates satisfied my inspiration and imagination: I need to invest in a global power company. Then I had to commit to finding the investment candidate: I then conducted research to uncover AES Corporation. After uncovering AES I had to engage in the deed by purchasing the investment. Amongst these steps, each was equal in importance. If I had failed to act upon any of the five manifestation steps then I would not have purchased AES Corporation.

Accord amongst the five manifestation steps is essential for manifesting what you want. As the following example demonstrates …

✦A Lack of Accord in the Manifestation Steps ✦

I want very badly to succeed by making a lot of money in my first post-college job. I imagine that being a stockbroker is a quick way to satisfy my inspiration, as well as utilize my economics education. I state this to all of my friends, to my family and to anyone who will listen. I work nearly 80 hours per week for a year and a half. Yet, I am a failure as a stockbroker.

At the core of my being as I was trying to sell people investments, I was saying to myself, "I am just a glorified used-car salesman." My thoughts were not in accord with my inspiration, my imagination, my words, or my deeds. I felt no pride in what I was doing; I felt ashamed to be a salesman, and so naturally, I failed. But words are important, too.

Everyone has had "friends" who said they care about you, yet their deeds continually did not match their words. At some point they shared their real thoughts about you. It turns out that their thoughts and deeds were in alignment, but not their words. That is, they didn't like you and their actions communicated just that. However, the words confused the issue until your "friends'" words were in accord with their thoughts and deeds. Then the energy of the situation moved effortlessly and the friendship either repaired itself or ended.

I discussed earlier that if the ego, and its emotional defenses, enters the process of manifestation then inspiration never takes shape within your imagination. This is just like when I scoffed at my initial inspiration to write a book back in 2002.

Most importantly, if you are not inspired in the first place to do something then the manifestation process is equally impossible. Many people scan the investment landscape looking for opportunity, but find nothing inspiring. Nonetheless they engage their powers of imagination to arbitrarily and artificially come up with an investment thesis. Then they begin thinking about the investment, its benefits vs. its costs. Next, they commit themselves to buying the investment. Finally, they purchase the investment. While it is possible that this investment results in money being made, it is much less likely than had inspiration been present from the beginning. This is because

Inspiration is information!

If you want something in your life and it just isn't happening, you need to spend some time examining if your inspiration, imagination, thoughts, words, and deeds are truly in accord. In all likelihood, at least one of the five steps is out of harmony or missing completely. Once you have discovered which step is missing then you can move the five steps back into accord with one another.

EQUALITY

Now a new wrinkle of the *Action* principle can be introduced since you now have the lens of manifestation present. Principle IV, Action, is "effects follow causes;" and that suggests one of the secrets of manifestation. Namely, if you want a million dollars worth of effect then you must give a million dollars worth of cause/action. Many people fail when they try to use the power of manifestation because they are trying to get their money for nothing, so to speak. It just doesn't work that way.

Remember Isaac Newton's version of Principle IV, his Third Law, which is often stated as: "For every action there is an equal and opposite reaction." Thus, if you want something then you must give something *equal* in return. That giving/investment on your part might be $1 million of inspiration, or $1 million worth of imagination, or $1 million of thought, or $1 million of word (commitment), or $1 million worth of action. To receive, you must give. It's that simple.

EFFICIENCY

The universe operates efficiently. That is, it conserves energy and does not waste it, and in fact the universe's preference is for new things that contribute to its growth and overall health. So the greater the efficiency of something or newness of something then the greater is its probability of it continually being supported by the universe.

Thus, when manifesting you must acknowledge that there are already efficient manifesting solutions that have been discovered, such as being a doctor, lawyer, accountant, inventor, or entrepreneur. These successful manifesting paths have survived a Darwinian process and have proven to contribute value to the universe. This doesn't mean that there aren't new ways of manifesting what you want. No, that's missing the point. The point is that manifestation must work with, not against, the universe because of Its preference for efficiency. That's why doing a $1 million worth of television viewing, web-surfing or video game playing is less likely to result in $1 million coming back to you. There is less value contributed so there is less efficiency and consequently, less support.

SPECIFICITY

When using the power of manifestation people usually get exactly what they ask for—even if it's not what they want. The universe is like a tricky djinni fulfilling your wishes literally. Because the universe keeps its accounts in generic energetic terms you need to master the art of specificity. This is why it's important that your inspiration, imagination, thoughts, words and deeds are harmonious and focused. If discord is present then the manifestation signal sent out to the universe is full of static. Consequently, you receive disharmony in return.

To avoid poor manifestation you take care to be specific with each portion of the manifestation process. That is, you make sure you are inspired. You make sure that you have utilized your imagination and minimized the contribution of your ego. Your thoughts are pure and exactly what you want.

When you translate your vision into commitment you make sure you are precise in voicing your intentions (i.e., the Words). Lastly, you do not take action (Deeds) until you are clear about the correct path.

Think of inspiration, imagination, thought, word, and deed as lenses that you project your energy through. If any of the lenses is out of focus then the energy coming through the other side is also out of focus. Likewise, if the lenses do not work in concert with one another then the energy is also unfocused.

The Intuitive Investor and You: Self-Assessment

Take a moment to remember an important accomplishment in your life. This may include getting a college degree, getting married, having a baby, surviving a life crisis, growing as a person, etc. Consider how each of the five steps of manifestation was either present or not. How did this affect your ability to manifest your goal?

Exercises

AN ACCOMPLISHMENT INVENTORY Take a moment to reflect back on the investments you have made in your life. Write one down in your notebook. Now spend some time identifying each of the five steps of the manifestation process within your decision to invest. To review, they are: inspiration, imagination, thought, word, and deed.

Now describe how each of the steps was either present or not present in your process. Were there any portions of the manifestation process missing? If so, how did it affect the investment decision for you? Did you get what you wanted from the investment? How long did it take?

Now that you know the process for manifesting, is there anything that you would change? Does this process feel more, or less, complete than the process you used before? Place any observations in your notebook.

REVIEW

The ultimate investment skill is manifestation. That is, knowing what you want and going out and getting it. Manifestation is the four principles worked forward from *Infinity* to *Action*. More specifically, the process of manifestation is: inspiration, imagination, thought, word and deed.

Inspiration is the initial, radical spark that literally inspires your life. Imagination is a merging of inspiration with your knowledge to create something wonderful and new for yourself. When inspiration and imagination work together logical structures begin to form. This allows you to think about and investigate your inspiration. Thought is the stage where substance and form meet in equal measure. Word refers to your commitment to make real your original inspiration and the structures necessary to realize them. Lastly, deed means that you must act if you want to manifest your inspiration.

Refinements to manifestation include gravity, accord, equality, efficiency, and specificity. Gravity means that you have to make your inspiration as dense as possible through focus, continuance and persistence. Accord and equality mean that all five steps of the manifestation process must be present in order for radical manifestation to take place. Efficiency draws your attention to the universe's preference for supporting what works and what will help it to grow, too. Lastly, specificity means that you must stay absolutely focused in order to achieve your dreams.

14

Reports from the Field— Real World Stories

What follows are reports from the field. These are real world stories from my continuing investment career. It's one thing to imagine scenarios and invent outcomes, but you need hard evidence of the efficacy of creativity and intuition, in action.

Devon Energy, Part I

It is 1999. Devon Energy (ticker symbol: DVN) is one of the largest independent oil and natural gas producers in the United States. They are renowned for their ability to make excellent acquisitions to grow their oil and natural gas reserves. They are also well known for their unusual production of natural gas from coal bed methane deposits. Typically natural gas wells are very expensive to drill because natural gas is found deep in the earth. The weight of all that rock over the hydrocarbons causes them to turn into natural gas. So a natural gas well might be drilled over 12,000 feet into the earth, whereas an oil well might be less than 1,000 feet. That's why Devon's coal bed methane technology is important. This gas is found as bubbles in water inhabiting coal seam deposits. And these coal deposits may only be 100-200 feet below the surface of the earth. This is a significantly cheaper well to dig, so the potential for economic returns is higher. The trick is extracting the natural gas from the bubbles. This is Devon's specialty.

I am in Denver for the "Rocky Mountain Natural Gas Investment Forum." Devon publicly says its future cost of extraction will be much lower because of their huge coal bed methane properties in central Wyoming (near Gillette). This is a huge competitive advantage. Because there are coal-bed methane deposits throughout the world, every analyst and portfolio manager wants to know where Devon will invest next. Over the course of the day I watch countless numbers of folks ask a variation of this same question, "Where else are you looking?" But Devon doesn't want folks to know where they are looking. Any leak of their interest is valuable information for any competitor. So understandably, Devon's management has developed quite an intellectual fortress around this information. Through a skillful combination of creativity and intuition I get the information nobody else gets.

First of all, Devon has a large number of executives at this smallish conference. This is unusual. During most conferences only the upper management attends and each of them is very skilled at playing matador with an analyst's bull question. So my first essential observation is that potentially non-savvy executives are participating in the conference.

Importantly, I notice that Devon's upper management is accompanied by second-tier executives at the conference. This distinction is because of my accord with Principle II: *Paradox*. Next, using Principle I: *Infinity*, I identify which executive to target for my questioning.

I decide to focus on Devon's executive in charge of worldwide exploration because he is in charge of the information I want to know and because he is potentially unsavvy. I begin by sitting on the periphery of the group of questioners surrounding him. The question, "where else are you looking?" is asked in every possible permutation over the course of an hour and a half. No one gets the goods. I am waiting for the right moment.

With my intuition I feel the energy of the conversation relax. At this particular moment the exec only has two Wall Street analysts around him. They are discussing: "How're the wife and kids," and "How's your [golf] handicap?" Blah, blah, blah. I have an inspiration and know that the time is right to move in. One of my preparations is that I have masked myself by *harmonizing* with the energy of someone young, ignorant and naïve so that I am underestimated. I am a wolf in sheep's clothing.

I walk up to the three men and say, "So this coal bed methane thing sounds like a home run, yes?" The two Wall Street jokers laugh heartily at my naïveté as the exec answers my question. This means my trap is properly baited. Devon's exec then goes on to explain to me all about their coal bed methane prospects. All the while I nod as if he is delivering revelations to me. I then ask another naïve question that I already know the answer to: "Where in the world are coal-bed methane deposits?" Before Devon's exec has the chance to answer, the two Wall Street analysts have another condescending moment at my (supposed) expense, and say almost in unison, "Everyone knows that. They are in lots of places, like the former Soviet Union, Czech Republic, Poland, Canada, Kazakhstan ..." I feel via my intuition that Devon's exec is vulnerable and I go in for the kill. I speak through the verbal cacophony of the two Wall Street pumps and ask: "And what foreign languages are you studying?" Devon's exec replies without suspecting: "Czech and Pol ... i ... sh." I say, "Thank you," and walk away with my Treasure. The Wall Streeters' mouths are agape.

How my intuition contributed to this success is fairly obvious as I noted these moments above. I had set my intention to, "When he is weakest." When I felt the "empty spot," that is the Devon executive's moment of vulnerability I moved in to fill the vacuum of the empty spot.

The real magic was how my creativity joined everything together and worked together with my intuition. I pieced together many disparate pieces of information—a creative process that included my left brain's store of coal-bed methane knowledge. I also harmonized with the exec's life and realized he traveled a lot. I also knew Devon's company culture and knew that their execs work for the company for a long time. Thus, there was a high probability that the exec was expected to stay overseas for long periods of time. As the exec in charge of worldwide exploration he was likely to be studying foreign languages to ensure that any important transaction details didn't escape him. I also spent almost the entire afternoon in a meditative state because I realized the answer to this one question was more valuable than any other I could possibly uncover.

How my right brain made these connections I do not know, nor will I ever know. The right brain's functioning is natural, and beyond words, *but it does respond to process.* I followed the very same processes I have outlined for you and tapped my creativity and intuition, and a magical, unique piece of investible information was the result.

Devon Energy, Part II

Devon Energy was one of my largest holdings over the course of my entire portfolio management career. There were many reasons behind my choice, but one was their management team. By my reckoning they were among the finest management teams in the United States. There was a lot of evidence for this, but one was Devon's brilliant way of pulling off the merger or acquisition that nobody else could seem to pull off.

> It is 2001 and Devon has bought two large competitors in a little over a month. The first deal is a complete and utter shock and its most recent deal is blowing the minds and gaskets of Wall Street even more. There is a huge outcry that Devon is just "an Empire Builder" that will pay any price to grow itself.

First, note the use of the archetype "Empire Builder." Like all archetypes it has a whole bunch of presumed "facts" associated with it that mean analysts and money managers don't actually need to do analysis. They just need to know that Devon is an "Empire Builder."

> Wall Street's fear is that Devon is willing to pay any price for a competitor because they want to be big for big's sake. This charge is partially credible because Larry Nichols, the CEO of Devon, is a very charismatic man whose intelligence has a way of making other people feel stupid. I think he is brilliant and my kind of executive. Another reason folks are uncomfortable with Devon's acquisitions is the company has put, by normal standards, huge amounts of debt on the balance sheet. And there is an unwritten Wall Street rule (prejudice) that exploration and production businesses should not have more than

40% of financing coming from debt and Devon has exceeded that level.

Well the "Empire Builder" charge is quite serious and the price of Devon precipitously falls. I owe it to my shareholders to find out if Devon Energy is just an Empire Builder. The right moment is coming soon because I am scheduled to be in New Orleans for the Howard-Weill energy conference. Larry Nichols, Mr. Emperor, and his company Devon Energy are going to be at the conference also. On one of the nights after the daily proceedings I am scheduled to be sharing dinner with Devon along with a number of other Investors. But because our firm, Davis Selected Advisers, is Devon's largest shareholder I get to sit at Larry's table for dinner.

So how did I ask that Empire-Builder-question of the CEO and actually get an honest answer? Larry is one of the smartest executives in the United States, and by the time I asked him this question it was several months after the acquisitions. In the interim he had answered this question more times than Bill Clinton was asked about Monica Lewinsky. Larry knew all the angles and all the ways of answering all of the angled questions. Devon denied the charges, but "Are you an Empire Builder?" is the sort of question that every executive knows they should answer "no" to. I really need to know if they are Empire Builders. What was I to do? I engaged the creative and intuitive process to get my answer.

The way to ask the question occurs to me on my flight to New Orleans. In effect, my entire trip boils down to the moment when I ask my question and get my answer. The right answer and subsequent choice on my part will potentially make my shareholders tens of millions of dollars. So all of the other conference moments are superfluous in comparison. As before, I plot my strategy. Again, I decide that the appropriate time to ask Larry the question is at the end of the evening when business is not the center of the conversation. "How're the kids?" "Are you still skiing?" Blah. Blah. Blah. Before I ask my question I mask myself by harmonizing with an air of "fond remembrances." Then I ask Larry Nichols, "Ten years ago, did you have any idea that Devon would be where it is today?" He answers, "No. Opportunity has smiled very kindly on us." And that is that. Devon is not an Empire Builder. I take advantage of the depressed value of Devon and buy more.

How did this question guarantee me that I had an honest answer to the Empire Builder question? First, my question was a variation of "Are you an Empire Builder?" But it was different. You see, Empire Builder has the whiff of a decided, concerted, effort full of guile on the part of the Empire Builder. This *is* true for any Empire Builder. Because of that guile it suggests a plan is in place to build an Empire from the beginning.

The only way to get through Larry's defenses was to reminisce about the good ole days to see if his original intention was Devon becoming as big as they ended up becoming. If he said "yes," it wouldn't have necessarily meant that he was an Empire Builder, but it would have meant that he had the capacity to "reach" for a deal to serve the plan of getting bigger. Instead, he answered "no." My question worked because I played with context. The context of the conversation was our personal lives. The context of the conversation was the past, not the current or future state of the Empire. My question avoided the context of "big" and "Empire" and focused on a generic result. This process came about because of my right brain. No computer or amount of linear analysis could have generated this combination of timing and question.

General Growth Properties

It's 2004 and I am in Chicago with several of my Davis Selected Advisers colleagues, Andrew Davis, Chandler Spears, and our intern at the time, Richard Selim. I am here to meet with Morningstar, the mutual fund evaluation company. My fund has just gone through a name change and names are very important in the mutual fund industry. If you say that you are a growth and income fund then your fund must adhere to the official criteria for a growth and income fund. And Morningstar determines what fund category you are in, and thus who your competition is, by your name. So Andrew and I are here to talk about the name of the Fund.

After Morningstar we head to the offices of Chicago's General Growth Properties (GGP) to meet with the CEO, John

Bucksbaum, and the CFO, Bernie Friebaum. GGP is the largest owner of shopping malls in the United States. This position was attained by using a lot of debt to purchase malls around the country. Many analysts are afraid this leverage is dangerous for the long-term health of the Company. So Andrew and Chandler, the guys responsible for real estate, want to talk with GGP to gain greater comfort with their financial reasoning. Richard and I are just passengers.

First up is the very likeable John Bucksbaum, son of the Company's founder. But John defers most of the finance questions to Bernie Friebaum upon his arrival. Bernie arrives and I sit through an hour of questions, asking only one question at the end. Afterward we hop in the car for the airport. Andrew asks me my opinion of the meeting. I answer vociferously, "I hated that watch!" I am referring to Bernie Friebaum's wrist watch. He has the most massive watch I have ever seen. Its face is approximately 2.5-3 inches across and has pretty sparklies everywhere. What's more, he intentionally positions his suit jacket and shirt-sleeves to show it off. And Bernie makes sure you see it, too. In fact, he contrives his hand movements like a Hindu dancer to show off the damned watch. My intuition tells me "the watch" means Mr. Friebaum is not interested in serving us as shareholders, but instead in his own aggrandizement.

That was all it took. After harmonizing with the personality behind The Watch and knowing the facts about the company I knew GGP was very likely a poor investment. In the fall of 2008 Mr. Bucksbaum and Mr. Freibaum were both asked to leave General Growth Properties by the Board of Directors. GGP was in tremendous trouble, as brought on by their heavy load of debts, and the rabid creditors trying to protect their interests in that same debt. And in the spring of 2009 the company declared bankruptcy.

The examples from my career so far all feature one distinct advantage that the average Investor seemingly does not have. Namely, I had direct access to management. However, because of Principle I, Infinity, and the fact that everything is interconnected, everyone has access to the answers to these questions via intuition.

Now that I am a retired portfolio manager, I manage my own investments, publish a blog and am an investment author, yet I no longer have access to management. So *my intuition is even more important now than it was then*, and more importantly, I have continued to have success employing my intuition, as my blog's regular readers can attest to. The next several examples are examples of creativity and intuition in action sans personal access to management.

Enron

I am at my alma mater, the University of Colorado, giving a talk about my investment methodology. The year is 2002. During the "question and answer" session I am asked if I was an investor in Enron. I believe the questioner is trying to test the power of my methods and wants to see if I followed the herd and invested in Enron like many money managers.

Everyone remembers the baddies of Enron. They were the natural gas and energy trading company that went bankrupt after massive corporate malfeasance. Its executives were either imprisoned or died awaiting prison. And many of its employees lost all of their retirement savings.

I answer quite honestly and say, "No." He follows up with, "Why not?" I tell him it's really quite simple. I am a very sophisticated reader of financial documents and yet, I could never figure out Enron's financial documents. To me that meant they were trying to hide something. Not only that, but also their executives were so arrogant that you felt you had to wash your hands after you *saw* them.

My creativity allowed me to make the necessary connections between disparate parts of my knowledge. I connected together "Byzantine financial statements," "faith in my accounting skills," and "arrogant behavior." I remember sitting at my desk trying to comprehend Enron's financial statements. I even took out a piece of paper and tried to diagram what was happening and I could not figure it out. I thought about calling their VP of Investor Relations, but I didn't. Instead, I trusted my intuition and went into a meditative state that allowed me to creatively connect the above pieces together. I also tuned into their arrogance. Enron's brand of arrogance was the ugly, aristocratic kind, not the bravado-kind of an amazing athlete. So it was in that moment I declined to invest in Enron because I was confident that they were intentionally trying to screw people over.

All of the pieces of information I used to understand Enron's information are available to the general public. The financial statements are a matter of public record at the SEC's website. Everyone has the capacity to learn how to read financial reports. And lastly, almost all publicly traded firms in the United States allow you to listen to their conference calls via the Internet. What's more, the replays of conference calls are frequently available for several weeks after the call.

More importantly though, each person's creative and intuitive process can lead to the same conclusion yet use entirely different information. The truth about Enron was there for everyone to see. Everything Enron did was a reflection of itself, thus everything it did was potentially evidence of its corruption. There were many others who avoided owning shares in Enron and each of them had their own reasons. Take confidence that "there is a why" and endeavor to discover its Truth.

Dot.com Bubble Bursting

It's 1999 and I am in San Francisco to attend a technology conference, starting the next day. It is the dot.com era and I am in the belly of the beast, San Francisco and Silicon Valley. It's the time of heady business valuations with some tech businesses trading at 100+ times earnings! The investment climate is even headier than the punch bowl at a San Franciscan, Haight-Ashbury party of 1967. Many in the investment business are utterly confounded because there are a number of very smart people stating the world is changed forever. That the way to examine businesses has changed forever. That investors shouldn't be concerned with price-earnings ratios, but price to eyeballs (I kid you not). My intuition tells me it's all madness, but I am confused why no one else can see what I see. I am relatively new to this elevated level of investment management and am vulnerable to claims that I am ignorant and just don't "get it."

But right now I am taking a taxi from the airport to my hotel. It is late at night and I am a little sleepy and without a conscious intention to, I enter a meditative state. And then I see a billboard for Stream.com featuring a little boy peeing and photographed very artfully, at that. It's all I need to see to know that the dot.com era is about to end and soon. It's all coming down like a house of cards. I vow to avoid most technology investments and proceed to earn outsized returns for years.

What was it about that billboard that communicated to me that the dot.com era had already ended? I am not entirely certain. But something about the decadence of the image, the lack of self-consciousness of Silicon Valley businesses such that they could erect and tolerate such a billboard, told me all that I needed to know. But it was my intuitive inspiration that jolted me and said, "Hey, did you notice that! Huh, did you?" It was one of the most crystalline moments of my entire life and it throbbed with the sensation of the Truth I have described.

So what did I do with this insight? Even though there was pressure on me from many outsiders to invest more of the cash the Fund was accumulating, I maintained a healthy cash position. I also avoided most technology businesses. I knew whole-heartedly that most stocks were massively overvalued and that there would be a correction in price. Dissecting my performance record you would discover I earned most of my outsized returns in the years post the bursting of the dot.com bubble.

Note: The taxi moment was happenstance. I was not consciously trying to tap my intuition. Nonetheless, it was an intuitive moment brought on by my meditative state and intention. I had flown to San Francisco to try and understand the dot.com story better because I was very confused. That was my intention. And there I was in the back of the taxi in a meditative state. And it happened. I saw what I needed to see. Again, this information was there for anyone to see, on the side of the highway, but seeing the billboard in a meditative state, coupled with my knowledge about the world and its people, was all I needed to see. This was not secret information, but my intuitive understanding was.

Calling the Financial Market Bottom

I call a bottom to the autumn 2008 stock market collapse days after the big market sell-off of November 20, 2008. The collapse is brought about by the liquidity crisis brought on by the real estate bubble bursting. I spend the days after the huge selloff continually entering a meditative state trying to intuit whether the financial market participants have exhausted their anxiety. I feel that the anxiety has massively abated. I therefore conclude that the sell off is over.

But I am also nervous, because I cannot sense real and necessary changes occurring at the regulatory level. I post on my blog that I feel the market has bottomed but that I am still nervous because real change has yet to begin. My prediction holds up until March of 2009.

So, in the midst of the massive financial market meltdown of November 2008, what gave me confidence that a bottom had been reached? I entered a meditative state with the intention of finding the answers to "is this the bottom?" and "is everyone done with panic-selling?" I received a definitive answer of "yes" to both questions. And over the next three exceptionally turbulent months, my prediction held up with levels skittering just above the bottom quite a few times.

This may sound like a failure, but it isn't. Instead, it's a cautionary tale. The caution is to remember that intuition reveals a likely resolution of currently entangled structural threads as they play out over time. In other words, intuition demonstrates the natural effect given a set of causes—no matter how complicated the causes are. However, because we all have free will, the global causes do change over time. So the real test of whether your intuition continues to work is whether you are able to adjust your original predictions to reflect new causes coming into play.

Again in March there is panic-selling that takes market valuations well below my initial call of the market bottom, culminating with a terrifying slide on March 9, 2009. Again I enter a meditative state. Again I sense that the energy of anxiety has exhausted itself. Again I call a market bottom on March 12, 2009, and publish my prediction on my blog.

This bottom is different because deep, systemic shifts are underway in the U.S. economy and the regulatory structures are shifting. For the first time in almost four years I buy, and recommend my blog readers buy, U.S. equities.

As of early fall 2010 the original prediction still stands.

Ground Covered and Action Steps

Congratulations. You have completed your journey through *The Intuitive Investor*. I began the book by highlighting the most important investment skill: understanding information. I then went on to discuss the limitations of the traditional, linear descriptions of the world, numbers and words. To fill this information gap I offered a non-traditional, non-linear source of information: feelings. Feelings are an unbelievably rich source of information, but they can only be accessed when the obstructions of the ego are either controlled or removed. One such obstacle can be emotional states when your feeling-senses are corrupted by preferences and prejudices.

Next I shared with you Principle I, Infinity which is about the unlimited vastness and interconnectedness of the universe. It's about possibilities. Next I explored with you two primary sources of emotional obstructions that erect artificial boundaries around you: ignorance and anxiety. These boundaries prevent you from experiencing Principle I, Infinity and consequently limit your understanding of information.

Following up, I described Principle II, Paradox which acknowledges how most people perceive the universe, with distinct probabilities. Separating out information from the vast information landscape requires three skills: contexts, scales and continuums. Contexts are equivalent to choosing micromaps from amongst the macrocosm map. Scales determine how close you want to be to the information; this aids in understanding. Last, continuums are in accord with paradox as they illustrate graphically how two opposite concepts can be in harmony/truth with one another. This is a paradox.

At this juncture all of the skills shared were about externally mapping the world. Yet, for a true understanding of information investors need an internal map, too. The natural course was to discuss the what, why, who, where and when of investing. The "what" of investing is to consciously expend energy (resources) so that the benefits of the expended energy exceed the costs of the expended energy. The "why" is so that benefits of an investment decision exceed its costs. Investors are detectives; this is the "who" of investing. In order to know "where" to invest you must see your world differently, through an investment lens. Lastly, you invest when you feel that you understand the information about an investment and when you are confident that benefits will exceed costs.

Much of the work up to this point was about ridding yourself of the slate of distortions present in each person that restrict access to the feeling-self. With the old slate firmly discarded, a new slate was needed that could serve as the grounds for your feeling experience and your ability to understand information. So Principle III, Harmonizing, was introduced, which is all about becoming one with information to understand it. To harmonize with this new slate required the introduction of the Seven Essential Investor Attitudes.

The Seven Attitudes are: focusing on risks before opportunities; having comfort with uncertainty; recognizing that a good decision is often greater than or equal to the perfect decision; forgiving yourself for not being perfect; knowing that you are holding investment interviews for limited positions with your investment portfolio; asking yourself why an investment has to be the One; and being cautious of false prophets, including analogies, adjectives and archetypes.

With a new investment slate, new chalk had to be added to the slate in the form of the Seven Essential Investor Behaviors. Each of these behaviors required that you make choices, by Principle IV, Action. The Seven Behaviors are: choosing full responsibility; honesty; balancing intelligence and wisdom; judging, but not pre-judging; having courage; having conviction; and assuming that there is a why.

All of these skills were then brought together to form an Investor Toolkit. This toolkit featured three tools that addressed different moments in the life-cycle of an investment. "Your Cousin Vinny" helped create the proper context for evaluating an investment before you buy it. "The Investment Thesis" was the right context for continuing to evaluate an investment while you own it. Finally, "The Lessons Learned List" provided an excellent context for you to learn from your mistakes after you sell an investment.

While each part of the book up until this point helped you to understand information, it was necessary to de-secularize and combine the four principles. By unshackling the Four Principles from a secular understanding, the boundaries of what is possible to do with them was dramatically expanded. In particular, when the Four Principles are used in sequence, either forward or backward, the full powers of the right brain become accessible: meditation, creativity, intuition and manifestation.

I next shared with you that meditation is the vehicle for accessing the full power of your mind. Meditation is a natural mind state and is where both the left brain and right brain merge to become One Mind. A powerful analogy for understanding the meditation practice is: Meditation is like cutting a pathway through the jungle to an ancient temple to find treasure. Pathway is equivalent to your meditative practice. Jungle is another word for your ego. The Temple is a metaphor for the meditative state. Treasures are the inspirations and understandings you bring back from the meditative state. In short, meditation is the four principles worked backwards.

Creativity is the four principles worked backward, but grounded in the knowledge of your left brain. The steps of the Creativity Process are: doing your research; having a point of focus; creating time and space for yourself; relaxing; entering a meditative state; putting the problem into your mind's eye; relaxing more; not forcing an outcome; recording the information; understanding the information; and choosing to do something with the information.

Intuition is similar to creativity in that it is the four principles worked backward, but instead, it is grounded in the right-brain's feelings. In effect, intuition is tuning into the cosmic radio station. First you choose the station. Then you must tune in by turning off your ego. Next, you hear the signal by surrendering to the feeling of the station. Then you have to allow that feeling-sensation to enter your mind. Next, you must translate the feeling-sensation into a linear form so that your left brain can understand it. Then you have to evaluate the information to understand what the information means. Finally, you have to decide what to do with the information.

Manifestation is the four principles worked forward. The manifestation steps are: inspiration, imagination, thought, word and deed. To manifest wealth all five steps must be in accord with one another and be given equal treatment.

I ended with anecdotes from my career that demonstrated how I have used the techniques to make money for myself, Davis Funds shareholders, and to help my blog readers understand information better.

Because of the persistence and strength of both egoic structures and dogmatic science, I conclude by asking you to try the techniques I have shared for yourself. Everything I have shared is something that I have personally experimented with and experienced. What's more, every technique has been used to make good investment decisions.

Let a sense and spirit of adventure serve as your guide. Good luck and good skill!

ACTION STEPS

Now that you have come to the end here are some suggested action steps to help you become a better investor:

1. Evaluate what you have just read. Find out where there are gaps in your understanding. Know what information you absolutely agree with and what information you absolutely disagree with. Explore the source of the differences. Allow yourself the power to reject anything that you have read.

2. Re-read the book to ensure that you understand each of the skills and techniques.

3. Do each of the self-assessments and exercises.

4. Keep a method for recording your insights with you going forward.

5. Relate your investing history to the material of the book. This takes advantage of Principle III, Harmonizing, and helps you to become unified with the information.

6. Put the information to the test with your investment portfolio.

7. Gain conscious awareness of your mind.

8. Gain conscious awareness of your ego and the ways in which it separates you from a valuable source of information: your feeling-self.

9. Begin honoring your meditative state by doing the things that rejuvenate you.

10. Begin experimenting with the material, especially that of creativity, intuition and wealth manifestation. Ideally, you begin to expand your boundaries.

11. Talk with other people about your experiences. This aids in understanding.

12. Attend an Intuitive Investing Workshop. Details about them can be found at my business partner's and my website: www.intuitiveinvestingworkshop.com.

13. Read some of the books on my Recommended Readings list.

14. Persevere!

Appendix: Sample Investment Thesis and Lessons Learned List

THE INVESTMENT THESIS	
Company Name	Thesis Date:
Investment Time Horizon	Purchase Date:
STRENGTHS	How Long:
1. Devil's Advocate	
2. Devil's Advocate	
3. Devil's Advocate	
4. Devil's Advocate	
5. Devil's Advocate	
WEAKNESSES	How Long:
1. Devil's Advocate	
2. Devil's Advocate	
3. Devil's Advocate	
4. Devil's Advocate	
5. Devil's Advocate	

Issues That Make Me Feel Ignorant:
1.
2.
3.
4.
5.

Issues That Make Me Feel Anxious:
1.
2.
3.
4.
5.

I Feel Like Buying an Interest in This Investment Because:
1.
2.
3.
4.
5.

Things That *Would* Cause Me to Sell This Investment Immediately:
1.
2.
3.
4.
5.

Things That *Might* Cause Me to Sell This Investment Immediately:
1.
2.
3.
4.
5.

PRICE VALUATION:	PRICE PAID/COST BASIS
	price after 0.5 year
	price after 1 year
	price after 1.5 years
	price after 2 years
	price after 2.5 years
	price after 3 years
	price after 3.5 years
	price after 4 years
	price after 4.5 years
	price after 5.0 years

THE LESSONS LEARNED LIST

Here are the actual Lessons Learned that I created after my first year as a Portfolio Manager:

Lessons Learned 2000-2001
(in no particular order)

1. Lesson: Firm specific risk must be minimized in selecting stocks.

   Discussion: Declines in stock price that are the result of broad macroeconomic trends, terrorist attacks, etc. can be forgiven. What cannot be forgiven is misunderstanding a firm's: industry, management, strategy, or financial statements.

2. Lesson: If you trust your models to make your buy decision then you should trust them to make your sell decision, too.

   Example: Not selling IRF, PWR, and KM when high model-based target prices had been reached.

3. Lesson: Money on the table is money on the table. That is, selling is the only way to lock in the fruits of good stock picking.

   Example: IRF, PWR, and KM.

4. Lesson: The cost basis of a purchase is irrelevant in making a sell decision. The reason is that, like the buy decision, the sell decision is based on forward-looking information and not past information. The market is a discounting mechanism.

5. Lesson: it is better to miss out on some gains and buy securities on the way up from the bottom rather than buy under uncertain conditions.

   Example: PVN pre-announced their third quarter numbers and I bought prior to the full disclosure that would come with their conference call. I anticipated positive factors to be talked about on the call and thought these factors would stabilize or propel upward the stock. The factors were in fact discussed on the conference call. But, after the conference call, the stock tanked. I had thought that the bad news was already baked into the stock and had bought because I did not want to miss out on potential gains that would be lost if I was "late."

6. Lesson: Buying a security without creating your own fundamental model is indefensible.

   Example: I bought TXN last fall based on the fact that its stock was inexpensive on a P/E basis relative to its 52 week P/E. Because I did not create my own model and relied upon a "rule of thumb" I got burned by not understanding the negative factors that would affect TXN's revenues. This would have been prevented by having created a fundamental model.

7. Lesson: Never underestimate the irrationality of the market in volatile times.

   Example: PVN's stock should not have collapsed the way it did.

8. Lesson: The window of opportunity for a seasonal business's stock price to appreciate is the length of their operating season. After the operating season the stock is dead money. Perhaps more important to recognize, the shortened window of opportunity amplifies any bad news for a seasonal business. For while the size of the rock that hits the pond is the same size as for a non-seasonal business, the pond it hits is much smaller so the ripples are larger.

   Example: When PKS has bad news the magnitude is always disproportionate to its relevance.

9. Lesson: Every stock purchase should be accompanied with a brief thesis entitled: "What Would Cause Me to Sell This Stock?" Knowing ahead of time what factors would cause you to sour on a name would help shift the sell decision from an emotional decision to an analytical one. (Note: This is the beginning of the Investment Thesis.)

10. Lesson: The only people with a more positive skew on a company than sell-side analysts, is a company's management team.

    Example: IMAX

11. Lesson: Peter Lynch was right: whoever turns over the most rocks wins. Time invested in seeking out stocks rewards well the critical eye.

    Example: the purchases of IRF, PWR, AES, and URI were the result of much hard research work.

12. Lesson: To properly evaluate management takes many years and many interactions. Management doggedness and nimble-

ness is best demonstrated by the negotiation of a complex obstacle course that only time and uncertainty can create for them.

13. Lesson: When a management grows its company through acquisition, the appropriate metric for them to use when evaluating prospective targets is price to cash flow less capex. Price per tower or price to EBITDA overlook either the cash flow generation of an asset or overlook the capital investment necessary to bring the asset up to the acquiror's growth standards.

    Example: AMT, CCI, PKS, and maybe PWR.

14. Lesson: Anything can and will happen and everything cannot be foreseen. Hence, you must forgive yourself and move on for not being a seer.

    Example: the events of September 11th and their effect on the portfolio. [Note: this is the beginning of "Forgiving Yourself for Not Being Perfect.]

Encouragingly, other than buying TXN without an analytical opinion in place, I don't believe any of my mistakes this year were financial analysis mistakes, but portfolio management mistakes.

Suggested Readings and Resources
for Intuitive Investors

Because understanding information is the most important investment skill, I highly recommend each of the following sources of investment information:

- The U.S. Securities and Exchange Commission EDGAR website. This site is located at: www.sec.gov/edgar. This is the greatest free service of the U.S. government and contains every publicly traded company's audited financial data. In particular, focus on the 10-K document. This is the annual report that each company is required to file. Each 10-K contains almost every piece of data you would need in order to understand a business.

- My investment discernment blog which can be found at: jasonapollovoss.blogspot.com.

- *The Wall Street Journal* newspaper and website. In my opinion, the single greatest newspaper on the planet. Reading this daily is highly recommended because of its delivery of pertinent business information. Read each headline and then let your intuition guide you into which individual stories to read in full.

- *Business Week* magazine. It's important that you read a business weekly. This ensures that you do not miss any of the crucial features of the information landscape.

- Stratfor.com website. Basically this is a private intelligence organization that analyzes geopolitical events and material. Stratfor's approach to the information landscape is similar to my own. A subscription to their service is expensive, but in my opinion, worth it.

- *The Economist* magazine. A wonderful resource for global political, economic, and business news. You will learn a lot about those three important subjects by reading this magazine.

- Grant's Interest Rate Observer. Dry humor and dry analysis and always very prescient and intelligent.

- The Berkshire Hathaway annual report. Warren Buffett is an essential read. There is no single greater processor of information on the planet than Buffett.

- Wikipedia

I highly recommend the following investment books:

➤ Bernstein, Peter L. *Against the Gods: The Remarkable Story of Risk.* New York: John Wiley & Sons, 1996. An overview of how humanity has dealt with the "there is no such thing as a future fact" issue.

➤ Brigham, Eugene F. and Louis C. Gapenski. *Financial Management: Theory and Practice, Eight Edition.* New York: The Dryden Press, 1997. Brilliant overview of how to conduct business operations from the point of view of a finance professional. I especially love their "Additional Funds Needed" analysis which is a huge aid in valuing a business.

➤ Cassidy, Donald L. *It's When You Sell That Counts.* New York: McGraw Hill, 1997. A book that addresses some of the emotional aspects of investing. The particular focus is on when to sell an investment.

➤ Cottle, Murray, Block. *Graham and Dodd's Security Analysis, Fifth Edition;* New York: McGraw Hill, Inc, 1988. In my opinion, the best book ever written about left brain financial analysis.

➤ Duggan, William. *Strategic Intuition: The Creative Spark in Human Achievement.* New York: Columbia University Press, 2007. One of the few business books written about intuition and a fine introduction to the worth of the topic.

➤ Goodspeed, Bennet W. *The Tao Jones Averages: A Guide to Whole-Brained Investing.* New York: Penguin, 1984. A much needed book about the importance of using both the left, and right brain as an investor.

➤ Hooke, Jeffrey C. *Security Analysis on Wall Street: A Comprehensive Guide To Today's Valuation Methods.* New York: John Wiley & Sons, 1998. A fine overview of valuation. I appreciate the details of how to value specific types of businesses that fall outside of the normal manufacturing business model.

➤ Pollan, Stephen and Mark Levine. *Die Broke: A Radical Four-Part Financial Plan.* New York: HarperBusiness, 1998.

➤ Zukin, James H., editor. *Financial Valuation: Businesses and Business Interests.* Boston, MA: Warren, Gorham, Lamont, 1990. The single greatest valuation book ever written. Very obscure, expensive and hard to find. However, your local business school library or library may have it. Well worth the difficulty in understanding its contents.

I highly recommend each of the following sources of scientific information:

➤ New Scientist website

➤ Ford PhD, Kenneth W. *The Quantum World: Quantum Physics for Everyone.* Cambridge, MA: Harvard University Press, 2004.

➤ Gleick, James. *Chaos: Making a New Science.* New York: Penguin Books, 1987

➤ Goswami, Ph.D., Amit, with Richard E. Reed & Maggie Goswami. *The Self-Aware Universe: How Consciousness Creates the Material World.* New York: Tarcher Penguin, 1995.

➤ McTaggart, Lynne. *The Field: the Quest for the Secret Force of the Universe updated edition.* (New York:) HarperCollins Publishers, 2008.

➤ Radin, Ph.D., Dean. *The Conscious Universe: The Scientific Truth of Psychic Phenomena.* New York: Harper San Francisco, 1997.

➤ Sheldrake, Rupert. *The Sense of Being Stared At: And Other Unexplained Powers of the Human Mind.* New York: Crown Publishing, 2003.

➤ Talbot, Michael. *The Holographic Universe.* New York: Harper Perrenial, 1992.

➤ Vilenkin, PhD, Alex. *Many Worlds in One: The Search for Other Universes.* New York: Hill & Wang, 2006.

I highly recommend the following spirituality sources of information:

➤ Eager, Bill. *Thrive Inside: Transformative Secrets of Spiritual Masters, Gurus and Shamans.* Evergreen, Colorado: Chakra Systems, 2010.

➤ Patanjali and Chip Hartranft. *The Yoga-Sutra of Patanjali: A New Translation with Commentary.* Boston, MA: Shambhala, 2003.

➤ Pollan, Stephen and Mark Levine. *It's All in Your Head: Thinking Your Way to Happiness.* New York: Harper, 2006.

➤ Selby, John. *Seven Masters, One Path: Meditation Secrets from the World's Greatest Teachers;* New York: Harper San Francisco, 2003.

➤ Yogani. *Deep Meditation: Pathway to Personal Freedom.* Nashville, TN: AYP Publishing, 2005.

➤ Yogani. *Samyama: Cultivating Stillness in Action Siddhis & Miracles.* Nashville, TN: AYP Publishing, 2006.

I highly recommend the following general sources of information:

➤ The Internet

➤ Aburdene, Patricia. *Megatrends 2010: The Rise of Conscious Capitalism.* Newbury Port, Massachusetts: Hampton Roads Publishing, 2005.

➤ DeBecker, Gavin. *The Gift of Fear: and Other Survival Signals that Protect Us from Violence:* 10th Printing. New York: Dell Publishing,1998.

➤ Gelb, Michael J. *How to Think Like Leonardo da Vinci: Seven Steps to Genius Every Day.* New York: Dell Publishing, 2000.

➤ Poundstone, William. *Labyrinths of Reason: Paradoxes, Puzzles and the Frailty of Knowledge*. New York: Doubleday, 1988.

And of course, do not overlook the obvious...

➤ My homepage: www.jasonapollovoss.com
➤ The book's homepage: www.intuitiveinvestor.com
➤ Workshops homepage: www.intuitiveinvestingworkshop.com

Index

About the Author

Before retiring at age 35, Jason Apollo Voss was co-Portfolio Manager of the Davis Appreciation and Income Fund (DAIF), one of the nation's largest money-management firms and among the largest shareholders for several familiar brands. During his tenure he bested the NASDAQ, S&P 500 and DJIA by staggering percentages. Lipper Analytical Services named the Davis Appreciation and Income Fund a "Lipper Leader" and it was ranked number one in its investment category. The Fund was also a regular Morningstar "Analyst Pick."

An active speaker and presenter in the realms of finance and academia, Jason now resides in Santa Fe, New Mexico with his wife Dawn Jacobson, who is well known in the fashion world for her work as a makeup artist.

For more information please visit www.jasonapollovoss.com